A New Perspective

Rethinking the History and Myths of the Past

by

Richard Lawson Singley

Prometheus

A NEW PERSPECTIVE

Copyright © 2020 by Richard Lawson Singley

All rights reserved. This book or any portion thereof may not be reproduced or used in any manner whatsoever without the prior written permission of Richard Lawson Singley except in the case of brief quotations embodied in critical reviews and certain other noncommercial uses permitted by copyright law.

Published by Prometheus Educational and Business Consultants, Germantown, MD, 20876

ISBN 978-1-7321844-1-1

Amazon: https://www.amazon.com/Richard-Singley/e/B07FC71R87?ref=sr_ntt_srch_lnk_fkmr0_1&qid=1563812520&sr=8-1-fkmr0

Medium.com: https://medium.com/@richardsingley

Email: rich.singley5234@gmail.com

LinkedIn: https://www.linkedin.com/in/richard-singley-a7218332

RETHINKING THE HISTORY AND MYTHS OF THE PAST

Cover design by Adrian Christopher Singley and Richard Lawson Singley

Cover Image: A collection of pictures from Public Domain unless otherwise specified and follows Wikipedia Commons' guideline of usage. From top to bottom, left to right

1. Malcolm X's only meeting with Martin Luther King Jr., March 26, 1964, in Washington DC
2. First Reading of the Emancipation Proclamation of President Lincoln by Francis Bicknell Carpenter (1864)
3. Homer's Odyssey: The Cyclops' Curse Delays the Homecoming of Odysseus
4. Surrender of General Lee to General Grant at Appomattox Court House
5. JFK with His Mother Rose
6. Christ Crucified (c. 1632) by Diego Velázquez. Museo del Prado, Madrid
7. Death of Caesar by Vincenzo Camuccini.
8. Galileo with His Telescope
9. Charles Darwin with an Ape or Monkey Body Symbolized Evolution
10. Scott Joplin, 1903
11. Nefertiti Berlin Museum
12. Thomas Alva Edison
13. Gaius Julius Caesar. Vatican Museum
14. Toussaint Louverture
15. Napoleon Bonaparte
16. Suleiman the Magnificent of the Ottoman Empire
17. Alexander Pushkin by Orest Kiprensky
18. Senusret I (Sesostris I)
19. The Pyramid of Menkaure, the Pyramid of Khafre and the Great Pyramid of Khufu. By Ricardo Liberato—All Gizah Pyramids, CC BY-SA 2.0, https://commons.wikimedia.org/w/index.php?curid=2258048
20. The Arab Slave Trade
21. Last Supper by Leonardo da Vinci

A NEW PERSPECTIVE

RETHINKING THE HISTORY AND MYTHS OF THE PAST

Dedication: To my wife Jeanne, thanks for everything!

Special thanks to my good friend, Gene Limb, for his help in, editing and reviewing parts of this book and for helping me to develop my writing skills.

Author's note:
Many have asked why I include my middle name, Lawson, on everything that I write. It is to honor my father Lawson Singley. He told me once that he did not want to name any of his kids after him, but since I was born just before Father's Day, he decided to give me his name as a middle name.

A NEW PERSPECTIVE

RETHINKING THE HISTORY AND MYTHS OF THE PAST

Contents

Introduction 1
Abraham Lincoln and the Civil War 5
    Abraham Lincoln and the Hope for America 7
    Abraham Lincoln and Emancipation 17
        The Great Emancipator? 18
        Aftermath 20
    West Point and the Civil War 23
        West Point 23
        The Civil War 25
Antiquity 35
    Ancient Egypt 37
    Predynastic Egypt 39
        The Gift of the Nile 40
        Before the Pharaohs 42
        Nubian Roots 45
        Unification of Egypt 47
    Dynastic (Pharaonic) Egypt 49
        The Old Kingdom 50
        The First Intermediate and the Middle Kingdom 51
        The Second Intermediate (Hyksos) 53
        The New Kingdom 54
        The Third Intermediate Period and the Nubian Dynasty 59
        The Greco-Roman Era 60
        List of Dynasties in Ancient Egypt 63
    Greece and Rome 65
        The Origins of Greece: Minoan, Mycenaean and Egyptian Influence 67
        The Roman Republic and the Rise and Fall of Julius Caesar 77
        The Roman Republic 77
        The Rise of Julius Caesar 79

A NEW PERSPECTIVE

    The Fall of Caesar 80

    The Legacy of Rome 82

Religion 85

    Christianity 87

    The Makings of the Gospels 89

    The Evolution of the New Testament 97

        The Formation of the Catholic Church 97

        Church Dogma 99

    Islam 105

    A Brief History of Islam 107

        Early Islam 107

        Rightly Guided Caliphs 110

        Umayyad Caliphate (661–750) 112

        Abbasid Caliphate (750–1258) 112

        Mongol Invasion 114

        The Ottoman Empire (1299–1922) 114

    The Nature of Our Existence: Science Confronts Religion 117

        The Celestial Realm 117

        The Terrestrial Realm 121

Technology 125

    The Dawning of the Electrical Age (Part I): The Story of Two Towns and Two Luminaries 127

        Let There be Light: Roselle, Thomas Edison and Electricity 128

    The Dawning of the Electrical Age (Part II): The Story of Two Towns and Two Luminaries 137

        Wireless Communication: Roselle Park, David Sarnoff and the Radio 137

        Legacy 143

Cybersecurity 147

    A New Threat to Our Freedoms 149

Music 155

RETHINKING THE HISTORY AND MYTHS OF THE PAST

Fundamentals of Music 157
   The Development of Scales 157
   Chords 161
   Modulation 162
   The Cycle of Fifths 162
   Music and Mathematics 164
Roots: The Impact of Black Music on America and the World 169
Black History **185**
Origins of the African Slave Trade 187
   Arab Slave Trade 187
   Origin of the Trans-Atlantic Slave Trade 189
   Differences Between the Two Slave Trades 193
   Conclusion 193
Haiti and the Louisiana Purchase 195
   The Slave Revolt in Haiti 195
   The Louisiana Purchase 198
   Fear of Slave Revolts in America 200
Black Literary Giants: Dumas and Pushkin 203
   Thomas Alexander Dumas 203
   Alexander Dumas 205
   Abraham Hannibal 207
   Alexander Pushkin 208
The Rise of the Nation of Islam and Malcolm X 213
   Noble Drew Ali and the Moorish Science Temple 213
   The Founding of the Nation of Islam 216
   The Influence of Malcolm X on the NOI 219
   Malcolm's departure from the NOI 222
   Assassination 224
Politics **227**

A NEW PERSPECTIVE

First Mothers: The Relationship Between American Presidents and Their Mothers 229
    The Matriarchs 229
    Kennedy and Nixon 232
    The State of the Union 239
Appendix 243
Relevant Notes 247
References 265
Acknowledgments 277

RETHINKING THE HISTORY AND MYTHS OF THE PAST

List of Illustrations

All illustrations are in the Public Domain unless otherwise specified. Illustrations from Wikipedia Commons are in accordance with usage guidelines

1. March on Washington, August 28, 1963 (Library of Congress)
2. Gordon, a Louisiana Slave, 1863 (National Archives)
3. Lincoln and McClellan at Antietam, September 1862 (Library of Congress)
4. Chain and Shackles at the Feet of the Statue of Liberty (National Park Service)
5. March on Washington, August 28, 1963 (National Archives)
6. First Reading of the Emancipation Proclamation of President Lincoln by Francis Bicknell Carpenter (1864)
7. Abe Lincoln's Last Card; Or, Rouge-et-Noir (Red and Black)", a cartoon by John Tenniel
8. Emancipation Statue Lincoln Park, Capitol Hill—Library of Congress
9. Surrender of General Lee to General Grant at Appomattox Court House
10. Fort Sumter 1861; Flying the Confederate Flag
11. Ulysses Simpson Grant, 18th President of the United States
12. General Custer and James Washington
13. Jefferson Davis President of the Confederacy
14. George McClellan
15. James McPherson
16. Robert E. Lee, Commander of the Army of Virginia
17. William Tecumseh Sherman
18. The Sphinx: Taken by the uploader, w:es:Usuario:Barcex, CC BY-SA 3.0, https://commons.wikimedia.org/w/index.php?curid=4483211
19. Map of Ancient Egypt By H.Seldon—The map was made from file Ancient_Egypt_map.svg. This file was made by Jeff Dahl. For Faiyum_oasis.svg was used information from book: Ian Shaw: Dějiny starověkého Egypta, ISBN 80–7257–975–4., CC BY-SA 3.0, https://commons.wikimedia.org/w/index.php?curid=3948636
20. A Geographical Map of Africa, showing the ecological break that defines the Saharan area.
21. The Sahara Desert
22. The Rosetta Stone (ca 196 BC)
23. Afterlife Scene of Horus Leading the Deceased to the God Osiris
24. Scorpion macehead (detail) (Ashmolean Museum) By Udimu—Own work, CC BY-SA 3.0, https://commons.wikimedia.org/w/index.php?curid=10353240
25. Exhibit in the Oriental Institute Museum, University of Chicago, Chicago, Illinois, USA
26. The Narmer Palette Depicts the Unification of Upper and Lower Egypt

A NEW PERSPECTIVE

27. The Pyramid of Menkaure, the Pyramid of Khafre and the Great Pyramid of Khufu. By Ricardo Liberato—All Gizah Pyramids, CC BY-SA 2.0, https://commons.wikimedia.org/w/index.php?curid=2258048
28. The Pyramid of Djoser
29. Mentuhotep II
30. Senusret I
31. Foreigners Entering Egypt. By NebMaatRa—Own work, CC BY-SA 3.0, https://commons.wikimedia.org/w/index.php?curid=4390535
32. Statue of Ahmose I, Metropolitan Museum of Art
33. Queen Hatshepsut
34. Nefertiti Berlin Museum
35. Statue of Akhenaten in the early Amarna style. CC BY-SA 2.5, https://commons.wikimedia.org/w/index.php?curid=505800
36. The Boy King Tutankhamen (Tut)
37. Queen Tiye. By Einsamer Schütze—Own work, CC BY-SA 3.0, https://commons.wikimedia.org/w/index.php?curid=16320509
38. Abu Simbel By <a title="User:Pepaserbio" href="//commons.wikimedia.org/wiki/User:Pepaserbio">Pepaserbio</a>—Own work, <a title="Creative Commons Attribution-Share Alike 4.0" href="https://creativecommons.org/licenses/by-sa/4.0">CC BY-SA 4.0</a>, <a href="https://commons.wikimedia.org/w/index.php?curid=72663874">Link</a>
39. Nubian Pyramids, Meroe.
40. Cleopatra VII's Head as Displayed at the Altes Museum in Berlin
41. Homer's Odyssey: The Cyclops' Curse Delays the Homecoming of Odysseus
42. Mask of Agamemnon Discovered by Heinrich Schliemann in Mycenae in 1876 By Xuan Che—Self-photographed (Flickr), 20 December 2010, CC BY 2.0, https://commons.wikimedia.org/w/index.php?curid=15165017
43. Heinrich Schliemann
44. Colossus of Memnon
45. Death of Caesar by Vincenzo Camuccini.
46. Lucius Junius Brutus
47. Gaius Julius Caesar. Vatican Museum
48. Marc Antony's Oration at Caesar's Funeral as depicted by George Edward Robertson
49. Statue of Augustus Caesar
50. Last Supper by Leonardo da Vinci
51. Relationship Between Synoptic Gospels. By Original: AlecmconroyDerivative work: Popadius—this file was derived from: Relationship between synoptic gospels.png:, CC BY-SA 3.0, https://commons.wikimedia.org/w/index.php?curid=27903558
52. Pope Sylvester I and Emperor Constantine
53. Imperial Coronation of Charlemagne, by Friedrich Kaulbach

RETHINKING THE HISTORY AND MYTHS OF THE PAST

54. Statue of Isis Nursing Horus
55. Christ Crucified (c. 1632) by Diego Velázquez. Museo del Prado, Madrid
56. A Persian Miniature Depicts Muhammad Leading Abraham, Moses, Jesus and Other Prophets in Prayer
57. Main Tribes and Settlements of Arabia in Muhammad's Lifetime
58. Age of the Caliphs Expansion
59. Suleiman the Magnificent of the Ottoman Empire
60. Cristiano Banti's 1857 painting Galileo facing the Roman Inquisition
61. Galileo with His Telescope
62. Newton in 1702 by Godfrey Kneller
63. Hubble Deep Field
64. Charles Darwin with an Ape or Monkey Body Symbolized Evolution
65. The Hominoids are Descendants of a Common Ancestor
66. Forensic Reconstruction of an Adult Male *Homo erectus*. Reconstruction by W. Schnaubelt & N. Kieser (Atelier WILD LIFE ART)Homo_erectus.JPG: photographed by User:Lillyundfreya—Homo_erectus.JPG, CC BY-SA 3.0, https://commons.wikimedia.org/w/index.php?curid=9503611
67. The Bright Lights of Coney Island 1905
68. Thomas Alva Edison
69. Sir John Ambrose Fleming
70. Lee De Forest and His Vacuum Tube
71. The ENIAC
72. Nikola Tesla
73. The World's First Demonstration of the Transmission of Radio Signals Over Open Sea, May 13, 1897 (Wikipedia) By Cardiff Council Flat Holm Project - Cardiff Council Flat Holm Project, CC BY 3.0, https://commons.wikimedia.org/w/index.php?curid=4012156
74. Sarnoff Speaking at RCA's Roselle Park station,1921 http://www.davidsarnoff.org/gallery-radio/DS_WDY-1.html
75. David Sarnoff
76. Inventors of the transistor: John Bardeen, William Shockley and Walter Brattain at Bell Labs, 1948
77. The Pentagon, a Symbol of our Might, in the Wake of the 9/11 Attacks (U.S. Navy).
78. Anne Vallayer-Coster, Attributes of Music, 1770.
79. String Vibrations as a Function of Length
80. Piano keyboard By Tobias R.—Metoc—Own work, CC BY-SA 2.5, https://commons.wikimedia.org/w/index.php?curid=1256764
81. Bernhard Ziehn's 1907 list of, "diatonic triads", diatonic seventh-chords," and two examples of, "diatonic ninth-chords," the "large" and "small" ninth chords; all from the C major or the C harmonic minor scale

A NEW PERSPECTIVE

82. The Cycle of Fifths By Just plain Bill—Own work, CC BY-SA 3.0, https://commons.wikimedia.org/w/index.php?curid=4463183
83. Bass Guitar Time Signal of an Open String A Note (55 Hz)
84. Fourier Series (Wikipedia)
85. The Old Plantation, ca. 1785–1795, the earliest known American painting to picture a Banjo-Like Instrument
86. Bert Williams (Library of Congress)
87. Scott Joplin, 1903
88. Billie Holiday at the Downbeat Club in New York City
89. Leadbelly
90. Young Louis Armstrong
91. Duke Ellington at the Hurricane Club 1943
92. Charlie Parker, with Dizzy and a Young Miles in the Background
93. Chuck Berry
94. Ray Charles
95. Jimi Hendrix
96. Isaac Hayes, 1973
97. Donna Summer in a Recording Studio, 1977
98. The Arab Slave Trade
99. Arab Slave-trading Caravan
100. A Slave Market in Cairo. Drawing by David Roberts, circa 1848
101. Prince Henry the Navigator
102. Mansa Musa Sitting on a Throne and Holding a Gold Coin
103. A Map of Prester John's Kingdom as Ethiopia
104. Stowage of a British Slave Ship (1788)
105. Louisiana Purchase Stamp Bureau of Engraving and Printing—U.S. Post Office
106. Toussaint Louverture
107. Napoleon Bonaparte
108. Pushkin Exam at Lyceum
109. General Thomas-Alexandre Dumas, Father of Alexandre Dumas
110. Alexandre Dumas
111. Abraham Hannibal. By Ludushka—Own work, CC BY-SA 3.0, https://commons.wikimedia.org/w/index.php?curid=19010606
112. Alexander Pushkin by Orest Kiprensky
113. Duel of Pushkin and Georgesd'Anthès
114. Paul Robeson
115. Nation of Islam Members at Speakers' Corner in Hyde Park, London, March 1999. By No machine-readable author provided. Nrive assumed (based on copyright claims).—No machine-readable source provided. Own work assumed (based on copyright claims)., CC BY-SA 2.5, https://commons.wikimedia.org/w/index.php?curid=1449313

RETHINKING THE HISTORY AND MYTHS OF THE PAST

116. 1928 Moorish Science Temple of America in Chicago, Drew Ali dressed in white in the center
117. Madame Blavatsky
118. Master Fard
119. Elijah Muhammad
120. Malcolm X before a 1964 press conference
121. Muhammad Ali, 1967
122. Malcolm X's only meeting with Martin Luther King Jr., March 26, 1964, in Washington DC
123. Mary Ball Washington, Mother of George Washington
124. FDR and His Mother Sara
125. JFK with His Mother Rose
126. Nixon and His Mother Hannah (Richard Nixon Library)
127. Union Army Flag, 1863–1865

RETHINKING THE HISTORY AND MYTHS OF THE PAST

Introduction
My Literary Journey

"To find a common future we must find a common past."

Manning Marble

This is my second published book. My first book entitled: *In a Nutshell* is a collection of popular English phrases. This book, however, is a collection of articles and essays. It is a compendium of history, technology, religion, science, music and politics. Many of the articles are excerpts from my forthcoming series of books on the history of Western Civilization. In this book, I explore the following: was Lincoln the Great Emancipator? West Point and the Civil War, the origins of Greece, why Brutus killed Caesar, Ancient Egypt, the making of the Gospels; the evolution of the New Testament, the history of Islam, the origins of the African slave trade, Thomas Edison and the lightbulb, Sarnoff and wireless communications, Haiti and the Louisiana Purchase, Nixon and Kennedy, Dumas and Pushkin, the emergence of Malcolm X, the fundamentals of music, Cybersecurity, Astronomy, Anthropology, emerging technologies and other topics of interest.

I have always been interested in history and the origins of things. Because of my engineering background, I am also interested in technology and its impact on our daily lives. I was fortunate to have been born during interesting times in an interesting town, Roselle, NJ, that was the first town in the world to have an electrical infrastructure whose story is contained within.

My literary journey began in January of 1989 when, at the age of 34, I was hospitalized due to a rare growth that led to the temporary failure of my kidneys. This was a particularly difficult time for me because my sister, 16 years my senior and my surrogate mother, died of kidney failure after giving birth to her only child. I was five years old then and my earliest and fondest memories were of her kindness and love. She took me everywhere she went, and I was the only child of ten children in our family whose godparents were her friends and not the friends of our parents. Her sudden death hurt me deeply and became an early example of the uncertainty of life. Death castes such a dark shadow over the living; and there I stood a frightened little boy in the darkness with only the light of her sweet memories to illuminate the path of my future. Sorrow had paid me a visit at an early age, and for most of my life, I could not chase the deep sadness of her death away.

A NEW PERSPECTIVE

Those days in the hospital made me confront some of my deepest fears and in my nocturnal solitude, the specter of gloom brought tears, once again, to a little boy that had now become a man. I knew what it was like to lose someone you loved at an early age and I did not want that to happen to my little boy. I had a major operation and was in the hospital for several weeks. During that time, my wife brought my son to the hospital to see me in hopes that it would cheer me up. But with him came fear, as I saw my life, not through my eyes but his. I was a man in body, but a child in spirit, and I found myself once again afraid of the darkness of the unknown.

While in the hospital, my wife brought me a book entitled: *The African Origins of Civilization, Myth or Reality* by the late Dr. Cheikh Anta Diop in the hope that it would lift my spirits. Ironically, while in college, I befriended James G. Spady, a graduate student at the University of Pennsylvania who was the first American scholar to bring Diop's work to the fore. This book, more than any other, opened my eyes to the contributions of African people to civilization. I began to see a purpose for my life. Thus, my journey toward recovery began when I read the first page of this book. In it, I had found something to live for as if my destiny was being revealed to me. And the more and more I continued to read, the more and more my fears began to recede, and the light of my faith began to enter my dark room, and it released me from my cloister of gloom.

Although the seeds of my articles and books were planted in a Maryland hospital bed decades ago, the germination and cultivation of it came later. After my health was restored, I was determined to investigate and record the origins of things and contributions of African people to Western Civilization. I continued to work fulltime as an engineering manager while writing and researching history in my spare time. In 2011, I started writing and researching fulltime. Although my professional engineering career had come to an end, I never lost my love for engineering and technology.

As far as writing was concern, I was a novice. Prior to this time, I had never written a book of any kind and I was perfectly content being an Electrical Engineer and taking on home projects such as Astronomy, Photography, Music, etc., from time to time. While in high school; I told my father that I wanted to study History in college, but he suggested that I study Engineering and buy history books on the side. My mother, on the other hand, always told me that my purpose on this earth was "to tell the story that others couldn't tell." Perhaps Eleanor Roosevelt said it best: "I don't know what kind of a future life I believe in, but I believe that all that we go through here must have some value."

RETHINKING THE HISTORY AND MYTHS OF THE PAST

I was always closer to my father than I was to my mother. But when she died, I felt far more sorrow. I felt that I had disappointed her. Engineering had brought me financial success and prestige in the eyes of my father. But even as a child I had an inquisitive mind and a passion for stories and storytelling. My mother would always say: if you run away from who you are, you will never find what you can be. This is something that she clearly understood. It was my mother that brought home for me a telescope, books, and other items that the people she worked for as a maid discarded. It was her that sent me to piano lessons at the age of eight. She was a lover of the arts, her garden and stray animals and made Mother's Day flowers. She once told me that "you never know what instrument God will choose as a means to your salvation."

All of this was part of my heritage and I was molded from the clay of the black experience during the turbulent 60s and I had a desire to write the stories from a new perspective, one that embraced my blackness and my humanity and engineering experiences. Many proclaim that history is not the chronicles of what happened in the past, but rather, "his" story or the interpretation of what happened. Since it is often written by the victors, it seldom does justice to the times or those that do not write it. I wanted to give a voice to those that were muted by time and circumstance so that their stories could be heard. If the past is indeed prologue, we must understand it as it was and not how we wanted it to be. Because the future is the prodigal son of the past, our prospective is only as good as our perspective.

Armed with this conviction, I began to ask questions of which I had no answers. I decided to explore the origins of things not based on what I was taught or told in the classroom, but rather, on the information available. Libraries and bookstores became my sanctuaries. Reason, commonsense and perseverance were my vehicles, as I moved from the dawn of man's consciousness and his place in the cosmos, to reflections on the present day.

My articles and books are the chronicles of my literary journey, told from a person of African ancestry who learned not only to love his race but the human race as well. In the final analysis, the only race that we should be concerned about is not one of color, but instead, the race to save humanity.

Richard Lawson Singley

A NEW PERSPECTIVE

RETHINKING THE HISTORY AND MYTHS OF THE PAST

Abraham Lincoln and the Civil War

A NEW PERSPECTIVE

RETHINKING THE HISTORY AND MYTHS OF THE PAST

Abraham Lincoln and the Hope for America

March on Washington, August 28, 1963 (Library of Congress)

What's past is prologue. The Civil War was more than a nineteenth-century epic encounter; it was the gateway to America's prosperity and greatness. Though we have laid down our swords and shields, we have yet to lay down our burdens—we are still fighting the Civil War. It is most unfortunate that there is so much that we can learn from the Civil War if only we would stop fighting it.

Abraham Lincoln and the Civil War are inextricably linked and etched into our collective memory. Because of this inseparable link, it is nearly impossible to discuss one without the other. The Civil War's oft description as the "American Iliad" testifies to its enduring mystique as a fratricidal war. While the graveyard of history is littered with civil wars, the American Civil War not only transformed a nation but christened the world into modernity by decisively resolving the issue of slavery.

We have draped in the cloth of myth and, at times, canonized America's sixteenth president. But if we are to be true to ourselves for the sake of posterity and the good of the nation, we must not look to angels and saints to adorn this earth with their wings and halos but rather look within ourselves and learn from the prologue of our past. To better face the torrents of our times, we must honestly assess the American president behind the Civil War and the truth of why we created—and needed—the myth of Abraham Lincoln.

A NEW PERSPECTIVE

The story of Abraham Lincoln is one of mythological proportions. Born poor in the back roads of a young nation, he emerged from the wilderness to become America's greatest president. He was the first president not born in the original thirteen colonies and the first to be assassinated. F. Scott Fitzgerald, the author of *The Great Gatsby*, once wrote, "Show me a hero and I will write you a tragedy;" like most martyrs, in death, he became larger than in life. He became the icon of an age to which he belonged and a seminal figure to which future presidents would aspire.

Although all American presidents are endowed with the responsibilities of commander-in-chief, Lincoln was the first to truly embrace that mantle—the first, many argue, to define the role of the modern presidency. Father Abraham, as he was so often called, was not a Founding Father but the heir apparent—indeed, the son—of the Founding Fathers. And while the founders had enshrined a system of government in the Constitution, they deliberately postponed the issue of slavery for another day.

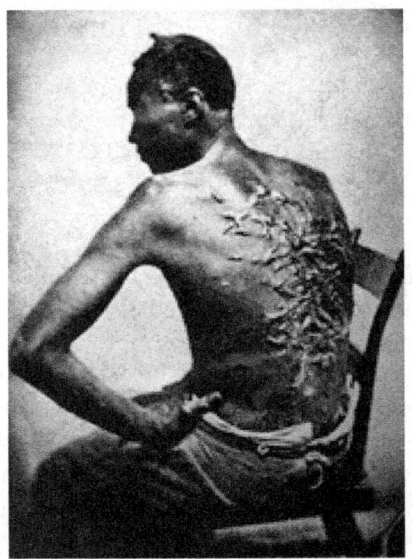

Gordon, a Louisiana slave, 1863 (National Archives)

By the time Lincoln came of age, the scourge of slavery and all that it entailed had muddied the waters of a hypocritical nation, mired in sin. The United States had professed ideals and beliefs that were antithetical to its actions to such an extent that the nation, as it stood, could no longer endure. The reckoning of such hypocrisy was the true cause of the Civil War. Lincoln believed, however, that even if "every drop of

RETHINKING THE HISTORY AND MYTHS OF THE PAST

blood drawn [should] be paid by another drawn with the sword," justice, in the eyes of God, would still not have been served.

In his display of character, Lincoln set a precedent of moral leadership to which all those who would take the highest office in the land would be compared. Though clothed in immense power as president, he never put himself over the good of the nation. In *Presidents of War*, historian Michael Beschloss recounts one among many such stories:

One evening, a few weeks after Ball's Bluff, Lincoln and his Secretary of State, William Seward, came to see him and were told that the General was out. They waited for an hour; when McClellan arrived, he went upstairs and let his visitors wait for another half hour before having them informed that he had gone to bed. "Better at this time not to be making points of etiquette and personal dignity," Lincoln told John Hay. "I will hold McClellan's horse if he will only bring us success."

Lincoln and McClellan at Antietam, September 1862 (Library of Congress)

Lincoln possessed an extraordinary capacity to show strength and humility in dire circumstances. Reserving judgment until the end, he listened closely to different points of view, including those he did not agree with. He applied his wit, sharp as a knife and cutting through any situation, to defuse tensions or to emphasize a point. He was always willing to share credit for his successes with others but also to take the blame for their failures. Above all, he controlled his emotions in the most dire straits to comfort a nation at war.

A NEW PERSPECTIVE

Throughout his public life, he mingled freely with the common folk. With a soft but clear voice, he spoke to their hearts and minds, often employing stories from his life as allegories to a more profound meaning. During the war, he visited the sick and wounded and wrote compassionate letters to the families of those that gave to the nation their "last full measure of devotion." Despite his meteoric rise to the highest office in the land, he never forgot where he had come from nor where the nation had to go.

Lincoln's political and strategic genius, for which generations have admired him, was the product of a leader who was not ignorant of his own ignorance. Amidst the maelstrom of the war, whose early catastrophes challenged his competence as commander-in-chief, Lincoln exploited every available resource to remedy his inexperience. A veteran autodidact, who had studied on his own to become a lawyer, he diligently examined all manner of knowledge, from firsthand accounts of soldiers to the wealth of literature in the Library of Congress, to gain a complete strategic and tactical understanding of the conflict through which he was to lead the nation.

To ensure that he retained a diversity of honest opinions, he kept advisers who not only openly opposed each other but also not so secretly opposed him. He deliberately chose not to correct his cabinet members' impression, many who boasted of their pedigree from America's upper classes, that he was little more than a rail-splitting prairie lawyer, who would only act as a figurehead which they could undermine for their political ambitions. But at critical junctures, Lincoln abandoned his homely facade to reveal exactly who was being manipulated: when he refused to accept the resignations of his cabinet secretaries Seward and Chase, Lincoln delivered a blunt reminder, with an illustration harking to his childhood in rural Indiana, that they were merely pumpkins to be balanced at each end of his saddlebag.

We revere Abraham Lincoln for his genius with words, which resonate through the ages. We remember his speeches, through which he addressed a nation divided North and South, not only for their clarity but for their reverence, worthy of a Homeric poem, for his allusions and for his audience. Sworn into a presidency which, within weeks, would be consumed by civil strife, he ended his First Inaugural Address with the following invocation:

We are not enemies, but friends. We must not be enemies. Though passion may have strained it must not break our bonds of affection. The mystic chords of memory, stretching from every battlefield and patriot grave to every living heart and hearthstone all over this broad land, will yet swell the chorus of the Union, when again touched, as surely they will be, by the better angels of our nature.

RETHINKING THE HISTORY AND MYTHS OF THE PAST

By evoking in the phrase "better angels" the figurative language of Shakespeare and the Bible, two cornerstones of his life-long love of literature, Lincoln elevated his speech to a spiritual plane. Painting for the audience a picture of understanding, he employed, as he often did, his gift for metaphors to be subtle and succinct all at once.

Lincoln's two-minute address at Gettysburg two years later completely overshadowed Edward Everett's two-hour oration. Both speakers compared the American Civil War to the Peloponnesian War of Ancient Greece as a conflict to defend their country's character. Everett's analysis was stark and overbearing and spoke to the intelligentsia. Lincoln, a smith of words, simply invoked the sentiment of Pericles's funeral oration and directly called on the people to preserve the United States as a "government of the people, by the people, and for the people."

In the stories we tell and his words we quote, we see how the myth of Lincoln has held Americans spellbound generation after generation. But it is when we peek behind the mythic veil that we glimpse a portrait of a man who is inconsistent with his myth, a man whom Stephen A. Douglas had once accused as being "two-faced." African-American historian W. E. B. Du Bois would later characterize Lincoln as a man big enough to be inconsistent: "Cruel, merciful; peace-loving, a fighter; despising Negroes and letting them fight and vote; protecting slavery and freeing slaves. He was a man—a big, inconsistent, brave man.*"*

The pages of history reveal that Abraham Lincoln is a riddle wrapped up in an enigma. He struggled throughout his life with severe bouts of depression, and he was married to a woman whose behavior, at times, bordered on insanity. Yet he never lost his clarity of purpose in preserving the union and upholding the idealistic vision of the Founding Fathers. He had been called Honest Abe since childhood and was renowned for his diligence in his duty (As Lincoln once described himself, he walked slowly but never backward). As president, however, one of the few consistent threads in his web of thinking was pragmatism.

Through his life experiences and quest for knowledge, he became the embodiment of Plato's philosopher-king perhaps not seen since the days of Marcus Aurelius. But behind the homely image of his stovepipe hat and deep-set eyes was a mind that could be tyrannical, draconian, even Machiavellian. In an action as a great stain to his legacy, he arrested members of the Maryland legislature to prevent them from voting to secede from the Union by arrogating, on account of a burgeoning war, the exclusively congressional powers of suspending habeas corpus.

Lincoln was a man who understood his times so well but was so misunderstood in his time. Save for his Second Inaugural Address, the end of the Civil War, and the

A NEW PERSPECTIVE

passage of the Thirteenth Amendment, the monumental accomplishments that characterized his presidency were largely made before the election of 1864. Yet in 1864, the country was so uncertain about his leadership that his second term was anything but guaranteed. It was only after his tragic death and the retrospect of ages that the picture of the man, and the nature of his genius, began to emerge.

Today his herculean achievements continue to have great resonance in what has come to define America. Amid the strife of civil war, he established the Transcontinental Railroad, the Congressional Medal of Honor, the first federal income tax, the issuing of greenback dollars, a college for the deaf, and Thanksgiving as a national holiday. But over a century and a half after his death, the enigma persists, and the puzzle remains incomplete. Over sixteen-thousand books have been written about Lincoln, more than any other person in history except Christ. Many, including those looking inward from faraway lands, have sought the hidden secrets of his mystique and allure.

But when the British author Jan Morris went in search of the sixteenth president of America, she instead discovered a greater understanding of America. In the centennial of Lincoln's birth, Leo Tolstoy, the Russian author of *War and Peace,* wrote:

Of all the great national heroes and statesmen of history, Lincoln is the only real giant... Lincoln was a man of whom a nation has a right to be proud; he was a Christ in miniature, a saint of humanity, whose name will live thousands of years in the legends of future generations.

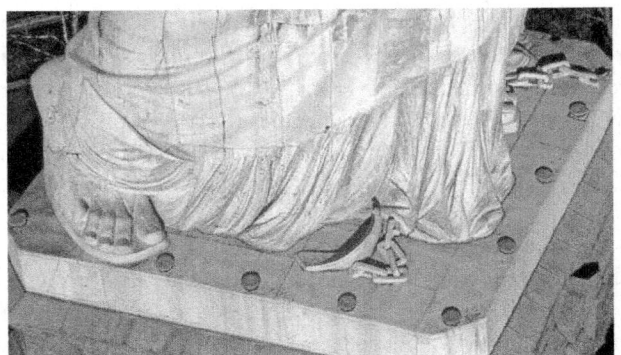

Chain and Shackles at the feet of the Statue of Liberty (National Park Service)

After the abolition of slavery, Lincoln became synonymous with America to many across the world. They saw, as Lincoln did, that by granting freedom to the slave, America had assured it to the free. France was so enamored with Lincoln that in 1886 it gifted a Statue of Liberty—a burning torch as a symbol of American freedom and

RETHINKING THE HISTORY AND MYTHS OF THE PAST

democracy in one hand, and in the other, according to French sculptor Frédéric-Auguste Bartholdi's original design, a broken chain commemorating the eradication of slavery (Fearing that he would lose the critical support of his American financiers, Bartholdi ultimately relegated the chain and broken shackle to the statue's feet, which we can observe today). The world began to look at America as a beacon of hope or perhaps, as Lincoln himself once said, "the last best hope of earth."

The veneration of Lincoln as the Great Emancipator, however, came to overshadow a more candid perspective of the man behind the American myth. More than anyone, Lincoln was knowledgeable of the frailties of man and the judgment of history upon his failures. Yet in folklore and in legend, Lincoln had borne the cross of the nation's sins through which the nation was cleansed and resurrected (Of the many analogies made between him and Christ, the one most noted is that they both died on Good Friday). But the narratives that dared to remove his saintly robes, especially those written by his law partner William Herndon and Elizabeth Keckley, Mary Lincoln's friend and confidante, were heavily criticized and fell on deaf ears.

History attests to the danger of myth when it is mistaken for the truth, and quite often, a myth is exploited in the service of one group at the expense of another. The Radical Republicans, wearing the blood of a martyred president, used the myth of Lincoln to propel the passage of the reconstruction amendments, which laid down the constitutional protections of former slaves. Others, in need of a pretext, used the myth of Lincoln to equate emancipation with equality and usher in nearly a century of Jim Crow. The plagues of "separate but equal," literacy tests, and black codes, reversed the gains achieved by the 14th and 15th amendment, stripping the laws of all its power.

But when Martin Luther King, Jr. delivered his *I Have a Dream* speech in 1963, he invoked the myth of Lincoln once again. At the steps of the Lincoln Memorial, with the likeness of America's sixteenth president behind him, King alluded to the promissory note issued to African-Americans "that all men, ...black men as well as white men, would be guaranteed the inalienable rights of life, liberty, and the pursuit of happiness." The promissory note embodied America's legacy of injustice and the Emancipation Proclamation and the constitutional amendments that should have addressed that injustice for good. The note, signed by Lincoln a century before the March on Washington, had been returned, time and time again.

But on that hot day in August 1963, Americans; from sea to shining sea; of all religions, colors, and creeds; marched together, arm and arm, to demand immediate payment. To the disenfranchised masses clamoring for the restoration of their civil rights, the myth of Lincoln served, once more, as a symbol of the hope that would

A NEW PERSPECTIVE

christen the nation into the future. The civil rights movement, which had galvanized a generation, would struggle to complete, "the unfinished business of the Civil War." The descendants of the freed slaves, joined by their allies, called upon the nation to cleanse itself once more of its sins to assure the equality for all.

March on Washington, August 28, 1963 (National Archives)

Today, the United States is a cosmopolitan melting pot, a microcosm of the world. Perhaps more than any other on this earth, we are a nation constituted of people of every religion, creed, and color—forged together out of many as one, as the Great Seal of the United States attests in *E pluribus unum*. Despite our shortcomings, we continue to represent, echoing the vision John Winthrop and the puritans hoped America would be, "a city upon a hill."

Yet it was Lincoln who declared that a house divided against itself cannot stand. He warned that "if destruction be our lot, we must ourselves be its author and finisher. As a nation of freemen, we must live through all time, or die by suicide. More than anyone, Lincoln was aware of the frailties of man and the judgment of history against those who succumb to them. As the face of America continues to change, the warts of slavery, prejudice, and injustice remain visible. The struggle for true equality continues to this day; the civil war, in muted skirmishes, is still being waged.

In the temple of the Lincoln Memorial, we have seated the sixteenth president as the oracle of a more perfect union. But the depiction of the man in the marble figure is as likely to be profound as the depiction in his myth. When we examine Lincoln's true face in the pages of history, we observe, reflecting his own, the face of the nation. We see the flaws that undermine an expressed commitment to equality and justice for all, yet we also see the tenacity to endeavor to persevere, the ability to overcome obstacles, and the capacity to lead in times of great strife—the enduring story of America.

RETHINKING THE HISTORY AND MYTHS OF THE PAST

If we are to truly assume the mantle as *the last best hope of the earth*, if we are to embody, as President Ronald Reagan reiterated three-and-a-half centuries later, a shining "city on a hill," we must first see the myth of Lincoln for what it is—a myth. Though the power of myth may be formidable and enchanting, it is necessary that we speak truth to that power. For us to carry on the inspirational legacy of Lincoln into the future, we must bravely face the truth of our past and the imperfect nature of the enigmatic man that has bridged the past to the present. Only then, in the immortal words of America's greatest president, may we embrace, "with malice toward none and charity toward all," the better angels of our nature.

A NEW PERSPECTIVE

RETHINKING THE HISTORY AND MYTHS OF THE PAST

Abraham Lincoln and Emancipation

First Reading of the Emancipation Proclamation of President Lincoln
by Francis Bicknell Carpenter (1864)

In 1889, William Herndon, Abraham Lincoln's close friend and law partner at Springfield, published a three-volume biography on Lincoln, which would provide one of history's most brutally honest contemporaneous accounts of America's sixteenth president. Many years in the making, it was a work borne out of Herndon's repulsion that the American public had effectively deified the slain president as a martyr and out of the fear that the memory of Lincoln, the man, would be forever lost, dwarfed by the stature of Lincoln, the myth.

In the biography's preface, he wrote:

If the story of his life is truthfully and courageously told—nothing colored or suppressed; nothing false either written or suggested—the reader will see and feel the presence of the living man…, live with him and be moved to think and act with him.

If, on the other hand, the story is colored or the facts in any degree suppressed, the reader will be not only misled, but imposed upon as well. At last the truth will come, and no man need hope to evade it.

Following this spirit, let us, but for a moment, take a look – truthfully and courageously – at the issuing of the Emancipation Proclamation and the circumstances that compelled it.

A NEW PERSPECTIVE

The Great Emancipator?
Abraham Lincoln is known as "the Great Emancipator," but is such a title an applicable moniker or a misnomer?

As American students, we were fervently taught that he had issued the Emancipation Proclamation, effective January 1, 1863, but what did that proclamation proclaim? It was announced on September 22, 1862, five days after the battle at Antietam, giving the South 100 days to return to the Union or to lose its slaves.

Abe Lincoln's Last Card: Or, Rouge-et-Noir (Red and Black)", a cartoon by John Tenniel printed by *Punch* after the *London Times* wrote in October 1862 that Lincoln had played his "last card" in issuing the Proclamation

Several historians point out the ambiguity and double-talk of the document: "…shall be then, thenceforward, and forever free." Lincoln knew he had no such power to make this statement without a Constitutional amendment. If ever there was a document that had the devil in its details, this was it. Not a single slave in any state was freed by the Emancipation Proclamation. They were only freed once each individual state decided to free its slaves, which culminated in the ratification of the thirteenth amendment on December 6, 1865. So, the sting of the whip felt the same in Maryland on New Year's Day of 1863 as it did scores and scores of years before.

The paradoxical nature of this document was recognized by those who understood its true intent, its meaning, and the circumstances in which it *had* to be released. Karl Marx reported in a European newspaper, to an audience who could consider the conflict more objectively, that it was a summons sent by one lawyer to another. At home, perhaps Secretary of State William H. Seward said it best, "We show our

RETHINKING THE HISTORY AND MYTHS OF THE PAST

sympathy with slavery by emancipating slaves where we cannot reach them and holding them in bondage where we can set them free."

In effect, the proclamation was a warning shot fired at the South and a signal to Europe not to intercede in the war on behalf of the South. Lincoln said on many occasions that he was not for eradicating slavery where it presently existed but that he was against the expansion of slavery into western territories. This distinction is seldom emphasized in history, but the vicissitudes of the war made Lincoln's former point subordinate to the latter. Contrary to popular opinion, he never claimed to be an abolitionist, and he scorned abolitionists such as John Brown.

The American Civil War was a war fought against the expansion of slavery into the territories acquired after the Mexican-American War. It was not about the moral rectitude of Lincoln or the North. Although he personally found slavery abhorrent, he believed in the innate superiority of the white race. His paramount goal was not the freedom of over four million black slaves but to save the Union at all costs. He once said:

My paramount object in this struggle is to save the Union, and it is not either to save or destroy slavery. If I could save the Union without freeing any slave I would do it; and if I could save it by freeing all the slaves, I would do it; and if I could save it by freeing some and leaving others alone, I would do that. What I do about slavery and the colored race I do because I believe it helps to save the Union, and whatever I forbear, I forbear because I do not believe it would help to save the Union.

In fact, Lincoln vehemently pursued the deportation of people of African descent, until it proved to be too impractical to implement. As a scion of Henry Clay, Lincoln viewed deportation as a method of purging the United States of its blackness and its original sin. Furthermore, he did not believe in the miscegenation of the races nor the equality of the races. For example, he thought that paying white Union soldiers more than black soldiers was fair. This position angered many prominent blacks: Harriet Tubman was so outraged over it that she refused an invitation to the White House. Indeed, Lincoln is quoted as saying publicly:

I am not, nor ever have I been, in favor of bringing about in any way the social and political equality of the white and black races… I as much as any man is in favor of having the superior position assigned to the white race.

In the end, like most of his contemporaries, he placed white people above all other races. In fact, one of the reasons why Lincoln opposed slavery and its spread into territories to the west was that he believed slavery served as a catalyst for

A NEW PERSPECTIVE

miscegenation, which thereby would pass on the superior white intelligence to an inferior black race.

Aftermath
Within ten years after his death, Lincoln's persona had migrated from a hero to a saint. And so, began the legend of the black race being freed by his merciful hand, and the resemblance of the man was eradicated by myth, as best exemplified by the Emancipation Memorial Statue located in Washington, DC. At the unveiling of the statue on April 14, 1876, the centennial year of the Declaration of Independence and the eleventh anniversary of his death, Frederick Douglass, a man who had several candid conversations with Lincoln and knew him well, said the following in front of President Grant, Supreme Court Justices, and members of Congress:

Lincoln Park, Capitol Hill—Library of Congress

It must be admitted, truth compels me to admit, even here in the presence of the monument we have erected to his memory, Abraham Lincoln was not, in the fullest sense of the word, either our man or our model. In his interests, in his associations, in his habits of thought, and in his prejudices, he was a white man. He was preeminently the white man's President, entirely devoted to the welfare of white men.

Life is full of ironies. The person portrayed in the statue was a runaway slave Archer Alexander, the last fugitive slave captured in Missouri. Ironically, his emancipation had been declared by John Fremont, only to have Fremont's proclamation revoked by

RETHINKING THE HISTORY AND MYTHS OF THE PAST

Abraham Lincoln, thus taking away Alexander's freedom and shackling him back into bondage.

Moreover, if Lincoln would have lived to serve a second term, his views on equality for black people may not have been any different from the Jim Crow South of the Gilded Age. In fact, if the South had offered him such a deal in those 100 days between the issuing and effective dates of the Emancipation Proclamation, America's sixteenth president would probably have been elated.

Lincoln's views on slavery are well documented, but his views on equality for all black people remain hidden behind the veil of his desire to place the white man first—and everyone else second. Although he now belongs to the ages, let's not forget that he was a man of his times and not judge him by our times. Like the Founding Fathers of the United States and most white men of the post-Columbian era, he believed in the innate superiority of the white race, and there was nothing in his collective experience to alter such a view. Above all, he was a pragmatist and therefore did not truly believe in the Jeffersonian declaration that all men are created equal but instead believed that some men are more equal than others.

A NEW PERSPECTIVE

RETHINKING THE HISTORY AND MYTHS OF THE PAST

West Point and the Civil War

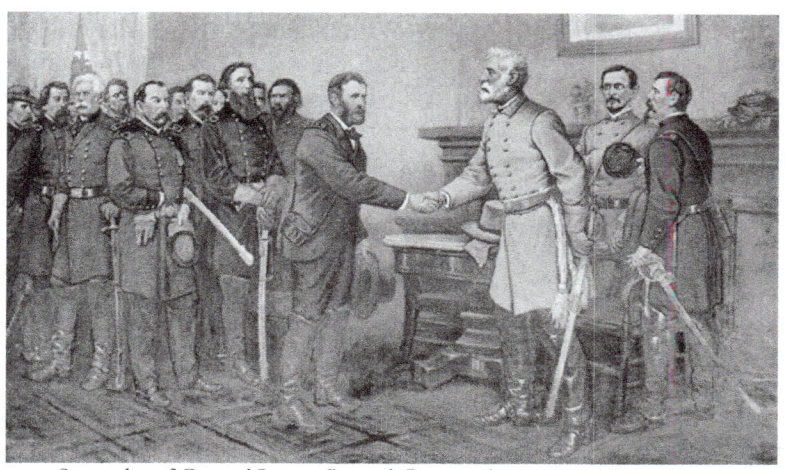

Surrender of General Lee to General Grant at Appomattox Court House

Many scholars of military history call the first two decades before the Civil War the "Golden Age" of West Point. Indeed, it was a transitional period from civilians that were directly commissioned and rose through the ranks into a professionally trained army. By the beginning of the Civil War, 75 percent of the officers were West Point graduates. The Civil War is often referred to as the first modern war. It was the largest war ever fought in the Western Hemisphere and it established the military traditions of West Point.

West Point

Located on the high west bank of New York's Hudson River and established by Thomas Jefferson in 1802, West Point was the site of a Revolutionary-War fort built to defend the Hudson River Valley from British attack. The commander of the fort was Benedict Arnold, America's most notorious traitor. Under his command was another famed American, Aaron Burr, who later was also labeled a traitor. West Point was conceived to be more than the nation's military institution. Jefferson was a man of science and he appointed Ben Franklin's grandnephew, Major Jonathan Williams, as the first superintendent with the instructions to emphasize science. Over the years, West Point had one of the best engineering schools in the world and it was from these seeds that the military tradition of the United States was established.

A NEW PERSPECTIVE

There was a cadet appointed from each congressional district along with some at-large appointees. Although all cadets were treated equally and abided by the same set of rules, some had advantages over others. Those from affluent families and educated at private schools such as McClellan and Lee were better prepared academically than those such as Grant and Stonewall Jackson that received only a basic education. Throughout the years, the curriculum and tradition of West Point matured. The academy was somewhat modeled after the French in general and Napoleon in particular. So much so that French was a required course for at least the first two years so that American officers could converse with French officers. Although in existence for decades, it was at the onset of the Mexican-American War that West Point began to come of age.

By the time of the Civil War, many of its cadets had been seasoned by the Mexican-American War. They had shed blood together on the battlefields as brothers of a sacred fraternity of men bound together by a Revolutionary War fort transformed into an institution of higher learning and honor. West Point made the Civil War, and the Civil War made West Point.

Because of the emphasis of professional soldiers, both the North and the South sent their future military leaders to this distinguished military academy. The military and engineering prowess displayed during the Civil War would become part of the culture ingrained in the nation. West Point was a revolving door, where every four years new bonds were formed that became links in a chain of brotherhood that stretched for decades. Friendship was also stretched across the blue and the gray as fellow West Pointers and comrades of the Mexican-American War were divided by the war. To what extent friendships both severed and maintained impacted the war effort is a question still unanswered.

Duty, Honor, Country—those hallowed words were ingrained in every cadet, but they struggled with which country that they would be loyal to. Secession came at a high price for the cadets and graduates of this noble military institution as many of them were forced to choose sides. This was extremely difficult to do amid an environment that thrived off comradeship and duty to each other. Few of them wanted war, but all would answer the call of duty if necessary. Although the enemy of my enemy is my friend has proven to be a wartime aphorism, in this case, the Civil War created enemies that had mutual friends and were friends among each other. The breakup of the band of brothers at West Point initiated a schism, not between maternal but fraternal brothers.

RETHINKING THE HISTORY AND MYTHS OF THE PAST

The Civil War

Unlike the Greek Peloponnesian War, which has gone down in the annals of history as the quintessential civil war, the Athenians and the Spartans had fought together against the Persians, but they did not train together. Therefore, personal relationships did not develop among the soldiers on opposite sides. On the contrary, from the beginning of the American Civil War, friendships were broken by an ideological line drawn in the sand that separated the North from the South.

The Civil War started with one West Pointer firing on another. On April 12, 1861, at Fort Sumter in Charleston, South Carolina, General P.G.T. Beauregard (Class of 1838), the former but temporal superintendent at West Point, attacked the Union commander at Fort Sumter Major Robert Anderson (Class of 1825), an Academy graduate who was an artillery instructor at West Point. Among Anderson's students were Beauregard (who became his assistant), Sherman, Bragg, McDowell, Meade, Hooker, and Early.

Fort Sumter 1861; flying the Confederate Flag

Furthermore, the men at West Point, for the most part, were taught by the same instructors in the strategies and tactics of war and it was not unusual for former cadets to oppose their instructors and former superintendents on the battlefield. For example, at the battle of Gettysburg, Union Brigadier General Henry J. Hunt later criticized the firing of one of his Confederate students and stated that his firing did not do justice to his instruction.

Ulysses "Sam" Grant (Class of 1843) and James "Pete" Longstreet (Class of 1842) were good friends at West Point. Grant was married to a distant relative of "Old Pete" as Longstreet would be later called. Longstreet went on to become Lee's second in command and Grant, Lee's nemesis. Yet, Longstreet and Grant remained close. One of the first things that the two did after Lee's surrender was to meet together, not

A NEW PERSPECTIVE

as enemies, but as friends. At the end of the war, Grant signed Longstreet's name to a pardon list after Longstreet refused to sign citing: he had done nothing wrong in defending his state.

Another close friend of Grant's was Simon Bolivar Buckner (Class of 1844) whose union with Grant was less pleasant as he was captured by Grant and became a prisoner of war. As the commanding officer at Fort Donelson, he asked Grant for terms of surrender, in which Grant replied those words that have echoed through history: "No terms except unconditional and immediate surrender can be accepted."

Ulysses Simpson Grant, 18th president of the United States

Battlefields of war, although long for men, are short terrains for fate. And once again it brought former classmates together on opposite sides. General George Armstrong Custer (Class of 1861) captured James Washington one of his classmates at West Point and they were photographed with each wearing different uniforms. Custer was one of the most popular cadets at West Point and he accumulated near-record demerits while at the Academy. During the Civil War, his popularity continued with his fellow Union soldiers and Confederates alike. As surrender talks were ongoing between Lee and Grant, Custer was likewise united with his West Point friend Robert V. Cowan now a member of the Confederacy.

During a battle between Union and Confederates, Custer sent a message to one of his Confederate friends not to expose himself so much in battle for fear of his life. Custer, like Pickett, (Class of 1846) graduated last in his class, yet he was the only one from his class to become a general. What is most ironic is that cavalry tactics was one of his worst courses. He would become one of the youngest generals in the Union army and his commanding officer, Phil Sheridan (Class of 1853) admired him so

RETHINKING THE HISTORY AND MYTHS OF THE PAST

much that he brought the table that Lee signed his surrender on and gave it to Custer as a sign of his appreciation.

A flamboyant soldier that designed his uniform, his post-Civil War demise at the Battle of the Little Big Horn still shines through the clouds of posterity. Custer loved the military and revered his time at the academy so much that he chose West Point as his final resting place.

General Custer and James Washington

There were some bonds of friendship that were not divided by the war. Early in the war, Sherman (Class of 1840) had helped to persuade one of his old West Point friends George Thomas (Class of 1840) a Virginian to abandon his state and to fight for the Union. Thomas paid a heavy price for his loyalty to the Union as he was ostracized by members of his family. As a child, Thomas' family had to move because of events stemming from the Nat Turner rebellion and some of them never forgot it. Yet, Thomas "known as the Rock of Chickamauga" became one of the Union's most successful and respected generals.

Likewise, Robert E. Lee (Class of 1829) and Jefferson Davis (Class of 1828) were at West Point together and during the war, they shared a close relationship. Joseph E. Johnston was also in the same class as Robert E. Lee. Davis: however, disliked and distrusted Johnston, a person that Grant thought was one of the most competent Southern generals. Some historians say that the feud between the two started at West Point over a girl, others say it happened while Jefferson Davis was Secretary of War.

A NEW PERSPECTIVE

One thing for certain is that the two did not like each other. Jefferson Davis was also at West Point with Albert Sydney Johnston (Class of 1826) and shared an amicable relationship with him. Yet, others parted peacefully and respectfully never to see each other again or to meet briefly on the field of battle. Robert E. Lee and George Meade (Class of 1835) faced each other at Gettysburg but were old friends from the Engineering Corps.

Jefferson Davis president of the Confederacy

Just before the start of the Civil War, Winfield Scott Hancock (Class of 1844) who also fought at Gettysburg held a dinner at his house with his West Point and Mexican War friends that would soon join the Confederacy. Among the guests were George Pickett, Dick Garnett (Class of 1841), and Lewis Armistead. They would all meet again on the battlefield at Gettysburg. Hancock would be seriously wounded; Armistead and Garnett would be killed, and Pickett's charge would go down in history as the most failed blunder of Gettysburg if not the war. Pickett was also good friends with George McClellan and Stonewall Jackson who were also members of their West Point Class of 1846 as was Jesse Reno from which the city in Nevada derived its name.

Like many West Pointers, McClellan had other friends that wore the gray uniform as he and A.P. Hill (Class of 1847) were roommates and both dated the same woman who eventually became McClellan's wife. McClellan would face his former roommate on the battlefields as the war turned friends into enemies. Also, good friends of Hill and McClellan at West Point were Henry Heth (Class of 1847) and Ambrose Burnside (Class of 1847). Burnside was popular with many Confederate soldiers. When he was

RETHINKING THE HISTORY AND MYTHS OF THE PAST

blamed for the loss at Fredericksburg, many Confederates felt sorry for him. After the war, Heth, a Confederate General and Burnside had a lasting friendship. In fact, Burnside lent Heth money to get back on his feet.

George McClellan also known as Little Mac

Robert E. Lee had a propensity to place West Pointers and Virginians in command of his forces. After Stonewall Jackson died of a wound that resulted from being shot by one of his men, Lee divided his army into three corps with A.P. Hill, Longstreet and Richard Ewell (Class of 1854) as corps commanders. Unlike McClellan, A.P. Hill was known for his courage on the battlefield and both Robert E. Lee and Stonewall Jackson in their delirium call for him on their deathbeds. McClellan would survive the war, but A. P. Hill would not be as fortunate. He died on April 2, 1865, less than a week before the war ended. He was the last Confederate West Point general to die in the war.

The West Point nepotism was apparent within Lee's ranks and not all of the West Pointers got along. For example, Armstead was expelled from West Point for breaking a plate over the head of Jubal Early (Class of 1837). Both became generals in Lee's army but the animosity between the two persisted during the Civil War. Similarly, A.P. Hill did not care much for Stonewall Jackson. Hill compared Jackson to a slumbering volcano that might erupt and wreak havoc at any moment. Lee often had to serve as an arbitrator between his generals. Competition was also fierce among West Pointers. During the war, some underclassmen at the academy became superior officers to upperclassmen. Yet, West Point remained an exclusive club on both sides

A NEW PERSPECTIVE

during and after the war. Some classes produced more generals than others. The class of 1846 was much like the later class of 1915, "The Class the Stars Fell On." The senior cadets had felt the winds of war breeze by them as the War with Mexico started in that same year. For many of that class, it was indeed baptism by fire. Forty–four of fifty-eight graduates would go on to fight in the Civil War.

The classroom was one thing, but the battlefield was another. For example, Pickett who was last in his class proved to be a much better soldier than Charles Seaforth Stewart who was first in his Class of 1846. Stewart never became a general and like many of his classmates would eventually serve under George McClellan the cadet that finished second to him. McClellan was viewed as the cream of the crop. Six classmates served under him in the Army of the Potomac as generals: Reno, Couch, Seymour, Sturgis, Stoneman and Gordon. Four fought against him as generals in the Army of Northern Virginia: Jones, Wilcox, Pickett and Jackson (A.P. Hill fell to the class of 47 because of an illness). Of the future generals in other classes at West Point during McClellan's years there, 19 served under him including Franklin, Burnside, Hancock, Smith, Stone, Gibbon and Pleasonton.

This class fought in three wars and produced 20 generals. Also, at the academy around that time were: Longstreet (Class of 1842), Sherman (Class of 1840), Grant (Class of 1843), William B. Franklin (Class of 1843) Richard Ewell, (Class of 1840) George Thomas (Class of 1840) and William Rosecrans (Class of 1842). Grant's class of 1843 also produced 20 generals although they were not as distinguished as the class of 1846. Most of these men served together in the Mexican-American War or the Indian Wars of the 1850s where bonds of friendship were further enhanced.

There were bonds of friendship of which war or time could not shatter. For instance, James McPherson (Class of 1853) graduated number one in his class and was the protégé of Sherman and Grant. Generals on both sides were deeply saddened by his death. Grant stated, "In his death the army lost one of its ablest, purest and best generals." Sherman echoed these sentiments when he stated, "I have seen [McPherson], in danger, in battle when every muscle and every tissue was in full action, when his heroic qualities shone out as a star in the darkest night."

Confederate General John Bell Hood (Class of 1853) the opposing general was a classmate and roommate of McPherson. McPherson, a brilliant student, tutored Hood and helped him get through West Point. Hood lamented:

"I will record the death of my classmate and boyhood friend, General James B. McPherson, the announcement of which caused me sincere sorrow…the attachment formed in early youth was strengthened by my admiration and gratitude for his conduct toward our people in the vicinity of Vicksburg."

RETHINKING THE HISTORY AND MYTHS OF THE PAST

McPherson was one of those rare people that was not only a good student and soldier but also exhibited those rare charismatic traits of leadership that would have made him a promising political figure. McPherson Square in Washington DC is named in his honor. It is important to note that all of the outside Civil War statues in Washington DC are monuments of Union soldiers—with the exception of Albert Pike who does not appear in uniform and is honored for his contributions to Freemasonry and not his actions during the Civil War.

James McPherson (November 14, 1828—July 22, 1864)

Philip Sheridan (Class of 1853) and John M. Schofield (Class of 1853) were also classmates of McPherson. Moreover, any cadet at West Point between the years of (1852–1855) would have had Robert E. Lee as their superintendent. As superintendent, Lee almost expelled Hood from West Point. Lee, like McPherson and McClellan, was an exemplary student graduating second in his class. While a cadet at West Point, Lee did not receive one demerit, a record that cannot be broken. In the minds of many of the cadets that went off to war, both North and South, Lee was the soldier's soldier. Such was the indelible stamps that West Point placed on its graduates.

The degree of which friendships and relationships established before the war, impacted the actions of the Civil War, has not been calculated and may be incalculable. For example, did Jefferson Davis' good relationship with Lee and dislike of J.E. Johnston impair his judgment? How valuable was the friendship between Lee and William Nelson Pendleton (Class of 1830) a clergyman, Virginian and West

A NEW PERSPECTIVE

Pointer? Pendleton provided spiritual counsel to Lee. Even though as an artillery commander he was mediocre at best, he was someone that Lee could speak candidly with and reveal his emotions and inner thoughts. Likewise, if Thomas and Sherman were not good friends would Thomas have fought for the South?

Robert E. Lee, Commander of the Army of Virginia

The circumstances of this war made it unique as a good friend may have been your foe and your comrade someone that you detested because of relationships forged before the war. In, *The Art of War*, Sun Tzu wrote: "Know thy self, know thy enemy; a thousand battles, a thousand victories." Grant said that his moves were often predicated by what he knew about his enemies and that some of the generals of the Civil War lost focus because of their relationships and split affinities during the war.

For instance, some of the Confederate West Pointers may not have liked the specter of treason that came along with secession, and some Union West Pointers may have believed in state rights but viewed secession as treason. If Lincoln was not immune to the personal sympathies of war, best exemplified by having his sister-in-law, a known Confederate sympathizer staying in the White House with him; how could he expect those on the battlefield that had friends on the other side not to be sympathetic to their friends? This was part of the fog of war that transcended the battlefield and into the homes and hearts of the American people.

RETHINKING THE HISTORY AND MYTHS OF THE PAST

During the Civil War, 286 West Pointers including 19 born in the North joined the Confederate ranks. It was truly a unique case of men being bonded by the fraternity of arms yet divided by the duty of war. Very few of the West Pointers wanted to see the disagreement between the North and the South come to war. In this regard, they were like children not wanting to see their parents' divorce because they loved them both. Few times in history have so many friends become enemies in such a short period, not because of their own doing, frailties or shortcomings but because duty pulled on them from different directions. The blood and treasure of the Civil War were painfully obvious. However, hidden amid the blood was the blood of family members and dear friends, forced into battle against each other by the fortunes of war. These are the invisible strings of the puppet master known as fate.

Time heals most wounds, yet the memories of the war and those friends that paid the ultimate price were invisible wounds undress by time. Such were the consequences of the Civil War that stretched, broke and bound the chains of friendship. After the war, there was union among West Pointers that fought on opposite sides. Some Confederates regretted raising arms against their country and others would fight for it again. Former Confederate Generals Joseph Wheeler (Class of 1859) and Fitzhugh Lee (Class 0f 1856) served in the Spanish-American War in 1898.

Sherman, the man that made Georgia howl

Sherman and J.E. Johnston, opponents during the war would become friends after the war. As part of the last surrender of the Civil War, Sherman, like Grant had done with Lee, offered Johnston friendly terms of surrender. They would meet again at Grant's funeral to pay homage to their fellow West Pointer and former President of the

A NEW PERSPECTIVE

United States. Johnston and Sherman along with Phillip Sheridan and Simon Bolivar Buckner were pallbearers at Grant's funeral in 1885. Two were from the Union and two from the Confederacy. J.E. Johnston would later be an honorary pallbearer at Sherman's funeral. Amid torrent tears and pouring rain, he refused to wear a hat citing that Sherman would refuse to wear one if the situation was reversed. He caught a cold and was dead within a month. At the funeral of Confederate General Cadmus Wilcox (Class of 1846), there were four pallbearers from the Union and four from the Confederacy.

War is such a terrible thing. Yet, as terrible as it is, there is something unexplainable about war that bonds men in ways that only those that have experienced it could understand. It forces men to embrace the trust necessary to place their lives in another man's hand. No sword ever forged could be made of the steel that bonds such camaraderie. It is well understood among them that each soldier owes the other a debt that neither could fully pay.

Uncommon valor, that is the willingness to sacrifice your life to save the life of another, like any good friendship is so precious, so rare and immune to color that it must be a gift from God. If there is anything beautiful in war, it is that it can bring out such qualities in men amidst the closest thing to hell experienced on earth.

RETHINKING THE HISTORY AND MYTHS OF THE PAST

Antiquity

A NEW PERSPECTIVE

RETHINKING THE HISTORY AND MYTHS OF THE PAST

Ancient Egypt

A NEW PERSPECTIVE

RETHINKING THE HISTORY AND MYTHS OF THE PAST

Predynastic Egypt

The Sphinx: Taken by the uploader, w:es:Usuario:Barcex, CC BY-SA 3.0, https://commons.wikimedia.org/w/index.php?curid=4483211

The Pyramids and the Sphinx stand as monuments of time in a land known for its antiquity. When Napoleon visited the Pyramids, it was two-thousand years after Alexander the Great's trip which was two-thousand years after they were built. The Pyramids of Egypt are the only standing monuments of the Seven Wonders of the ancient world. Egypt, however, is about more than pyramids. It is a land of mystery, of obscure origin that has captivated the world for almost five thousand years.

Ancient Egypt (often referred to as the gift of the Nile) was a gift to humanity bequeathed to Western Civilization by the Greeks, Romans and Hebrews. This great civilization shines through the Greco-Roman and Hebrew windows casting light on a much greater antiquity. Before the "Glory, that was Greece" and the "Grandeur that was Rome"; Egypt played a critical role in the development of the pillars of Western Civilization. For Abraham, Joseph and Jacob, it was the Land of Plenty where famine victims found food. For Moses, it was the Land of idolatry and of the enslaved wanting to be free. In this regard, it served as a canvas from which the portrait of greater antiquity was drawn.

The classical writers of Greece and Rome saw Egypt as a land of wonder, a paragon of technical excellence and a source of arcane knowledge and wisdom. Its pyramids continue to stand not only as a testament of time but to the greatness of the race and the people that erected them. Greece lasted five hundred years, Rome lasted a thousand years; but Egypt lasted for almost three thousand years. Even though Egypt has been studied in great detail since the hieroglyphics were deciphered almost two

A NEW PERSPECTIVE

hundred years ago, we are just beginning to understand the origins of this ancient empire.

The Gift of the Nile

In Africa, there is a great river known to us as the Nile. It rises from the heart of Africa, from the continent that gave birth to humankind. For thousands of miles, it makes its journey, through rocky terrain and desert sands flowing continuously through the land like time flowing through our existence; perhaps its journey is a metaphor for life itself. The waters of the Nile like all rivers seek the path of least resistance, and when it reaches the delta after its arduous journey of four thousand miles its spreads its wings like a majestic bird gliding to its final destination.

Just about everything in Ancient Egypt centered around the Nile River. The Nile, in many ways, is unique among the rivers of this earth. It covers one-sixth of the earth's circumference. It is almost twice as long as the Mississippi River. It is longer than the Tigris, Euphrates and Colorado Rivers combined. The Nile is so long that it could run across the continental United States and still have a thousand miles to go. For centuries, the source of the floods that gave the Nile its rebirth was unknown. The Ancient Egyptians believed the source to be the mourning of Isis for her murdered husband Osiris and that the shedding of her tears into the river made it overflow.

We so often associate the flooding of a river as a disastrous event often bringing destruction and death. Notwithstanding, the flooding of the Nile was a predictable annual event. Egypt was a land that was void of rain and therefore totally dependent, not only on its river, but its cyclic flooding to bring life to its inhabitants. In ancient times, the flooding of the Nile was inaugurated with the appearance of the bright star Sirius (Egyptian *Sopdet* meaning she who is—referring to Isis) on the horizon as if the gods had blessed this annual event. It was from watching the heliacal rising of Sirius (which took place around the Summer Solstice) for over 1,460 years that the Egyptians accurately measured the length of the solar year and developed a calendar that forms the basis of the calendar that we use today. However, instead of leaping a day every four years, they leaped an entire year every 1,460 years.

RETHINKING THE HISTORY AND MYTHS OF THE PAST

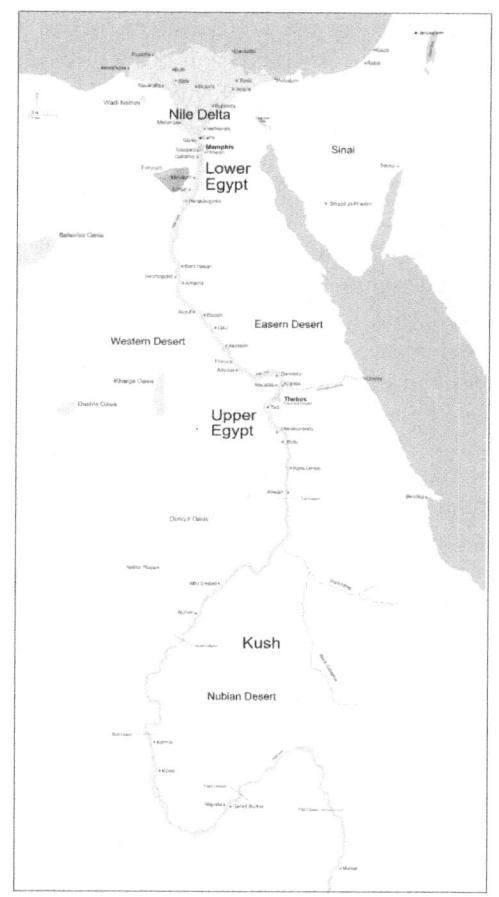

By H.Seldon—The map was made from file Ancient_Egypt_map.svg. This file was made by Jeff Dahl. For Faiyum_oasis.svg was used information from book: Ian Shaw: Dějiny starověkého Egypta, ISBN 80–7257–975–4., CC BY-SA 3.0, https://commons.wikimedia.org/w/index.php?curid=3948636

For centuries, the source of the flooding of the Nile was unknown. Scholars contend that the source was the heavy rains from the tropical regions to its south, from June to September, that caused the Blue Nile in the Ethiopian highlands and the White Nile in central Africa to rise to produce the annual flood of the Nile in which the Egyptians cherished as a gift from the gods. It could, therefore, be said that it was Ethiopia that gave geographical birth; to Ancient Egypt and throughout history; these two nations have been geographically and culturally linked. It was from this annual event that the religion of the Egyptians sprung like the crops that they planted in the rich soil. The flooding of the river not only brought water, but it also carried with it rich sediment that restored the fertility of the soil.

A NEW PERSPECTIVE

It is important to note that since Egypt was dependent on the flooding and the receding of the Nile River, its seasons were oriented accordingly. A twofold harvest was a general aim. As a result, the Egyptians developed methods for regulation and irrigation of the water supply. Unlike other areas, rain is particularly nonexistent in Egypt, and this created a dependency on the river that was uniquely Egyptian.

Before the Pharaohs
As more information regarding the predynastic period unfolds, we take deeper steps into the past in search of the beginning of this magnificent civilization. Although the waters of time have washed away some of its footprints, it has also washed ashore fragments of its greatness hitherto unseen or misunderstood. Unlike previous theories of its origins, which attributed the source of Egypt's greatness to outside influences, most scholars now believe that the origin of Ancient Egypt was indigenous to Africa.

In an attempt to detach Ancient Egypt from the African continent and its people, scholars of the Victorian era went in search of outside origins and ignored signs that it was an indigenous African civilization. For example, every kingdom, the Old, the Middle and the New emerged from the South and moreover form a contiguous cultural and technical chain (if the Intermediate Periods are removed).

Although Ancient Egypt's history is three thousand years, its story starts much further back. In the millennia after the last Ice Age (about 10,000 BCE), the Nile Valley was an area that attracted populations from the Sahara and North East Africa. We know little about the denizens of the-Ice Age Sahara. However, with the advent of recent technologies most noted various kinds of satellite imaging; we may be able to bring this picture into sharper focus. During the Pleistocene era (2,600,000–11,700 BCE) the Nile Valley was frequently swampy and the river levels much higher. As the Sahara dried up, it became less hospitable and as a result, more and more people migrated to the Nile Valley area.

On the periphery of the Sahara Desert, several sites date back as far as 15,000 years BCE. Furthermore, flint blades from Egypt and Nubia show traces that they were used for gathering grasses. This is probably the earliest indication of cereal consumption known in the world earlier than Syria-Palestine. We so often ignore the climate and geographical impacts that play such a vital role in the social, cultural and innovative developments of civilizations. Egypt is the progeny of the Nile, but it is also the progeny of events that led to the drying of the Sahara Desert.

RETHINKING THE HISTORY AND MYTHS OF THE PAST

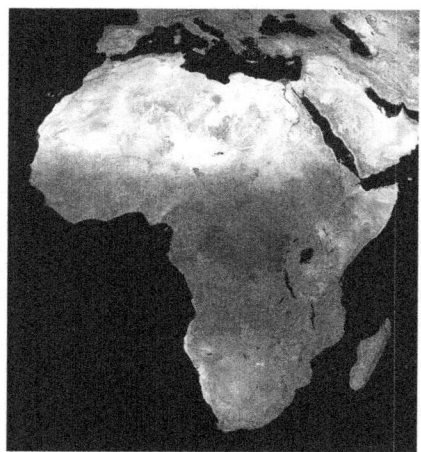

A geographical map of Africa, showing the ecological break that defines the Saharan area.
The Sahara Desert is so vast, so much so that the continental United States could reside in its borders

The predynastic culture of Ancient Egypt (now referred to as Dynasty 0) is identified as a necropolis north of Thebes known as Naqada. The predynastic period is traditionally assigned to the period between 4000 and 3100 BCE and broken into three chronological periods: Naqada I (4000–3500 BCE) Naqada II (3500–3250 BCE) and Naqada III (3250–3100 BCE). All three periods are contiguous and depict an evolutionary trail that led to Pharaonic Egypt. During the Naqada I Period, the South (Upper Egypt) was a cultural and technological monolithic society, while the North (Lower Egypt) was a patchwork group technically and culturally inferior to the South.

One yardstick used to determine the level of technology and culture of predynastic Egypt is to evaluate the pottery found at burial grounds. When scholars compare Naqada I and II of Upper Egypt with the coeval Maadi cultures (3750–3250) of the Delta region in Lower Egypt, it is clear that Upper Egypt was the innovator. It is also clear that the Delta region was influenced by Mesopotamia as their form of government was arranged around city-states and not a central government. It is at the end of Naqada II and the beginning of Naqada III that the vestiges of Egypt's dynastic system occurred five hundred years before the unification of Egypt.

The Ancient Egyptian state revolved around a semi-divine individual known as the pharaoh. And it is from this basic premise that it became the *Axis Mundi* of the Bronze Age world. Before Upper and Lower Egypt were unified, the South was united under one king. He is referred to as *Horus Scorpion*. The evidence seems to suggest that before the conquering of the North by the South militarily; most of the North was conquered socially via cultural diffusion from Upper Egypt to Lower

A NEW PERSPECTIVE

Egypt during the Naqada periods. Furthermore, no evidence suggests that pharaonic Egypt emerged from roots outside of the African continent as previously thought.

From the onset of its history starting with its first pharaoh, Ancient Egypt was a Theocratic monarchy based on ancestral worship. One in which the ruler was considered a god or a representative of god per the divine right of the monarch. The Ancient Egyptians thus believed that their pharaoh was both a god and a man. The etymology of the term pharaoh is *Per-aa* which means Great House and would be analogous to calling the president of the United States the White House. The Egyptians word for their leader was *nesewt*.

The Rosetta Stone (ca 196 BC) enabled linguists to begin the process of deciphering ancient Egyptian scripts.

One of the problems in understanding Ancient Egypt is that we often look at it from the eyes of an outsider. Many of the names, such as the Sphinx are Greek words, which are unrelated to its true name, in this case: (Horus on the Horizon). When the Egyptian name is used, the association is apparent. The sun has graced the face of this African carved in stone on the horizon every morning for almost five thousand years. It wasn't, however, until the Rosetta Stone was deciphered in 1822 by the French linguist Jean-Francois Champollion (with help from the Englishmen Thomas Young) that the Egyptian voice, silent for nearly two thousand years, was heard.

To the Ancient Egyptians, the power of their gods was absolute and divinely ordained. The pharaoh was the earthly embodiment of the god Horus, the son of Osiris who himself was a pharaoh that was killed by his evil brother Seth and then

RETHINKING THE HISTORY AND MYTHS OF THE PAST

deified. It was expected that when the pharaoh died that he (Osiris) would join his fellow gods in the hereafter and continue to rule his living subjects through the living incarnation of the pharaoh (Horus) who was the son of god. Scholars contend that this tradition could be traced to the Proto-dynastic (Dynasty 0) rulers of the South as th name Horus Scorpion indicates. Furthermore, Osiris is always shown wearing the white crown of the South as seen below.

Afterlife scene of Horus leading the deceased to the god Osiris to be judged

Nubian Roots

Nubia, (often referred to as Kush or Ethiopia) lies to Egypt's south and is a country much like Egypt divided between its upper and lower parts with a coeval yet different history. The history of Nubia can be divided into four major periods, Lower Nubia: The A-Group (3500–2900 BCE) which corresponds to Egypt's predynastic and early dynastic periods. Lower Nubia: The C-Group (2400- 1550 BCE). Upper Nubia: The Kerma State (2400–1500 BCE) which corresponds to the Middle Kingdom and Second Intermediate periods. Lower and Upper Nubia (1550–1050): which corresponds to the Egyptian New Kingdom, The Napata Kingdom (850–650): includes the 25th Dynasty that conquered Egypt.

The Egyptians called Nubia *Ta-Seti* "land of the bowmen". The bowmen of Nubia were expert archers and they were vital to the Egyptian army. Although Nubia, throughout most of its history, remained hidden in the shadows of Egypt's greatness; it had its own unique history. In fact, when Egypt was strong, Nubia was weak and vice versa. Many scholars believe that there was strong contact between predynastic and early dynastic Egypt with the Nubian A group. Although there was some borrowing, it is clear that the A group was distinct from Egypt with its own identity. The A group pottery consists of motif and shapes that are very different from those found in Egypt during this time. It is from this state that the Kerma culture emanated.

A NEW PERSPECTIVE

Discoveries in Nubia substantiate a common origin and strong nexus between Nubia and Upper Egypt during the predynastic and proto-dynastic periods. For example, the Royal Scene from Gharb Aswan and the Qustul Incense Burner clearly show iconography such as the white crown that became cornerstones first in Upper Egypt and after the conquest of Narmer of Lower Egypt and central to pharaonic Egypt throughout its long history.

The *Qustul Incense Burne*r is perhaps one of the most intriguing and contentious objects associated with the prehistoric Nubian culture. It was discovered by the late Professor Kevin Seele in 1964 and currently resides at the University of Chicago's Oriental Institute. Detailed analysis of this object began only after its restoration in 1977 by Professor Bruce Williams, who dated the object to the era of state-building in Upper Egypt and believed that it was evidence of the world's first kingship which originally evolved into pharaonic Egypt. It is interesting to note that the white crown depicted in the Qustul Incense Burner and Royal Scene from Gharb Aswan predates the white crown shown on the scorpion macehead which is considered the start of Dynasty 0.

Scorpion macehead (detail) (Ashmolean Museum)By Udimu—Own work, CC BY-SA 3.0, https://commons.wikimedia.org/w/index.php?curid=10353240

The Oriental Institute at the University of Chicago states the following regarding the Qustul Incense Burner:

This incense burner is distinctively Nubian in form. Carved in the technique of Nubian rock art, it is decorated on the rim with typical Nubian designs. It was found in the tomb of a Nubian ruler at Qustul and incorporates images associated with Egyptian pharaohs: a procession of sacred boats, the White Crown of Upper Egypt, a falcon deity, and the palace facade called a serekh. It appears to represent a ritual that involved a royal procession by boat to a palace. Scholars at the Oriental Institute assert that is now apparent that around 3600 BCE, Hierakonpolis (known in ancient times

RETHINKING THE HISTORY AND MYTHS OF THE PAST

as Nekhen) was a local center of power that probably encompassed part of Upper Egypt and into Nubia. This strongly suggests that the idea of kingship manifested in dynastic form happen at Hierakonpolis five hundred years before the Narmer Palette. [Teeter, Before the Pyramids]

Exhibit in the Oriental Institute Museum, University of Chicago, Chicago, Illinois, USA.

Unification of Egypt

It has been known for some time that prior to dynastic Egypt the South and the North were socially, culturally and possibly racially different. Although Egypt would be united as one nation; vestiges of the North and the South were apparent throughout its long history with the South being the most revered. The South referred to itself as (Kmt) Kemet (the black land) and the North was referred to as Dashre (the Red Land). In time, all of Egypt was referred to as Kemet and the white crown of the South although integrated with the red crown of the North was more symbolic of the union between the two than anything else. It is the South that placed its indelible stamp on Egypt, not the North as previously espoused.

The Narmer Palette is the world's first historical document. Many scholars believe that Narmer and Menes are the same Pharaoh called by different names. This is confirmed by the writings of Herodotus and Manetho. It was Menes that founded the great city of Memphis. The first name of this city was *Ineb-hedj* "White Wall" and late in the Old Kingdom, it became *Men-nefer* "Enduring of Beauty" which finally became the Hellenized Memphis.

The Narmer Palette displays in art form the conquest of the North by the South and the unification of the two kingdoms. On the first side of the Narmer Palette, the king of the South wearing the white crown of the South defeats his northern counterpart. On the reverse side, Narmer leads a triumphant parade wearing the red crown of the North.

A NEW PERSPECTIVE

The Narmer Palette depicts the unification of Upper and Lower Egypt

Egyptologists believe that the unification by King Narmer occurred somewhere around 3150 BCE. This would become a leitmotif throughout Egypt's long history. Through the ebbs and flows, it was always the South that restored Ancient Egypt to its greatness and continued to be the source of its great innovations.

RETHINKING THE HISTORY AND MYTHS OF THE PAST

Dynastic (Pharaonic) Egypt

From left to right, the three largest are: the Pyramid of Menkaure, the Pyramid of Khafre and the Great Pyramid of Khufu. By Ricardo Liberato—All Gizah Pyramids, CC BY-SA 2.0, https://commons.wikimedia.org/w/index.php?curid=2258048

When we think of Ancient Egypt, we often think of the age of the pharaohs, of biblical stories of its greatness and its oppression of Jews. In recent times, however, many scholars revisited its history based on excavations, stories and history written in their native tongue to extract the truth from myth and hyperbole. For instance, it has been reported on numerous occasions that Jewish slaves built the pyramids, but this is untrue.

The pyramids were built centuries before Abraham's trip to Egypt and over a thousand years before Moses. Moreover, they were not built by slaves, but rather, using organized work camps as part of a national work project. Egypt has long been misunderstood, hidden behind the mystique of mummies, the majestic pyramids and the stories written in the Bible. Its influence on Western Civilization obscured by the shadows of Greece and Rome. Dynastic or pharaonic Egypt primarily consists of three Kingdoms, labeled as Old, Middle and New with three Intermediate Periods. Kingdoms and Intermediate Periods consist of a series of dynasties.

A NEW PERSPECTIVE

The Old Kingdom

The predynastic or archaic period lasted from around 3150 to approximately 2686 BCE. The Old Kingdom lasted from 2686 to 2181 (3rd-6th dynasties). This was the first age of pyramid building. Djoser's step pyramid, at Saqqara, was the first to be built in stone and was constructed under the direction of the vizier, Imhotep. He was the world's first recorded polymath. Imhotep was not only renowned for his architectural achievements, but his knowledge of medicine and healing and is often associated with the Greek and Roman god of medicine Aesculapius.

The Pyramid of Djoser

The first true pyramid and the great pyramids of the Giza plateau were erected during the 4th dynasty which is often referred to as the Fabulous Fourth dynasty. It is also believed that the Sphinx was built at this time. However, there are some scholars that believe that the Sphinx predates the pyramids based on weather erosion patterns. During the reign of Snefru, three major innovations occurred that would have lasting impacts on the rest of Egyptian history. First was the building of the first true pyramid. Second, was the expansion of trade and an international presence and third was artistic and cultural standards. The future kingdoms that emerged from the south, always looked back to the Old Kingdom with great reverence.

It was also during the Old Kingdom that the pharaoh Pepi II of the 6th Dynasty ruled for over ninety-five years; one of the longest reigns in human history. Toward the end of his reign, there were signs of Egypt's decline perhaps best articulated in its literature. It was also during this period that foreigners flocked into Egypt mainly from the northeast. The southern base which had been its foundation was pushed further south. This decline is often referred to as the First Intermediate Period and it lasted from 2181–2055 (7th -11th dynasties).

RETHINKING THE HISTORY AND MYTHS OF THE PAST

The First Intermediate and the Middle Kingdom

The First Intermediate Period, like all seceding Intermediate Periods, was a time of chaos ruled by interlopers detached from a national and stable governmental structure and innovation that gave rise to Egypt's greatness. These periods are normally initiated by foreign influx into the Nile Valley. They represent periods of decline in the Egyptian infrastructure, emulation and exploitation of Egypt's past accomplishments. During the Intermediate Periods, the native rulers retreated to Egypt's South and would rise again to conquer the North and replenish and resurrect the nation, akin to the annual flooding of the Nile, bringing with it fresh ideas linked to the traditions of the previous kingdom.

The Middle Kingdom 2055 to 1650 (11th - 13th dynasties), like Egypt's legendary phoenix, rose from the ashes of the First Intermediate Period. This was the first resurrection of Egypt and a return to prosperity and pyramid building. In many ways, the Middle Kingdom looked back nostalgically at the Old Kingdom with its pyramids and stability. But it moved forward and developed a culture that can be uniquely identified. It bore the characteristics of continuity and change that would become the leitmotif of Egypt's resurrections.

Mentuhotep II

It was in the 11th dynasty under the rule of Mentuhotep II that the restoration process began. However, it was the 12th Dynasty that set the tone for the Middle Kingdom. The Middle Kingdom was the age of Amenemhats and Senusrets, with the

A NEW PERSPECTIVE

high-water mark of the dynasty being achieved under the reign of Senusret III. Many of these pharaohs ruled concurrently in the later years of the previous pharaoh with a string of Amenemhets and Senusrets alternating. They abandoned the capital at Memphis in favor of Waset (Thebes). Most scholars believe that Abraham's sojourn into Egypt happened during the Middle Kingdom.

The first great Pharaoh of the Middle Kingdom was Amenemhet I (1991–1962 BCE), and he set the standards that were followed by successive pharaohs of this dynasty. His son and their descendants ruled Egypt for two centuries. It is from this pharaoh that *The Instructions of Amenemhet* to his son are known to us. Although the author is unknown, most Egyptologists believe it was his successor Senusret I (Greek name, Sesostris) (1971–1926 BCE) who was also a great pharaoh and perhaps the first to erect an obelisk.

Senusret I. (Sesostris I) 1971–1926 BCE)

It is under this pharaoh that we get the expansion of Egypt into foreign lands. Senusret I was followed by Amenemhet II (1929–1895 BCE) who established foreign trade with artifacts found in the Levant. He was succeeded by Senusret II (1897–1878) who was seceded by Senusret III (1878–1853). He was a 6'6" military leader who dug a canal around the Aswan cataract. Senusret III was succeeded by Amenemhet III (1842–1797 BCE) who had expeditions to the Sinai and built two pyramids and an enormous labyrinth. The last of this series of pharaohs was Amenemhet IV (1798–1776).

RETHINKING THE HISTORY AND MYTHS OF THE PAST

A signature landmark of the Middle Kingdom was the obelisk (erroneously called Cleopatra's needles), a symbol, of resurrection and rebirth. This is a tradition that continued during the New Kingdom. The Romans were obsessed with them and Rome is now the home of the most obelisks in the world. Many reside in large cities around the world with the largest being the Washington Monument located in Washington DC.

The Second Intermediate (Hyksos)
The Middle Kingdom was followed by the Second Intermediate Period 1650 to 1550 BCE (15th -17th dynasties). Once again, a foreign influx led to the decline of the Middle Kingdom and the expulsion of its ruling class to the South. During this period, central power eroded. This was the age of the Hyksos who were foreign rulers, and many scholars think that this is a period contemporary with the story of Joseph in the Bible. The Hyksos were strengthened by the steady increase of immigration until their numbers were ripe for a full invasion or take over. The literature of Ancient Egypt is full of contempt and disdain for the Hyksos.

In the top picture, those on the left are foreigners entering Egypt and on the right Egyptians. By NebMaatRa—Own work, CC BY-SA 3.0, https://commons.wikimedia.org/w/index.php?curid=4390535

Many scholars believe that the Hyksos were Semitic and possibly the primogenitors of Jews in Egypt. Notwithstanding, a distinction was made along ethnic as well as cultural lines. Moreover, instead of worshiping Osiris; they worshiped Seth the evil one that killed Osiris by cutting him up into thirteen pieces. The Hyksos rulers assumed pharaoh's role and are credited with bringing the horse and the chariot into Egypt. In Egypt's long history, this appears to be one of the few times when an idea from the outside was adopted. Nonetheless, this was an age of decline and disunity much like the First Intermediate Period. Meanwhile, there was another set of

A NEW PERSPECTIVE

pharaohs that ruled at Thebes. This has led to problems with the interpretation of Manetho's list of Pharaohs.

The New Kingdom
The New Kingdom began with the 18th dynasty. This dynasty left some of the greatest artifacts as a testimony of their splendor, genius and greatness. It was the dynasty of some of Egypt's most famous pharaohs. They did not build pyramids, like the days of old, however once again; Egypt went on a massive building exercise this time at modern-day Karnak and Luxor. In addition to the building of edifices, Egypt expanded its borders and influence in the region. Throughout the major part of this dynasty, Egypt maintained control of the Mediterranean region. First, because of its military power and second because of its ability to govern using the Phoenicians and others as vassals.

Discoveries made by Egyptologist John Darnell indicate that the Theban dynasty in the south that preceded the New Kingdom was far more advanced than was previously thought. Although the revolution was spearheaded by his father Seqenenre Tao and older brother Kamose, it was the Pharaoh Ahmose I (1570–1546) that finally expelled the Hyksos and began the New Kingdom 1550–1069 BCE (18th–20th dynasties) and ended the Second Intermediate Period. Many scholars contend that he was the pharaoh referred to in the bible as: *There came a pharaoh that knew not Joseph*. Thereby aligning Joseph's reign with the Hyksos.

A fragmentary statue of Ahmose I, Metropolitan Museum of Art

The expulsion of the Hyksos brought a new period of prosperity, power and prestige. However, life under the Hyksos seemed to have taught Egypt a valuable lesson. In order to protect itself from foreign invasions, it needed to establish buffer states. The

RETHINKING THE HISTORY AND MYTHS OF THE PAST

beginning of this kingdom was led by a succession of strong military leaders. Amenhotep I (1551–1524 BCE) continued to expand the boundaries of Egypt. Moreover, during this dynasty, a professional army was raised, and Egypt expanded its influence into Palestine and Syria.

Queen Hatshepsut (1498–1483 BCE)

Although Amenhotep I left no heirs, he was succeeded by Thutmose I (1524–1518) another great military leader. He led a Mesopotamian expedition to the Euphrates River and south into Nubia to the fourth cataract. He constructed the first tomb in the Valley of the Kings which was to become a trademark not only of this dynasty but future dynasties. He was followed by Thutmose II (1518–1504) and then by Queen Hatshepsut (1498–1483 BCE) the first female pharaoh and the most powerful female in antiquity. She later co-ruled with Thutmose III (1504–1450). In later years, for unknown reasons, Thutmose III tried to destroy the legacy of Queen Hatshepsut.

Thutmose III was the greatest military leader in Egyptian history often called the "Napoleon of Egypt" (which is a misnomer since Napoleon should be called the Thutmose III of France). He was a natural-born leader and strategist who solidified Egyptian power throughout the Mediterranean. He was followed by another great warrior Amenhotep II (1453–1419 BCE) who was succeeded by Thutmose IV (1419–1386 BCE) who is often credited with the restoration of the Sphinx. He was followed by Amenhotep III (1386–1349 BCE). Amenhotep III was more of a diplomat and a great builder than a conqueror. He was responsible for constructing the two large statues known as *Colossus of Memnon*.

A NEW PERSPECTIVE

He was succeeded by Amenhotep IV (1350–1334 BCE) better known as Akhenaton "the Heretic King" or perhaps better yet "the husband of Nefertiti." He is often overshadowed by the bust of his wife Nefertiti and treasure of his son/ brother King Tut. It is important to note, that Egypt brought princesses from foreign lands, particularly under the reign of Amenhotep II, but they never sent their princesses to foreign lands. Some scholars believe that Nefertiti may have been a descendent of a foreign princess. Notwithstanding, Nefertiti and Akhenaton appeared to be inseparable.

Nefertiti Berlin Museum

Akhenaton is often called the world's first monotheist. He abandoned the worship of all gods including Osiris in favor of the God Aton (Aten). The birth of monotheism is often attributed to Abraham and the Jewish heritage. Notwithstanding, they believed that other gods existed but that their God was superior (known as henotheism). Akhenaton, however, did not believe in the existence of other gods (which is monotheism). He was a religious zealot that was not interested in foreign affairs. As a result, the empire built by his predecessors began to decline. He was succeeded by the boy- king Tutankhamen (Tut) more famous for his tomb than his tenure as pharaoh. The familial relationship between King Tut and Akhenaton has long been debated. It is now believed by some Egyptologists that King Tut was the son of Akhenaton and his sister.

RETHINKING THE HISTORY AND MYTHS OF THE PAST

Statue of Akhenaten in the early Amarna style. CC BY-SA 2.5,
https://commons.wikimedia.org/w/index.php?curid=505800

Unlike the aforementioned pharaohs, King Tut was an insignificant pharaoh virtually unknown before the turn of the 20th century. Many scholars contend that his tomb was not robbed because it was missed by grave-robbers in search of a larger treasure. Based on King Tut's short reign, and insignificance, one could only imagine the priceless treasure buried with other pharaohs. The boy-king, however, was not equip to handle an empire that was in religious transition. The 18th dynasty virtually ended with the death/murder of King Tut. The religious monotheistic revolution started by Akhenaton was over, and the worship of gods was restored.

The boy King Tutankhamen (Tut)

A NEW PERSPECTIVE

One aspect of the 18th dynasty was the reverence for women started by Ahmose I and continued throughout the dynasty. More than any other dynasty, the presence of powerful women is apparent. Perhaps best exemplified by the first female pharaoh Hatshepsut and the influence of his mother, Queen Tiye, and Nefertiti on Akhenaton's religious philosophy.

Queen Tiye. By Einsamer Schütze—Own work, CC BY-SA 3.0, https://commons.wikimedia.org/w/index.php?curid=16320509

The 19th Dynasty begins with Ramses I (1293–1291) *Ra moses* meaning son of Ra. His rule was brief and followed by his son Seti I (1291–1278). Seti which means: follower of Seth, the god that the Hyksos worshiped. He, like his father, was a vizier and a military man. Seti I was followed by Ramses II (1279–1212) known to us as Ramses the Great.

If ever there was a spin doctor in Egypt, Ramses the Great was one. For example, the battle of Kadesh with the Hittites was at best a draw but Ramses the Great much like Napoleon's later lost in Egypt turned this event into a glorious victory. He built temples all over Egypt the most famous is Abu Simbel and he ruled for 67 years. He ruled so long that most of the population upon his death could not remember a time when he was not pharaoh.

There are some Egyptologists that think that Rameses the Great was not so great when compared to some of the little-known pharaohs of the Middle and New Kingdoms. Some have gone as far as to call "the Great" a misnomer. They contend that other pharaohs, particularly the ones that started kingdoms, are the cornerstones of Egypt's restored greatness while Rameses and his descendants lived off the fat of the land and eventually drove the New Kingdom into decline. His popularity stems

RETHINKING THE HISTORY AND MYTHS OF THE PAST

from his longevity, his monuments, and the possibility that he was the pharaoh of the Exodus.

The date of the Exodus, however, is difficult to assess. Moreover, some scholars have a problem with the Exodus narrative and question if it really happened. Although the Egyptians constantly mention the reign of the Hyksos with disdain, there is not one word of a biblical Exodus as described in the Old Testament. Sigmund Freud, who was Jewish, in his last book entitled: *Moses and Monotheism*(1939) points out that the name Moses is Egyptian for *child* and goes as far as to proclaim that Moses was not Jewish, but rather, an Egyptian follower of Akhenaton who introduced monotheism to the Jews.

The next pharaoh was Menrptah, (1212–1202 BCE) the thirteenth son of Ramses. He was in his 60s when he assumed the throne. He only became pharaoh because he was the only living son of Rameses. He was succeeded by his son Amemesses (1202–1199 BCE), then Seti II (1199–1193 BCE) then Siptah (1193–1187 BCE), then another female pharaoh Twosret (1187–1185 BCE) who ruled for two years. The 19th Dynasty, however, did not follow directly in the footsteps of the 18th Dynasty. For instance, under Ramses the Great, they moved the capital from Thebes to Per-Ramesses outside of Avaris. This would prove to be problematic because it allowed the priest at Thebes to consolidate power and thus challenge the pharaohs of the 20th dynasty.

The 20th dynasty, often called the Ramessid pharaohs because of the number of pharaohs with the name Ramses, was founded by Setnakht, (Seth is victorious) (1185–1182 BCE). He was succeeded by Ramses III (1182–1151 BCE) and after him, Egypt is in a clear state of decline as succeeding Ramses came to the throne. Ramses IV (1151–1145 BCE) Ramses V (1145–1141 BCE) Ramses VI (1141–1133 BCE) Ramses VII (1133–1126 BCE) Ramses VIII (1126 BCE) Ramses IX (1126–1108 BCE) Ramses X (1108–1098 BCE) Ramses XI (1098–1070 BCE).

The Third Intermediate Period and the Nubian Dynasty
True to the leitmotif previously discussed, the New Kingdom was followed by a Third Intermediate Period from 1070–747 BCE (21st to 24th Dynasties). During the 21st dynasty, Egypt is divided once again. However, unlike the previous Intermediate Periods, Egypt would not emerge stronger than before. This was another protracted period of decline in which kings from rival dynasties ruled concurrently. The priests rule the South from Thebes and the North was invaded by the Libyans.

A NEW PERSPECTIVE

The 25th dynasty was the Nubian dynasty under Piy and his descendants and they first ruled southern Egypt from Napata while the Libyans ruled northern Egypt. However, unity was once again restored by men of the south as the Nubians conquered all of Egypt and found what is often referred to as the Kushite (Nubian) dynasty (747–671). The Nubians had great reverence for Egypt as they shared a similar history. In this regard, they tried to restore Egypt to its past greatness. They also built small pyramids in their native land that were used as burial sites.

Nubian pyramids, Meroe. Three of these pyramids are reconstructed.

The Nubians were not successful in their long-term restoration of Egypt's greatness and only lasted for one dynasty. Egypt was surrounded by emerging empires that would continue to challenge it. The Assyrians gained control over Egypt and ruled until 626 when they were defeated by the Babylonians. The Babylonians were defeated by the Persians who ruled Egypt for several dynasties before they were conquered by Alexander the Great in 332 BCE.

The Greco-Roman Era

The conquest of Egypt by Alexander the Great was the beginning of the Greco-Roman era and the spread of Hellenism throughout the Mediterranean region. When he died in 323 BCE, his empire was divided between his generals and Ptolemy inherited Egypt. It was the era of fourteen Ptolemies and one legendary woman, Cleopatra VII. The lover of both Caesar and Mark Anthony, she was not attractive (no Elizabeth Taylor). Notwithstanding, part of her allure and attraction was that she was a woman of power in control of a country something that was unheard of in Rome.

Her death in 30 BCE culminated the rule of the Greeks in Egypt and three millenniums of dynastic rule. This was the era of Cleopatra and Mark Anthony and as you can see, has little to nothing to do with the antiquity of the Ancient Egyptians

RETHINKING THE HISTORY AND MYTHS OF THE PAST

except for the continuation of Egypt's pharaonic system. During Cleopatra's reign, the Greeks in Egypt tried to hold on to the last vestiges of Alexander the Great's empire now under siege by the Romans.

Cleopatra VII's head as displayed at the Altes Museum in Berlin

Moreover, Cleopatra was the only Greek pharaoh that could read the hieroglyphics and she was by far the most Egyptianized. Cleopatra's relationship to Pharaonic Egypt has been grossly overstated. Like her forefathers before her, she was a *Macedonian Greek*. Long gone was the greatness that we associate with Ancient Egypt. For instance, the obelisks named after her (Cleopatra's needles) were first constructed two thousand years before her reign. After her death, Egypt fell into the waiting arms of Rome—as it made its transition from a Republic to an Empire three decades before the birth of Christ. It could, therefore, be said that Cleopatra is more related to Greco- Roman history than she is to the great pharaohs and edifices of Ancient Egypt.

There is much more to Ancient Egypt than, the bust of Nefertiti, the mystique of mummies and the pyramids, the treasure of King Tut and the stories in the Bible. Its greatness and contributions to the world are often trivialized or better yet misunderstood or misinterpreted. For instance, how did a society advance—in about five hundred years—from illiteracy to building three giant pyramids each consisting of 2, 500,000 perfectly cut two-ton blocks! Something that would be hard for the modern world to achieve with our current technology not to mention the tremendous

A NEW PERSPECTIVE

cost. Rather than sensationalize this ancient civilization, we should try to understand its beginning, its middle and its end. In doing so we may better understand ourselves.

RETHINKING THE HISTORY AND MYTHS OF THE PAST

List of Dynasties in Ancient Egypt

EARLY KINGDOMS (3200- 2800 BCE)

PRE- DYNASTIC PERIOD

NAQADA III DYNASTY 0

FIRST DYNASTY (Menes)

SECOND DYNASTY

THE OLD KINGDOM (2800–2250 BCE) (Pyramid Age)

THIRD DYNASTY

FOURTH DYNASTY (Great Pyramids)

FIFTH DYNASTY

SIXTH DYNASTY

FIRST INTERMEDIATE PERIOD (2250–2000 BCE)

SEVENTH, EIGHTH DYNASTIES

NINTH, TENTH DYNASTIES

MIDDLE KINGDOM (2000–1780 BCE)

ELEVENTH DYNASTY

TWELFTH DYNASTY

THIRTEENTH DYNASTY

SECOND INTERMEDIATE PERIOD (1780–1546 BCE)

FOURTEENTH and FIFTEENTH

SIXTEENTH and SEVENTEENTH (HYKSOS)

SEVENTEENTH (THEBAN)

A NEW PERSPECTIVE

THE NEW KINGDOM (1546–1085 BCE)

EIGHTEENTH DYNASTY (Thutmose I-IV) (Hatshepsut) (Amenhotep I-IV) (Akhenaten)

NINETIETH DYNASTY (Ramesses I, II)

TWENTIETH DYNASTY (Ramesses III-XI)

THIRD INTERMEDIATE PERIOD (1085–747 BCE)

TWENTY-FIRST

TWENTY-SECOND

TWENTY-THIRD

TWENTY-FOURTH (LIBYAN)

TWENTY-FIFTH (NUBIAN)(747–671)

LATE PERIOD (672–332)

TWENTY-SIXTH (ASSYRIAN)

TWENTY-SEVENTH (FRIST PERSIAN DYNASTY)

TWENTY-EIGHTH DYNASTY

TWENTY-NINTH DYNASTY

THIRTIETH DYNASTY (SECOND PERSIAN DYNASTY)

GREEK DYNASTIES (332–30 BCE)

MACEDONIAN (ALEXANDER THE GREAT)

PTOLEMAIC (CLEOPATRA VII)

ROMAN EMPIRE (30 BCE- 641 CE)

RETHINKING THE HISTORY AND MYTHS OF THE PAST

Greece and Rome

A NEW PERSPECTIVE

RETHINKING THE HISTORY AND MYTHS OF THE PAST

The Origins of Greece: Minoan, Mycenaean and Egyptian Influence

Homer's *Odyssey:* The Cyclops' curse delays the homecoming of Odysseus for another ten years

Greece was a child that had many midwives, born from a mother that resided in foreign lands.

Recently, much has been made about the tradition and influence of Western Civilization on the world. However, Western Civilization did not originate in Western Europe, but instead, in the eastern part of the continent and stands on the shoulders of older civilizations in Africa and the Middle East.

The debate over the origins of Greek civilization began in earnest with the release of two seminal works: Dr. Cheikh Anta Diop's (pronounced Jope) *The African Origins of Civilization, Myth or Reality* (1974) and Dr. Martin Bernal's *Black Athena* thesis composed in three volumes: The first was *The Fabrication of Ancient Greece 1785–1985 published in 1987.* The second: *The Archaeological and Documentary Evidence* (1991) and the last: *The Linguistic Evidence* (2006), In addition to these three volumes he wrote, *Black Athena Writes Back* (2001), which was a response to his critics. Their works were heavily scrutinized by scholars and Hellenophiles that sharply disagreed with their rendition of history.

A cursory investigation into the origins of Greek culture will trace its steps back to a much earlier non-Greek culture. One of the most prominent legends of the Greeks is about their hero Theseus who tied a cord to the entrance of the Cretan labyrinth and encountered the flesh-eating Minotaur in the middle of the labyrinth and slew him; thereby, freeing his fellow Greeks from the tribute of flesh demanded by the king of

A NEW PERSPECTIVE

Crete. However, in reviewing the history of Greece, we find another cord that freed them from their maze of ignorance and brought civilization to Europe. This cord could be traced, sometimes through the Phoenicians and other maritime nations, back to its source which was Ancient Egypt and Middle Eastern civilizations in existence thousands of years before the emergence of Greece. In the myths of the Greeks, we find the origins of its existence. The myth of the labyrinth on Crete, from which the Greeks trace their roots may lay in the legends of the great labyrinth of pharaoh Amenemhat III of the Egyptian Middle Kingdom.

The second millennium BCE witnessed two extraordinary cultures that were the precursors of Greek civilization. They were the Minoans on the island of Crete and Mycenae on the mainland. These two civilizations have left indelible traces across Greece and a nexus to earlier civilizations of Africa and the Near East. The Cretan culture was called *Minoan* from the legendary king of Crete Minos and the Mycenaean culture earned its name from the town of Mycenae in the Peloponnese.

Mask of Agamemnon discovered by Heinrich Schliemann in Mycenae in 1876 By Xuan Che—Self-photographed (Flickr), 20 December 2010, CC BY 2.0, https://commons.wikimedia.org/w/index.php?curid=15165017

When studying the history of Greece, a clear migration pattern from the Minoans to the Mycenaeans to the Greeks is readily apparent. Although the Minoan and Mycenaean cultures were both influenced by more sophisticated cultures to their south and east, the impact of the Minoans on the Mycenaeans can be seen in the imitation of Minoan culture and products. There is no doubt that Greece is the cornerstone of the Western world and there is also no doubt that the Greek accomplishments were significant. However, such accomplishments should not be viewed in isolation nor should we view the Greeks as a race of geniuses without any

RETHINKING THE HISTORY AND MYTHS OF THE PAST

reference to those antecedent civilizations that laid the foundation for Greece. We often start our history of Greece with Homer, Hesiod (c. 750 BCE) and the Archaic period (800–500 BCE).

The Archaic period, however, was an era of transformation; and the Greeks of that period looked back to the Mycenaean era (between 1600–1200 BCE) for their history and legends. For example, the Trojan War is believed to have been fought toward the end of this period around 1200 BCE. The pyramids and sphinx of Egypt were over 1000 years old and Egypt was in its 18th dynasty.

In Greek myth, the primogenitor was Hellen the man who should not be confused with the female Helen of Troy (The Face That Launched a Thousand Ships) and she was the cause of the Trojan War. He had three sons Dorus, Aeolus and Xuthus from which the main Greek ethnic groups originated. They were the Dorians, the Aeolians, the Achaeans and the Ionians. The Greeks became known as Hellenes and Greece as Hellas. According to the Greeks, the original inhabitants of Greece were the Achaeans and the Ionians, who fought in the Trojan War. The descendants of Dorus and Aeolus the Dorians and the Aeolians arrived just before the Dark Ages at the fall of the Mycenaean civilization.

The Ionians later migrated across the sea to settle the Aegean islands and found Ionia. Therefore, the Athenians could boast that they were the descendants of the first inhabitants of Greece. It is most apparent that Greek myths represent distorted memories of the Greek Mycenaean era. Before the rise of the Mycenaean civilization in mainland Greece, the Minoan civilization flourished on the large island of Crete from around 2000–1400 BCE. Although the legend of Troy had been around for millenniums, it was the excavation conducted by Heinrich Schliemann (1822–1890) that linked Mycenae to Troy. From childhood, Schliemann was fascinated by the Trojan War, and he dedicated his life to proving that the Greek legendary war was more than a myth.

Much of what we know about the Minoans could be attributed to the hard work and diligence of one man, Sir Arthur Evans (1851–1941). Like his predecessor Schliemann, Evans followed Homer and Theseus' Cord back to the island of Crete. Evans was not a professional scholar, however, like Schliemann, he was guided by the Greek tradition of recording the history of Crete in their legends. He was fascinated by clay tablets with deciphered script and he began to excavate Knossos located in central Crete.

A NEW PERSPECTIVE

Heinrich Schliemann

In 1900 CE, Evans came upon a building with nearly twelve hundred rooms. The similarities of the Minoan palaces to palaces in the Near East along with the sudden appearances of palaces around 1900 BCE strongly suggest cultural diffusion from the Near East and Egypt to the island of Crete. The objects found during excavations, such as seals, scarabs and rings show that the Cretans were in contact with Egypt. Between 1900 BCE and 1500 BCE, Crete was the western-most segment of the European Bronze Age world and was connected to the entire eastern Mediterranean. The inhabitants of this island were the first literate Europeans and are genetically close to the Myceneans.

Furthermore, the noted archeologist, Eduard Meyer, while excavating tombs in Thebes (Waset) in Upper Egypt, came upon paintings amazingly like those in the palace of Knossos. Meyer contends that the name Minoan assigned to the denizens of Crete is a misnomer and the real name of those inhabitants is Keftiu. Edward's name and assumptions were based on the trail of the Mycenaeans to the Minoans and their myths. Meyers, however, was the exact opposite, leading from the Egyptians directly to the Minoans (Keftiu). In Meyer's paradigm, the cultural diffusion from the Egyptians to the Minoans is more direct and pervasive. For example, he cites the Greek legend that Daedalus, the builder of the Knossan labyrinth modeled his structure on the then famous labyrinth of Amememhet III of the 12th Dynasty. Although this labyrinth was in complete ruins by the time of the Victorian Egyptologist, it was described by Strabo (Book XVII, I, 37 Bohn) and by Herodotus 448 BCE.

RETHINKING THE HISTORY AND MYTHS OF THE PAST

There has been a tendency to draw a distinct line between the Minoan and Mycenaean cultures, from which the Greek culture originated, and Ancient Egypt. However, Egypt's conservatism can serve as a link between the evolution and cultural diffusion of its great empire—to the rising age of the Greeks. Because of Egypt's conservatism, time seems to culturally standstill thus providing an excellent reference to compare and discern the evolution of the Hellenistic culture. Although it is well accepted that the Minoan and Mycenaean cultures were the primogenitors of the Greeks, they are also linked to the continuous cultural and linguistic streams of Ancient Egypt.

For example, the frescos found on Crete show the importance of cult games in Minoan life. This was a tradition that migrated to Greece in the form of religious festivals in honor of their heroes. This Minoan tradition can also be found in Mycenaean Greece in the mystery plays and festivals. Ancient Egypt also had mystery plays that outdated the Minoan plays. One significant difference between the Egyptian drama and Greek theater is that the Egyptians concentrated on the life of the god, and Greeks on the life of the hero.

Some theories link the King of Crete Minos to Menes (sometimes referred to as Narmer) the first Pharaoh of Egypt. It is interesting to note that Diodorus Siculus distinguishes Minos I from Minos II. Now there are not less than 200 years between Minos I and Minos II, which infers a dynasty not a single ruler. Furthermore, Diodorus Siculus claims that the Minotaur lived in the *labyrinthos,* a term which he also applies to an Egyptian tomb which he claims Daidalos saw in Egypt and imitated in Crete for Minos.

Since the Egyptians did not use vowels Minos and Menes are structurally the same. Just as Kaiser and Czar have their entomological roots in the great Roman emperor Caesar, Menes and Mino may have a similar relationship as Menes undoubtedly was the Caesar of his day. Now it is important to note that Minos is the son of Zeus begotten in Crete by Princess Europa. In other words, he is the son of god just as all Egyptian pharaohs were the embodiment of the son of god. A tradition that dates to the Old Kingdom. For example, the true name of the sphinx is *Hor-am-Akhet* (Horus on the Horizon). Horus was the son of the god Osiris. According to Egyptian myth, he was the first pharaoh.

There is also evidence that strongly suggests that the denizens on the island of Crete may have been in contact with the Egyptians as early as the Old Kingdom. Isis was the mother of Horus, the pharaoh of Egypt and likewise, Europa (from which Europe derives its name) was the mother of King Minos. She was raped by Zeus in the form of a bull. In Egyptian mythology, the holy bull, Apis, was linked with Osiris.

A NEW PERSPECTIVE

Moreover, according to Greek myths, the founders of Mycenae were the progeny of Princess Andromeda who was the daughter of an Ethiopian king. Both Minoan and Mycenaean primogenitors are princesses from foreign nations. What do these myths tell us about the origins of their civilizations? Thanks to the work of Evans and others, we now know that the Minoans were the predecessors of the Mycenaeans, and we can date their civilization to approximately 1450 BCE. The most active years of the Early Mycenaean Age are those from Egypt's New Kingdom from the rise of Thutmose III to the end of Amenhotep III about 1380 BCE.

The Minoans were a maritime nation traveling to Egypt, the Near East, the islands of the Aegean and Southern Greece. It is during these travels that the Minoans came in contact with the Mycenaeans on the mainland. The Minoans did not speak Greek but had extensive contact with Egypt and the Near East, particularly the Phoenicians who were also maritime people, and they passed this culture to the Mycenaeans. In this regard, they were conduits of culture and knowledge of the Egyptians and Near East providing indirect cultural diffusion to the Mycenaeans.

The deep influence of the Minoans on the Mycenaean culture is now clear. In 1954 CE, Michael Ventris demonstrated that the Linear B script was a form of Greek. When the Cretan places were destroyed around 1450 BCE, only the one at Knossos was rebuilt. The records from Knossos during the last excavation were recorded in Linear B, not in Linear A which indicates that Greek-speaking Mycenaeans occupied Crete in its last phase. These were Greeks from the mainland that occupied Crete for three generations and during that time absorbed, as the Romans would do later: the knowledge of a greater civilization now in decline.

The myth of Theseus' cord may be an allegory for the triumph of the mainland Mycenaean Greeks over the Minoans. This does not, however, exclude direct cultural diffusion as Mycenaean artifacts were discovered in Egypt by Sir Flinders Petrie (1853–1942). His breakthrough was helpful in the dating of the Mycenaean culture. Minoan and Mycenaean cultures ultimately became part of the oral tradition of the pre-Archaic Greeks. Legends such as those mentioned by Homer and Hesiod and possibly of Theseus on the island of Crete

Some of the legends, particularly the ones told by Hesiod, resemble the stories previously told by the Phoenicians. Historians and scholars have often pondered if the legends delineated in Homer's two epic poems were myth masqueraded as history or true events. It is believed by most historians that the Trojans were not Greeks, but vassals of the Hittites to the east of modern-day Turkey. However, to the Greeks and later the Romans, the Trojan War was real history of a Heroic age. Also, part of Greek legend is the presence of Ethiopians at the battle of Troy and the reverence for

RETHINKING THE HISTORY AND MYTHS OF THE PAST

Ethiopia during the Heroic period. In fact, Ethiopia was the place where the gods came to feast, and the Greeks often referred to them as the blameless race. An example from the Iliad states: *"Only yesterday Zeus went off to the Ocean River to feast with the Aethiopians, loyal, lordly men, and all of the gods went with him."*. Iliad 1.423–4 (Thetis is speaking to Achilles.)

Also recorded are noble warriors such as Memnon, the Ethiopian king, who was memorialized in art and poem. *"To Troy no hero came of nobler line; Or if of nobler, Memnon it was thine."* [Odyssey Book XI] So much so that centuries later, the twin statues of pharaoh Amenhotep III located in Egypt were named the Colossus of Memnon by the Greeks.

Colossus of Memnon

The word *Ethiopian* is the combination of two Greek words *burnt* and *skin* and thus does not only refer to a specific nation but rather to an ethnic or racial group located in other lands. During the Trojan War, Ethiopians (black people) may have lived in the vicinity of Troy. The Colossus of Memnon demonstrates that the Greeks, on occasion, associated Egyptians with Ethiopians. Furthermore, Herodotus wrote in his history centuries later: "The Egyptians said that they believed the Colchians to be descended from the army of Sesostris (Senusret). My own conjectures were founded, first, on the fact that they are black-skinned and have woolly hair."

Sesostris was a pharaoh of the Middle Kingdom who led a military expedition into Europe. The presence of Ethiopians at the Trojan War may shed some light on the demographics during the Mycenean era. One may ask the question: Why would Ethiopians travel thousands of miles to fight a war in Troy when they had no skin in the game? The Greeks celebrated this age in the poems of Homer and in the oral tradition prevalent before the Greeks learned how to read and write from the

A NEW PERSPECTIVE

Phoenicians. It is also important to note that during the Mycenaean period, the Phoenicians were under the Egyptian sphere of influence which gave them access to Egyptian expertise and products that they modified to make goods of which the Greeks emulated.

Furthermore, the Greeks associated papyrus paper and rope made from the stem of papyrus with the Phoenician city that was a port. The city of Byblos (which traded cedar for paper) was closely linked to papyrus, so much so that when the writings of the Hebrew prophets were translated into Greek, the city's name, Byblos, was given to the Bible. Both products were uniquely Egyptian, yet they entered Greece, not from the Egyptians, but through the Phoenicians. Since the Egyptians have never been maritime people, they relied on vassals such as the Phoenicians to be the conduit of their goods to what they viewed as the frontier. Moreover, it was a practice of the Egyptians to raise the son of the king of their vassals in Egypt, thus, molding its future leaders in the image of the Egyptians. Besides, princesses from other lands were also sent to Egypt and it is important to note that the Egyptians did not export their princesses to foreign lands.

Also significant is the profound influence that the Egyptians had over the entire Mediterranean region particularly the Levant during the Mycenaean era. During this time, the Phoenicians represented Egyptian power in the Levant. However, they were powerful in their own right and masters of the sea. This aspect of the Phoenicians was beneficial to Egypt and the region. However, for reasons unknown but often speculated, the Mycenaean culture collapsed around 1200 BCE and the period between 1200 BCE and about 800 BCE is often referred to as the Dark Ages of the Greeks.

The most common theory for the rapid collapse is a cataclysmic event such as a volcanic eruption. However, it could have also been an internal collapse or an external military invasion. It is also interesting to note, that the collapse of the Mycenaean culture corresponds to an overall decline in the eastern Mediterranean and the first mention of the state of Israel. However, this time also corresponds with the rise of the *sea people* some of which were the Philistines mentioned in the Bible from which the name Palestine emerged. As in the case of the Canaanites (Phoenicians), it is hard to obtain an unbiased opinion of the Philistines by reading the Bible because of the disdain that the Hebrews had for them.

The connection between the fall of the Mycenaean civilization, the Trojan War and the rise of Israel (or the possibility that the Philistines were perhaps responsible for the decline of the Canaanites) is seldom mentioned. During this decline, Israel produced three great kings, Saul, David and Solomon. The greatness of David and

RETHINKING THE HISTORY AND MYTHS OF THE PAST

Solomon may have been attributed to the incorporation of ideas that they inherited from the Philistines, who in turn inherited some of them from the Canaanites.

There is perhaps a nexus between the Mycenean myths told by the Greeks, the stories in the Bible and history as recorded by the Egyptians. According to (Exodus 12:41) the Israelites were slaves in Egypt for 430 years. Many historians associate Hyksos with the Jews in Egypt at the time of Joseph and the Exodus. Many historians interpret the phrase in the Bible: *"Now there arose up a new king over Egypt, which knew not Joseph"* (Exodus 1:8): as the end of the Hyksos domination and the rise of the New Kingdom under Ahmose I.

The Hyksos were expelled from Egypt in 1546 at the start of the New Kingdom. If you subtract 430 years from 1546, it equals the year 1116 BCE which is very close to the historical date of the establishment of the state of Israel, the decline of Mycenae and the New Kingdom. Toward the end of the New Kingdom, Egypt's influence and interest in the Levant waned, which created a vacuum of power in the region. Although there is no Egyptian historical record of Jewish slaves in Egypt, the biblical narrative could reflect the suppression of the Hyksos in Egypt and their presence in the Levant. This theme is consistent with the biblical narratives of Abraham and Joseph.

In the Levant, Solomon's greatest skill may have been his diplomacy which may also account for the worship of Canaanite gods in Israel. Some scholars believe that Israel was able to establish a temporary state because of the chaos and the weakness of its surrounding neighbors. Once their neighbors came out of this decline, Israel went into decline and was eventually divided and conquered by outside nations. After this time, there was a resurgence of an independent Phoenician state that established colonies all over the Mediterranean.

The collapse of Mycenae around 1200 was the end of the age of Greek legend. Yet their influence was remembered in the Homeric poems that have lasted for ages. *The Iliad* and *the Odyssey,* however, are only two parts of an eight-part known as "the Epic Cycle" of the Trojan War that emanates from a much older oral tradition. The others are as follows: the *Cypria,* which focuses on the first nine years of the war; the *Aethiopis,* which focuses on Troy's alliance with Ethiopia, the *Little Iliad* on the Trojan Horse, the *Iliupersis,* on the sack of Troy, the *Nortoris,* on the return of the Greek heroes and the *Telegony* a continuation of the Odyssey. Although the *Iliad* ends with the killing of Hector by Achilles, we learn of Achilles' death by Paris through other parts of the Epic Cycle.

A NEW PERSPECTIVE

The Greek City-States (*polis*) would emerge from the groundwork laid during the Heroic Age and the influence of non-European nations on Greece. Rome would later follow in the footsteps of the Greeks and bring civilization to the Western part of Europe. Thus, the pillars of Western Civilization stand on the foundation laid in foreign lands millenniums before.

The story of civilization is the story of humankind; Western Civilization, although sometimes used as a euphemism for European superiority, is just one piece of this evolving story.

RETHINKING THE HISTORY AND MYTHS OF THE PAST

The Roman Republic and the Rise and Fall of Julius Caesar

Death of Caesar by Vincenzo Camuccini.

The Founding Fathers of the United States used the Roman Republic as a model and viewed tyranny as an existential threat to democracy. As we follow in the footsteps of Rome, we must also remember, not only its glory and greatness, but how it rose and how it fell. Rome has left its indelible footprints on the roads of Western Civilization. Yet there is one Roman that stands above all, and his name was Gaius Julius Caesar. According to legend, he was born by the procedure that bears his name (cesarean) and some say he was destined for greatness. His life and death were memorialized by Shakespeare, so much so, that it is hard to discern the true history from Shakespeare's portrayal.

Roman leaders adopted his name, and his name lives on in the forms of Czar and Kaiser. Celebrated in monuments around the world, he is remembered not so much for how he lived but by how he died. *Et tu, Brute*, (Even you Brutus) were the Shakespearean words uttered by Caesar just before his demise. Yet, few understand the source or the reason why Brutus and his fellow conspirators betrayed and murdered Caesar.

The Roman Republic
When we think of Rome, we often think of an ancient empire that dominated the known world and the emergence of Christianity. As the scions of the Greeks and the conquerors of uncivilized Europe, Rome borrowed from others as much as it gave. According to folklore, Rome was a city that emerged from twin brothers Romulus

A NEW PERSPECTIVE

and Remus abandoned on the Tiber River and raised by a she wolf. Like the biblical story of Cain and Abel, one brother would shed the blood of another. Romulus killed Remus and henceforth the city would bear his name.

Rome rose from a section of Italy called Latium. This section was occupied by the Etruscan kings who oppressed the Romans. It was from the Etruscans that the Greek culture was introduced to Rome. Rome rebelled against the Etruscans and eventually gained its freedom. However, the Etruscans would leave their indelible mark on Rome, through its inherited Greek culture and the remembrance of past oppressive Etruscan kings. It was from such seeds that the Roman Republic (509 BCE) blossomed into an empire (27 BCE) that lasted (in various forms) for more than a thousand years.

Lucius Junius Brutus

The founder of the Roman Republic was Lucius Junius Brutus. Under his leadership, the Roman Republic established an executive branch, judiciary and a legislator that jointly controlled the reins of power. It was the Roman Republic that defeated Hannibal during the Second Punic War in 202 BCE. It was the Roman Republic that the Founding Fathers of the United States wanted to emulate in their form of government. In fact, America's capital city would be designed with Roman architecture in mind, the nation and its states often have Latin mottos and like Rome, the eagle is the symbol of its greatness. The greatest triumph of the Roman Republic was the defeat of Carthaginians in the Punic Wars which established complete dominance in the Mediterranean region.

RETHINKING THE HISTORY AND MYTHS OF THE PAST

The Rise of Julius Caesar

The Roman Republic, despite its success against foreign foes, was besieged by a series of domestic civil wars, and this was the environment in which Caesar rose to power. He did not ascend to power alone, but rather through the formation of the first triumvirate composed of: Caesar, Gnaeus Pompeius Magnus (Pompey), and Marcus Licinius Crassus. By their nature, triumvirates are temporal and ultimately one man will emerge as the sole leader. Of the three, Caesar was viewed as the weakest and least experienced. Yet in the end, he would prove to be the strongest. He first excelled as a military leader, and it was through his European campaigns that he gained the trust and admiration of his men.

Gaius Julius Caesar. Vatican Museum

While Caesar was away on foreign campaigns, Pompey solidified power at home, and Crassus soon became an insignificant figure in Rome. But it was Caesar's foreign success and local admiration that made the Senate and Pompey fear him. Although Pompey was married to Julia, Caesar's only child, it was not enough to forge a relationship between two men whose egos and quest for power exceeded any familial bond. And so, the stage was set for the epic battle between Caesar and Pompey.

There was a long-standing law that generals must disarm their army before entering Rome and the Senate decided to enforce it as a political tool to control Caesar. When he crossed the Rubicon River, without disbanding his army, the "die had been casted" and war was declared on Caesar. Pompey's military prowess was well renowned, and

A NEW PERSPECTIVE

he was therefore tasked with defeating Caesar. Caesar's army was small in comparison to Pompey's, but Caesar was swift and daring whereas Pompey was slow and hesitant. In the end, Caesar emerged as the sole survivor of the first triumvirate. As for Pompey, he was assassinated in Egypt and his decapitated head handed to Caesar as a means of currying favor with the new undisputed leader of Rome.

The Fall of Caesar
Lord Acton said: power corrupts, and absolute power corrupts absolutely. As power began to coalesce around Caesar, the Senate became even more fearful of his consolidated power and thus began to form cabals that secretly challenged and plotted against his rule. In public they were a group of sycophants, constantly giving him gifts such as a golden throne, praising him, naming a month (July) after him and so forth. For instance, in 46 BCE, he was made dictator for ten years, and in 44 BCE he was granted the title *Dictator Perpetuus* or "dictator for life. But, in private, their disdain for him could hardly be controlled, particularly among those that had supported Pompey.

In February of 44 BCE, a staged crown offering celebration was held planned to test the waters and see if the public would accept Caesar as king. He declined the offer several times. But it was this event that evoked the specter of the Etruscan kings among the Roman elite, including some of Caesar's loyal generals. It was seen as going too far and contrary to the ideals of the Roman Republic. Caesar had become more than a dictator; instead, he was now viewed by many as an uncontrollable tyrant. The Romans traditionally celebrated March as the beginning of the new year and the ides of March was typically viewed as the first full moon of the new year and thus was celebrated as a holiday. Ironically, it was Caesar that introduced a new calendar based on the solar year that started on January 1st in 45 BCE and introduced a leap year every four years. It was on the ides of March (March 15, 44 BCE) that the cabal of senators gathered to meet Caesar for the last time.

Among them was a young Marcus Junius Brutus of whom Caesar had treated like a son. Legend has it that when Caesar saw that Brutus was among them, he stopped defending himself against the traitorous blows of senators some of them crazed with power, others with envy but all united in the goal of ridding Rome of its tyrant: (*Sic Symper Tyrannis*) Death to tyrants: Thus, the climactic scene of the play was over and the Shakespearean omen given to Caesar by a soothsayer (beware the Ides of March) became a reality. According to legend, Caesar was stabbed twenty-three times and ironically fell dead at the feet of the statue of his nemesis Pompey.

Caesar's funeral was more of a trial than a memorial with both sides presenting their version of justice. The conspirators believed that his death was necessary to save the Roman Republic. They thought that the citizens of Rome would view them as

RETHINKING THE HISTORY AND MYTHS OF THE PAST

liberators and Caesar as the traitor to the Roman Republic. It was less about what Rome was, and more about what it would become. At his funeral, Brutus spoke for the conspirators. His argument was simple: Caesar had become too ambitious and they killed him to save the Roman Republic. After all, Brutus was a descendant of, Lucius Junius Brutus, the founder of the Roman Republic and although he loved Caesar, he loved Rome and the Republic more.

Marc Antony's Oration at Caesar's Funeral as depicted by George Edward Robertson

Yet, Mark Anthony's argument was more persuasive and perhaps more important, he had the last word. Anthony was one of Caesar's top generals and he spoke with a heartfelt passion that showed that he loved Caesar. He appealed to the crowd as fellow citizens; and he was able to use Brutus' words against him, while at the same time pointing to Caesar's accomplishments, his betrayal and his murder at the hands of men he had helped and, in some cases, forgiven. He did not cast the conspirators as bad men, nor Caesar as a saint, but instead as a man with human frailties. The Shakespearean version is as follows:

"Friends, Romans, countrymen, lend me your ears; I come to bury Caesar, not to praise him. The evil that men do lives after them; The good is oft interred with their bones; So let it be with Caesar"

The death of Caesar was a seminal moment in Roman history, and it changed its trajectory. It was both the end and the beginning. It was the end of the Roman Republic and the beginning of the Roman Empire. Under Caesar's adopted son and nephew, Augustus Caesar (Octavian), Rome became an empire. Augustus Caesar avenged Caesar's death, deified Caesar as a god and pronounced himself as the son of god (*divi filius*); decades before the birth of Christ.

A NEW PERSPECTIVE

Statue of Augustus Caesar

He established the *Pax Romana* (Roman Peace) which put an end to Rome's civil wars and established Rome as the dominant power in the region. He created a literary and historical tradition that produced magnum opuses such as Vergil's *Aeneid* and Livy's *The History of Rome*. Without the leadership of Augustus, Rome may have collapsed after the death of Julius Caesar. It was Caesar's goal to create an *Imperium Sine Fine* (an empire without end). Although Rome did not survive forever, it bequeaths to Western Civilization a heritage, in the form of its foundation, its laws and military prowess that continues to live on.

The Legacy of Rome

In the final analysis, Rome, like ancient Egypt, was strong because of what it had endured over its long history. The rise and fall of Caesar was just one defining episode in its turbulent history: from the defeat of Hannibal to the fall of Constantinople. Therefore, there is much that we can learn from the triumphs, resilience and failures of Rome. Time and time again, it was able to resurrect itself and when it could no longer rise from its ashes, through its leadership and adherence to its principles; it fell into the abyss of fallen empires. Perhaps the historian Will Durant's words serve as a warning to future empires:

RETHINKING THE HISTORY AND MYTHS OF THE PAST

"A great civilization is not conquered from without, until it has destroyed itself from within. The essential causes of Rome's decline lay in her people, her morals, her class struggle, her failing trade, her bureaucratic despotism, her stifling taxes, her consuming wars."

As we follow in the footsteps of Rome, we must also remember how it ended. Although Rome superstitiously placed its faith in the *Sibylline Books*, the Founding Fathers of the United States placed their faith in its Constitution to assure that their nation would not succumb to the pitfalls of Rome and other fallen empires. But instead, continue to endure and to strive toward a More Perfect Union. For over two centuries, America has basked in the reflective glory and grandeur of Rome, let us hope that it will heed the lessons of history and not succumb to the ill fate of Rome's demise.

The Founding Fathers viewed King George like the Romans viewed the Etruscan kings and therefore took a strong stand against tyranny. George Washington is quoted as saying: "I didn't fight George III to become George I." The Framers' safeguard against tyrants was impeachment by the House of Representatives and conviction by the Senate.

The greatest thing that Rome bequeathed to the Founding Fathers was the model of a Republic. But in the words of Ben Franklin: only if you can keep it.

A NEW PERSPECTIVE

RETHINKING THE HISTORY AND MYTHS OF THE PAST

Religion

A NEW PERSPECTIVE

RETHINKING THE HISTORY AND MYTHS OF THE PAST

Christianity

A NEW PERSPECTIVE

RETHINKING THE HISTORY AND MYTHS OF THE PAST

The Makings of the Gospels

Last Supper by Leonardo da Vinci

The Epistles of Paul, written between 49 and 64 CE, are among the earliest writings in the New Testament. They consist of letters written by Paul to various churches during his ministry. Paul viewed his letters as instruction and not as scripture, however, after his death they were combined and incorporated into the New Testament along with other epistles and the Gospels.

If the Epistles of Paul form the skeleton of the New Testament, then the Gospels form its body. Since Paul did not leave a biography of the life of Jesus, which is essential to any central figure of a religious group, one had to be included as the religion became more popular. Although Paul was more concerned with the post-Easter Jesus (after his resurrection), followers wanted to know more about Jesus the man and how he lived and died. Therefore, the Gospels, particularly the synoptic ones, are concerned with the pre-Easter Jesus (before his crucifixion).

When the history of Jesus' life is finally told, it is from the vantage point of four different writers. If a juxtaposition of the Gospels is conducted, we will see that many of the stories differ not only in content but in the order of events as the oral traditions associated with the life of Jesus were solidified into the written word. It is important to note that although names are attached to the Gospels, most scholars believe, they were written pseudonymously, with names of *Matthew, Mark, Luke* and *John* attached in the second century. Biblical scholars contend that it was important to attach names to Gospels, not only for posterity but for authenticity. From details in the Gospels,

A NEW PERSPECTIVE

clues of who the authors may have been were derived and names were assigned accordingly.

Matthew, Mark and Luke are called the Synoptic Gospels because they tell a common story. Most scholars also believe that the Synoptic Gospels originated close to the time of the destruction of the Jewish temple between 65–80 CE and John later around 90–95 CE. There are several methods of discerning such dates and the contemporary works of the Jewish historian Josephus, played an important role in chronicling the events surrounding the Gospels.

There can be no doubt that the Gospels deliver a powerful spiritual message. We should, however, not equate an ontological message with a literal one. Regarding the authorship of the Gospels, most Christians believe that the Gospels were written by, two of the disciples Matthew, the tax collector and John the beloved disciple, and by two friends of the Apostles, Mark the Secretary of Peter and Luke the traveling companion of Paul. However, nowhere in the Gospels are such claims made. The Book of Acts is also attributed to Luke and it is believed by many scholars that Acts and Luke were once one book. Moreover, the disciples were uneducated men from Galilee, and it is doubtful that they knew Greek, the language of the New Testament. Besides, there is evidence that the Gospels contain stories changed in the process of retelling. For instance, in the New Testament, the same story is told differently, and sometimes they contradict each other. Several examples could be cited, most notably is the discrepancy between John's Gospel and the Synoptic Gospels regarding the day of the Last Supper.

Many scholars argue that to understand the makings of the Gospels, it is essential that we independently investigate the historical background from which they emerged. The Gospels were written during a time of Jewish strife and during a literary age when stories about Rome and biographies of emperors were written by some of Rome's greatest writers. Rome went in search of its history perhaps best illustrated by the *Aeneid* written by Virgil. Many argue that the Roman *Aeneid* stands on the shoulders of the Greek *Iliad* and *Odyssey* in the same manner as the New Testament stands on the shoulders of the Old Testament.

It was during the Augustan era that Rome transformed from a Republic to an Empire and it incorporated many Hellenistic customs long in existence in the Near East. Chief among them was the construct of "the son of a god" as Caesar Augustus (27 BCE-14 CE) proclaimed to be the son of a god. Centuries earlier, Alexander the Great (356–323 BCE) traveled to Egypt over difficult terrain to see the oracle of Amon to confirm that he was the son of a god. In fact, being the son of a god appears

RETHINKING THE HISTORY AND MYTHS OF THE PAST

to be required to claim legitimacy in many Middle Eastern nations, a criterion adopted by the Greeks and later the Romans.

The New Testament was written during the *Pax Romana* or Roman Peace—a time of prosperity for many but not for all, when the denizens of the Roman diaspora were looking for spiritual alternatives. Many welcomed mystery cults that had at its core a crucified savior. One reason why Jews rejected Christianity, is because they viewed it as a paganized version of their religion. Consider this narrative often proposed by the biblical scholar Bart D. Ehrman: There once was a man that lived about two thousand years ago. Before he was born, his mother knew he would not be a normal child. An angel told her that her son would be divine. His birth was accompanied by miraculous signs. He was religiously precocious. He was an itinerant preacher. He gathered disciples and performed miracles. When he died, his followers claimed he ascended to heaven and that they had seen him alive.

Most people would think that Ehrman is referring to Jesus, but he is not. He is talking about Appollonius of Tyana whose life was recorded by Philostrantus in *The Life of Apollonius of Tyrana*. He lived around the same time as Jesus. Jesus was not the only man that was believed to be divine or the son of God. The simple fact that another man lived at the time of Jesus with essentially the same biography illustrates the environment that gave us Jesus. Therefore, one is left with the question: how much of the biography of Jesus written in the New Testament is historical? And moreover, how much of it is unique?

When one considers that the Gospels were completed several decades after the death of Jesus and were transmitted by word of mouth and in competition with men like Apollonious of Tyrana, the picture of Jesus as delineated in the Gospels may not represent the Historical Jesus but an archetype. Both are examples of the Messiah Motif; something Joseph Campbell (author of *The Hero with a Thousand Faces*) called a *monomyth*, common to Osiris, Dionysus, Mithras and a host of others that lay at the center of mystery cults. Many of them were born around the winter solstice and celebrated on Dec 25th, a date later ascribed to Jesus' birth. It was the crucifixion of the Historical Jesus along with his teachings that enable the alignment of his life and passion with those that had come before him. The esteemed historian Will Durant wrote: "Christianity did not destroy paganism; it adopted it."

I am not raising the question if the Historical Jesus existed or not; however, to ignore such a background and to accept Jesus as the "Only Begotten Son" based on the Gospels is a matter of faith and not necessarily one of history. There was nothing about the paradigm of a Mystical Christ that was not present in the pagan world and

A NEW PERSPECTIVE

both the Historical Jesus and the Mystical Christ emerged from the environment of the Roman Empire at the millennial end of Aries.

This raises a larger question regarding the Historical Jesus: Did Jews in Judea hand over Jesus to Pontius Pilate because he was teaching something "new"? Or did they hand him over to be crucified because he was teaching something different? Perhaps something that emerged and took root in the Jewish Diaspora among the gentiles? The fact that the Gospels were written in Greek by educated men; and the fact that Paul (a Roman citizen familiar with the Greek world) understood the significance of Jesus' death and resurrection better than the disciples of Jesus, seems to support this view. Of all of the apostles, it was Paul, someone who did not know Jesus in the flesh, that left his indelible stamp on Christianity.

Regarding the structure of the Gospels, biblical scholars have noted that the Synoptic Gospels consist of movable pericopes possibly based on anecdotes, some real some apocryphal, of the life and times of Jesus. These pericopes, such as the story of Martha and Mary in Luke 10:38–42, and other parables and miracles throughout the Gospels were part of the oral tradition of Jesus generated between his death around 30 BCE, and the writing of the Gospels thirty or so years later. They point to the fact that the final author moved pericopes because some units are in one context in one Gospel and another in another. Only gradually were pericopes assembled in books that purported to describe the life and times of Jesus as viewed by the author. However, decades had passed and the original context that inspired a given saying, action or belief may have been lost or distorted.

The consensus among biblical scholars is that Mark was written first, and that Matthew and Luke used Mark as a reference. This is based on similarities between Mathew and Luke that appear in Mark. This hypothesis is known as the *Markan priority*. Mark is the shortest Gospel and both Matthew and Luke incorporate most of Mark into their Gospels. Scholars have also questioned the ending of Mark which seems to make the Gospel feel incomplete. In addition to Mark, biblical scholars believe there was another document referred to as the Q document "Quelle" which means source in German. The writer of Q was more interested in the sayings of Jesus and not as much interested in his death and resurrection. They believe that both Matthew and Luke used Q as a reference in addition to Mark.

Biblical scholars also believe that the additions found in Mathew but not in Mark or Luke are referred to as (M) and those found in Luke are referred to as (L). Thus, the construction of Matthew could be written as follows: Mark plus (Q) plus (M) and similarly Luke: Mark plus (Q) plus (L) as illustrated below.

RETHINKING THE HISTORY AND MYTHS OF THE PAST

Relationships between the Synoptic Gospels

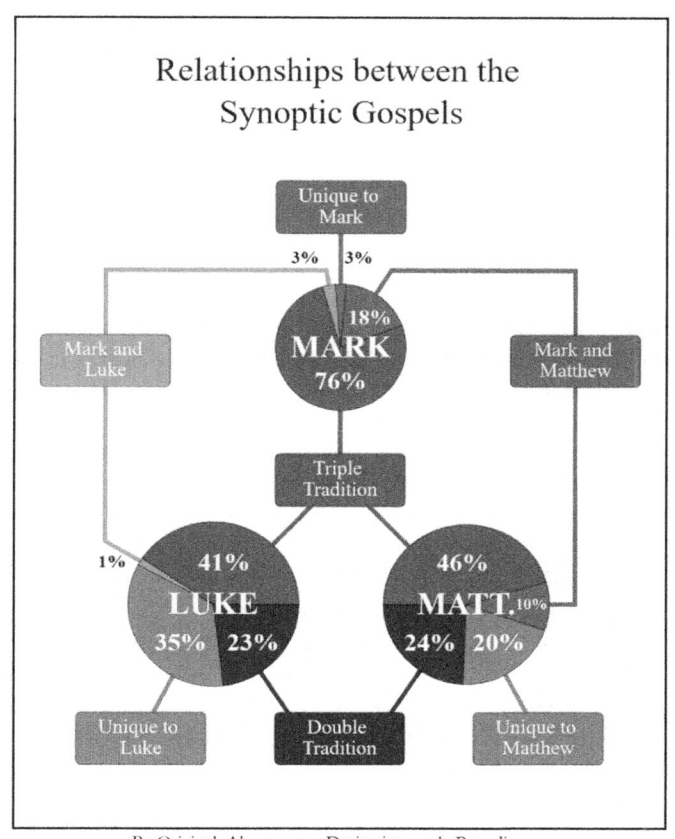

By Original: AlecmconroyDerivative work: Popadius—
this file was derived from: Relationship between synoptic gospels.png:, CC BY-SA 3.0,
https://commons.wikimedia.org/w/index.php?curid=27903558

John is a different Gospel. In some cases, the order of events is rearranged to support John's narrative at the expense of the other Gospels. Additionally, the narrative outline is different and so is the content. For instance, in John's Gospel, written 20–25 years after the first Synoptic Gospels, Jesus speaks about himself differently than he does in the other Gospels. It is only in this Gospel that all the "I am" statements are found, e.g., "I am the bread of life". It is only in John does Jesus say that "the Father and I are one." Another striking difference is the timeframe of Jesus' ministry. In the Synoptic Gospels, it is about a year in John it is slightly longer than two years. John's emphasis is Judea whereas the emphasis of the Synoptic Gospels is mainly Galilee, except for the final week of Jesus' life.

A NEW PERSPECTIVE

The Synoptic Gospels describe Jesus as being human particularly in Mark, however, the Gospel of John describes him as being divine. In the Synoptic Gospels Jesus visits Jerusalem one time at the very end, in John he visits it four times. In the Synoptic Gospels, the cleansing of the temple happens just before the crucifixion. In John, it happens two years before the crucifixion.

Perhaps the most striking difference that biblical scholars have tried to discern between the Synoptic Gospels and John is the day of Jesus' death which the Synoptic Gospels place on 15 Nisan and John places a day earlier before the Passover meal on 14 Nisan. Since the Gospel of John was written a decade or so later than the other Gospels, it could also represent the evolution of Christianity, or it could have been written to fill gaps that were not part of the Synoptic Gospels. For example, if the slaying of Jesus as the sacrificial lamb is associated with the Precession of Equinoxes, (every 2000 or so years) John may have seen it fit to end the era of Aries (the lamb) before the Passover as the Passover would esoterically and symbolically represent the beginning of the New Age of Pisces (the fish), i.e., the age of Christianity and an exodus from paganism.

It was said that the shed of blood of the lamb was the symbol that broke the power of death so that the lamb became the "agent of life." In the association with the lamb, John was not only looking back in time at Jewish tradition but using present events to shape the future. Perhaps John was aligning the story to correct what was written previously in the Synoptic Gospels. Since Jesus is the lamb, he had to be slain before the Passover meal not after the Passover Meal as stated in the Synoptic Gospels. In this regard, a clear analogy is drawn between Jesus and the New Israel and the Old.

According to the Gospel of John, Jesus never said the following at the Passover Meal: "This is my body" and "This is my blood" because he was already in his tomb at the time the Passover took place. Succinctly put, either the Synoptic Gospels are wrong, or John is wrong. Furthermore, it is in John that Jesus as the lamb is emphasized. For example, in John 1:29 John the Baptist sees Jesus and proclaims: *"Behold, the Lamb of God, that taketh away the sin of the world!"* Later in John comes perhaps the most powerful and widely quoted verse about Jesus in the Bible. John 3:16 *"For God so loved the world, that he gave his only begotten Son, that whosoever believeth in him should not perish, but have everlasting life."* (KJV)

Unlike other instances in the pagan world, Jesus is not the son of a god, but rather, the only Son of the only God. This may represent the merger of the gentile or pagan belief in the son of a god and the Jewish monotheistic belief in only one God. Hence, the Father and the son. Many gentiles had grown tired of the Roman pantheon of gods, therefore, the belief in one god was appealing to them. Furthermore, some

RETHINKING THE HISTORY AND MYTHS OF THE PAST

scholars that believe that the Book of Revelations and the Fourth Gospel both attributed to John were not written by the same author. They point to the fact that the Book of Revelation is Jewish poetry, whereas the Fourth Gospel is Greek philosophy. Others have pointed out that the Book of Revelations is a response to the persecution of Christians by Nero.

What is often ignored is that the image of Jesus that permeates Christianity is an amalgamation of all the Gospels in which stories from various Gospels are often intertwined to form a composite view of the life of Jesus. For example, the birth of Jesus is told in both Matthew and Luke, but they differ in content despite that they were possibly derived from the same Q pericope, yet they come to us as a composite. For instance, based on identifiable historical events, Luke places the birth of Christ around 6 CE based on the tax census and Mathew places his birth around 4 BCE based on the death of Herod who died in 4 BCE. It is also interesting to note that being born from a virgin or being impregnated by a god (as illustrated by Olympias the mother of Alexander the Great) was common among ancient pagan myths.

The genealogy of Jesus given by both also differs significantly. Only one of the two nativity scenes could be historically accurate. Such contradictions are often ignored in favor of a composite view of who Jesus was and what he preached. However, according to biblical scholars, the Gospel narratives are second hand at best—which may also account for some of the discrepancies. If by chance both Luke and Matthew were working from the same pericope, which in this case was to place the birth of Jesus in Bethlehem and to show that Jesus was a descendant of David, then it makes sense.

Although the storyline is basically the same, Matthew and Luke were writing from different perspectives. Matthew's genealogy has a Jewish flavor and traces Jesus back to Abraham. Whereas Luke's genealogy goes back to Adam which implies that Jesus' kinship is not limited to the Jews but to humanity. Some biblical scholars contend that just about all of the major stories in the New Testament have their Old Testament parallels, and, in some cases, are the amalgamation of Old Testament text as if the stories were reshaped to match the times. For instance, the betrayal of Christ by Judas is a new version of the selling of Joseph into bondage, in this case, Judas is substituted for Judah (notice the similarity in names) and 30 pieces of silver instead of 20. (Gen. 37: 26–28) Some scholars also contend that his hanging is a revision of the betrayal of Ahithophel's betrayal of King David (2 Sam. 15: 13–18).

Moreover, the hurling of silver back into the temple by Judas is a retelling of (Zech 11:13–15). All of these stories converge on the narrative of Judas and in fact, could be constructed without the existence of a Judas. Moreover, the 30 pieces of silver instead

A NEW PERSPECTIVE

of 20 in the Old Testament may have been intentional to comply with the number three associated with Jesus, e.g., three men on the cross; rose in three days, three wise men, etc.. When telling history, the details are important, however, in the realm of myth, the details are not as important as the moral of the story. Although Luke and Matthew paint a picture of Jesus' birth and early life, not contained in Mark, additional information is also contained in the Infancy Gospels which were ruled as non-canonical. Also, the authorship of some of the letters of Paul is called into question by biblical scholars. Chief among them are 2 Thessalonians, Colossians and Ephesians. The consensus among biblical scholars is that Hebrews, Timothy and Titus are certainly from another hand. Other scholars, however, have pointed out that although they may have been written by others it does not mean that they were not authorized by Paul. It is also important to note that Paul's letters to the churches are not arranged in chronological order, but rather, <u>in accordance with their length</u>.

This editorial is not an article of faith, but a consensus of biblical scholars on how the Gospels were developed and how they evolved over time. In many cases, it conflicts with the traditional view held by many Christians and taught in Sunday School classes., It is, however, consistent with the scholarly view taught at many universities and theological seminaries

RETHINKING THE HISTORY AND MYTHS OF THE PAST

The Evolution of the New Testament

Pope Sylvester I and Emperor Constantine

When Christianity was sanctioned as the official religion of the state by Constantine the Great (306–337), it needed a consistent dogma and orthodoxy, i.e., a book and it also needed to suppress competing sects. This was the genesis of the New Testament as we know it today.

The Formation of the Catholic Church

Before the conversion of Constantine to Christianity, a common testament did not exist and there were many Christian sects with different Gospels that were viewed as sacred. *Matthew, Mark, Luke* and *John* were accepted by the Catholic Church as canonical and the others rejected. In recent times, however, non-canonical gospels, known as *The Nag Hammadi* document have been uncovered and they shed a different light on the events of early Christianity. Although the life of Jesus comes to most of us through the lens of the four Canonical Gospels, up until the 4th century CE there were other Gospels available to Christians that the Church later viewed as non-canonical.

Among the more popular non-canonical gospels are the Gnostic Gospels of *Mary, Thomas, Phillip, Judas* and *Truth*. Like the canonical gospels, they were also written pseudonymously and were an integral part of the Christian movement before the Council of Nicaea in 325 CE. The apocryphal labeling of these scriptures, as viewed by the newly formed Church, may have had more to do with the politics of the day than the teachings of Jesus. Furthermore, the 27 canonical books of the New Testament were first enumerated by the Bishop (Athanasius) of Alexandria (298-373

A NEW PERSPECTIVE

CE) and are closely related to his overall theology. Those that did not subscribe to his theology (which became part of Church doctrine) were labeled as heretics. He was the gatekeeper and interpreter of what was inerrant and what was not.

While the four Gospels form a composite view of the life and times of Jesus, some have asked the following questions: Why four Gospels and not three or five, and why this group of four? Such decisions rested in the hands of one man, as the 27 books that Athanasius recommended were eventually accepted. It is also worthy to note that not all of the Canonical Gospels or the Epistles were *unanimously* accepted but instead ratified by consensus after the Council of Nicaea was convened. Scholars, past and present, have disagreed with Athanasius' assessment. Chief among them were Martin Luther and Thomas Jefferson. Jefferson wrote his own Bible in which he deleted the Epistles of Paul and the miracles of Jesus.

Before the Council of Nicaea, the two important rival sects were Marcionism and Gnosticism. Marcionism was centered on the letters of Paul and Gnosticism had several different Gospels. Both sects were viewed as heretical by the newly formed Church. To some within the Christian movement, Marcionism with its emphasis on Paul was viewed as a threat, not only to them but to their interpretation of the role of Jesus in the formation of the Christian faith. Christianity had to be seen as a religion of Jesus and not one of Paul in which Jesus was the subject of Paul's religion. The Gnostic movement was also seen as a threat and its Gospels rejected by the Church. Although Peter's influence on Christianity was not as great as Paul's, the newly formed Church was centered around Peter and not Paul.

Even though Christians were persecuted throughout the Roman Empire in the nascent days before Constantine, Christianity was not a monolithic religion organized around a Bible, as we know it today. It emerged as the result of a power struggle within the Christian movement, sanctioned by Constantine, as a means of developing a common orthodoxy and exegesis. Some scholars question Constantine's religious epiphany and motives and believe he saw Christianity as a means to gain control of an empire in decline. No longer the persecuted, the Church under Constantine became persecutors of others.

Rome eventually collapsed under the stress of its empire and when it did, it fell into the waiting arms of Christianity. When Constantine died and was finally baptized on his deathbed, the power transferred to the Pope and subsequent kings were subservient to him. The Pope became *Vicarius Christi* (Christ on earth) and had the power to excommunicate those that did not agree with his doctrine or exegesis. To quote the historian Will Durant author of Caesar and Christ:

RETHINKING THE HISTORY AND MYTHS OF THE PAST

"When Christianity conquered Rome the ecclesiastical structure of the pagan church, the title and vestments of the pontifex maximus… and the pageantry of immemorial ceremony, passed like maternal blood into the new religion, and captive Rome captured her conqueror."

The Roman Empire was transformed into the Holy Roman Empire. Christianity could not have spread without the monolithic structure of the Roman Empire. Its roads, its currency, its institutions and hegemony over foreign lands served as a catalyst for this new monotheistic religion center on one God and his begotten son. The transformation was completed with the coronation of Charlemagne (748–814) on Christmas Day, 800 CE, by Pope Leo III.

Imperial Coronation of Charlemagne, by Friedrich Kaulbach

Church Dogma

Some scholars contend that the New Testament represents a nexus between Jewish religious belief and prevalent Greek (Hellenistic) thought which draws upon pagan religious practices. The more and more the Catholic Church evolved, the more and more it became pagan in its motifs, ideology and its rituals that were present in the popular mystery cults throughout the Roman Empire. So much so that it was difficult to discern statues of Horus and Isis from Jesus and Mary. Moreover, some scholars believe that the tradition of the Black Madonna (Madonna and child) prevalent within the Catholic Church and worshiped as one of its most sacred icons has its origins in the Isis and Horus motif. Titles and attributes of Isis such as the *Virgin Mother* and *Queen of Heaven* were also assigned to Mary.

A NEW PERSPECTIVE

Statue of Isis nursing Horus

Many biblical scholars argue that Jesus' siblings and his parents viewed Jesus as human and not the son of God. Over time the siblings of Jesus were reduced, and Mary was raised to the mother of God untainted by sin. After Jesus' death, his brother James became the leader of the Christian church, yet three hundred years later we find his role greatly reduced. In Mark, the first gospel written, (65 CE) Jesus dies a lonely death without any of his disciples present, and it is left to a Roman centurion a pagan to watch Jesus die. In Mark's original conclusion, the disciples are never informed of the resurrection and thus are never reconciled with Christ.

In reading the Canonical Gospels, in the order that they were written according to biblical scholars, Jesus becomes more divine as the Gospels progress. In Mark, he is the "Son of God", a person that mediates God's will on earth and not a divine being. In Mark, the assumption is that Joseph is the father of Jesus and Jesus has sisters and brothers. Mark's Gospel is the only one in which the people who should understand him best, his family and his disciples, fail to recognize him as the Messiah.

Moreover, some ignore or fail to recognize that from the beginning, according to the virgin birth narrative in Luke, Mary knew that she was impregnated by God. So why is she surprised to find Jesus in the temple and his response that it is logical for him to be found in his Father's house? (Luke 2:39–52). For example, Alexander the Great believed that he was the son of god because his mother Olympias constantly told him so. Why is Mary surprised to see Jesus do something that she knew he was born to do?

RETHINKING THE HISTORY AND MYTHS OF THE PAST

By the time John is written, about 60 years after Jesus' death, the evolution of Jesus into a divine God is complete. To put it succinctly, the progression is as follows: human in Mark, a demigod in Luke and a God in John. This progression is perhaps best illustrated in the different crucifixion scenes in Mark and John. In John, the Son of God is in complete control and carries his cross and dies in the company of the beloved disciple. He accepts his death (John 19:17–42) In Mark, and the other Synoptic Gospels, he is too weak to carry his cross and dies in despair and without any disciple present. He cries: *"Eli, Eli, lama sabachthani? that is, "My God, My God, why have You forsaken Me?"* (Mark 27:46) Perhaps this progression indicates a movement within Christianity that is more consistent with the belief of the gentile (Hellenistic) populace and as we have seen in the development of Paul's theology a need to appease and appeal to the gentile community by removing such restrictions as kosher food and circumcision.

The pseudonymous writers of the New Testament were not only familiar with the Old Testament, but with Hellenistic philosophy and the Greek mind. Many scholars have pointed to the similarities between Christianity and mystery cults (pagan practices). The cult of Isis was the most popular cult in the Roman Empire and the Virgin Mary assumed the role of Isis. What many Christians fail to realize is that a different story could be told around the same idea or motif. In fact, this is what myth is often about. When one idea precedes the other, it is logical to assume the former influenced the later and not the other way around.

Many scholars contend that in support of their ideologies, the New Testament writers used the Old Testament as a reference and a prophetic tool for the prognostication of events to be fulfilled in the New Testament. This was particularly true of Matthew and Luke and was germane to the final product because it gave Christianity a history far beyond its times. Hence, the different versions of the genealogy of Jesus used in Matthew (Matthew 1) and in Luke (Luke 3:23–38) to confirm the prophecy of the Old Testament, and Isaiah 7: 14 regarding the birth of a child from a virgin.

Some scholars have pointed out that the verse in Hebrew says "young woman" which was interpreted in the Pentateuch as an "unmarried woman" which is later interpreted in the Septuagint and King James Version as "virgin". It is important to note that the Septuagint was the Greek version used by Luke and most of the elite Jews within the diaspora, many of them were unable to speak Hebrew. Moreover, the use of virgin instead of a young woman aligns Mary with Isis and the virgin motif prevalent throughout the Hellenistic world.

A NEW PERSPECTIVE

In this regard, being born of a virgin may have been a prophecy in search of a home and the book of Isaiah was used to give the virgin birth a home. Furthermore, some scholars have argued that the words in Isaiah apply to a contemporary messiah and not someone that would be born centuries later. What is often overlooked is that the Gospel writers wrote Jesus' biography in the shadows of the Old Testament. The fact that the Jews were looking for a messiah is confirmed by contemporary sources. However, exactly who was the coming messiah remains uncertain, but we must remember that the Persian king Cyrus the Great was referred to as a messiah by Jews.

Furthermore, during the reign of Pontius Pilate (26-36 CE), there were several Jews in Judea that claimed to be the messiah. Moreover, the unrest in Judea best exemplified by the uprising recorded by Josephus illustrates that Jews were not satisfied with Rome. In this regard, Christianity could also be seen as a rebellion of a different kind, one in which martyrdom was integral to its movement and a promise of eternal life was offered. As Tertullian (160–240 CE) would later state: *"The blood of the martyrs is the seed of the church."*

Christ Crucified (c. 1632) by Diego Velázquez. Museo del Prado, Madrid

Many biblical scholars have argued that although the New Testament and the Old Testament are similar in many ways; the God and the prophets differ in the way they behave. For example, the God of the Old Testament at times is jealous and at other times brings His wrath on the enemies of Israel and its people when they do not obey

RETHINKING THE HISTORY AND MYTHS OF THE PAST

His laws. Contrary, the God of the New Testament does not frequently bring His wrath, and Jesus, unlike Moses, prefers to turn the other cheek. Examples such as God telling the Israelites to murder all their enemies in Jericho (1 Samuel 15:2–3) and the God of Jesus teaching to love thy enemies (Matthew 5:44, Luke 6:27–36) Elisha calling out bears to kill all of the children (2 Kings 2:23–25) and Jesus saying: "Let the little children come to me, (Matthew 19:14) can be cited to illustrate the contradictory nature of the two Gods. This was a key point made by Maricon.

Furthermore, Moses was assumed to be the author of the Torah; Christ was not the author of the New Testament but rather its subject, symbol and article of faith. Moses brought God's wrath upon the Egyptians. Jesus surrendered to the Romans without a fight. It was clear that Jews were looking for a savior (messiah) with the attributes of a Moses or a Cyrus the Great and probably when the Historical Jesus failed to act in the same vein of Moses or Cyrus, they offered him up to be crucified. Additionally, if Jesus was not crucified, he would not have fit into the Crucified Savior motif (death and resurrection) of Dionysus and Osiris prevalent throughout the gentile population. Moreover, his resurrection would be inconsequential. The belief that a man could be born of a "human mother" and still be a god is a Hellenistic idea that was established with Dionysus which has its roots in Osiris.

Without such beliefs in place for centuries along with an established paradigm in the form of the Old Testament, it is doubtful that Christianity would have succeeded. So, few Christians are aware of the background from which their religion emerged or the antecedent paradigm based on a Crucified Savior or Redeemer that died and was resurrected. Moreover, Jesus died like Socrates and the cross became his hemlock. Like Socrates, he didn't leave any written words but left it up to others to interpret his message. In this regard, Paul was to Jesus what Plato was to Socrates. The Hellenization of the Roman Empire and the incorporation of motifs conceived millenniums ago in the pagan world and reinforced by Greco-Roman history were essential to the acceptance of Christianity as a universal religion. With Jewish dietary and circumcision restrictions removed by Paul, this new religion, founded in the name of Christ gained traction throughout the Roman Empire.

Gentiles recognized that in Christ, there was a contemporary figure that matched the savior motifs of the past. Was Paul, like a good politician, telling the gentiles of the Roman Empire something that they wanted to hear? Unlike the disciples, Paul was uniquely qualified because he knew the Jewish and the Hellenistic worlds. Many argue that although the Historical Jesus provided the clay, it was in the hands of Paul that the Historical Jesus was molded into the Mystical Christ.

A NEW PERSPECTIVE

What is interesting is that although Paul spoke little about the life of Jesus in his writings and was much more concerned with the meaning of Jesus' death, the author of Acts knowing of the death of Paul does not write about it at all. Instead, he ends his narrative with Paul spreading the word under house arrest as if to indicate that the word cannot be bounded, nor can it ever die.

Unlike the other Gospel writers, Luke is the only one that provides a biography of Jesus (The Gospel of Luke) and a history of the early Church (Acts: which is essentially a biography of Paul). Little is told about the acts of the twelve disciples, except for Peter, who knew Jesus in the flesh and were taught directly by him. Many scholars contend that Christianity is the product of two men, born about two years apart in two separate parts of the Roman Empire under the reign of Augustus Caesar. These two men, Jesus and Paul, were products of their time and they altered the course of world history for over two thousand years. One taught for three years the other for thirty years. They lived in a time that was about two thousand years after Abraham. Their gift to the world was the 27 books of the New Testament.

This essay is not an article of faith, but a history of how the New Testament was developed and how it evolved over time. Some may argue that the power lies not so much in the history, but in the story.

RETHINKING THE HISTORY AND MYTHS OF THE PAST

Islam

A NEW PERSPECTIVE

RETHINKING THE HISTORY AND MYTHS OF THE PAST

A Brief History of Islam

A Persian miniature depicts Muhammad leading Abraham, Moses, Jesus and other prophets in prayer.

Before Islam, the Arabian Peninsula was a region torn by centuries of tribal warfare. Before the birth of Muhammad, its people were aware of both Jewish and Christian faiths, yet they embraced neither. They were, however, painfully aware that their God, Allah, had never sent them a revelation or a prophet of their own.

Early Islam

Some Arabs that encountered Jews and Christians began to feel that God had left them out of His divine plan because they had not received a revelation that spoke specifically to them. However, all of that changed on the 17th night of Ramadan in the year 610 CE when Muhammad (570–632) received his first revelation. While sleeping in a mountain cave, he was visited by the angel, Gabriel that commanded that he recite *(iqra)*. The summons to his mission as a prophet is known in Islam as *Laylat Al Qadr* (the Night of Power). Like so many prophets before him, Muhammad did not think he was worthy. The word of God had been spoken for the first time in the native Arabic language and the holy book would be called the Koran (the Recitation). Four the remaining twenty-two years of his life, Muhammad continued to receive revelations.

A NEW PERSPECTIVE

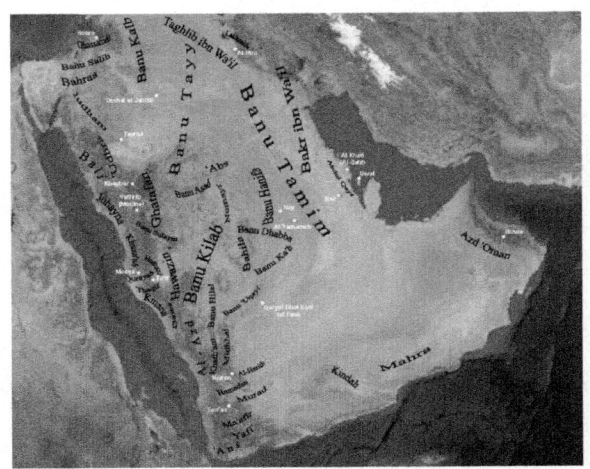

Main tribes and settlements of Arabia in Muhammad's lifetime

Muhammad was one of the most astonishing historical figures in world history. Born Muhammad ibn Abdullah in Mecca around 570 CE, he was orphaned at the age of two and was raised by his uncle Abu Talib. He married a rich widow named Khadijah and together they had four daughters: Umm Kulthum, Ruqayah, Zainab, and Fatimah. Khadijah was the first convert to Islam, and as a result, she is highly revered. Muhammad's leadership can be divided into two periods: The Mecca years (610–622) and the Medina years (622–632). It was in 622 that a small community of Muslims migrated from Mecca to Medina. This is known as *Hijrah* and marks the turning point in the development of Islam.

The year, 622, is the first year of the Muslim calendar. Although, Mecca is the holiest city within Islam, Medina and Jerusalem (where Muhammad ascended to heaven on his Night Journey) are also sacred to Islam. During his lifetime, he was able to communicate a religious vision that united not only his people but people around the world. The religious scholar Karen Armstrong in her book ***Muhammad*** explains:

If we view Muhammad as we do any other important historical figure, we would surely consider him to be one of the greatest geniuses the world has known. To create a literary Masterpiece, to found a major religion and a new world power are not ordinary achievements. But to appreciate his full genius we must examine the society into which he was born and the forces which he contended. When he descended from Mount Hira to bring the Word of God to the Arabs, Muhammad was about to attempt the impossible…….. Yet, Muhammad set out to make the Arabs achieve this major change in a mere twenty-three years!

RETHINKING THE HISTORY AND MYTHS OF THE PAST

Although Muhammad was an extremely charismatic and gifted person, he never professed to be a god in any way but rather, the Messenger of God. Nor did he profess to perform miracles such as raising people from the dead. Even though his name is perhaps the most popular in the world, the religion does not bear his name and he is subordinate to the Koran and Islam.

Muslims believe that the Koran was revealed to the Prophet Muhammad in a series of chapters (suras) and organized according to length with the longest first and the shortest last. The shorter suras are from the Mecca years. It was in 630 that Muhammad led his forces against Mecca and from 630 to 632 the remaining tribes of Arabia accepted Muhammad's mission and the Islamic faith. The life and achievements of Muhammad would change the lives of Muslims forever and leave an ingrained mark on human history for centuries after his death.

The holy book that he left, the Koran, is the fruit of Islam that nourishes nearly a billion people every day. Islam, like Judaism and Christianity, is a monotheistic religion that claims Abraham as its primogenitor through his son Ismael. Most scholars agree that the Jewish and Christian faiths had a profound influence on Islam; and Muslims refer to them as *People of the Book*. Many of the Prophets of the Old Testament are in the Koran, e.g., Adam, Noah, Isaac, Joseph, Moses, David, Solomon, Jonah, and John (the Baptist); and Christians would be surprised to find how many times Jesus (Isa) and Mary (Maryam) are mentioned in the Koran. Moreover, the Koran contains a chapter, 19, Surah Maryam, that is named after Mary.

The Following are used as sources for guidance within Islam:

Koran (Qur'an): The Word of God as revealed to the Prophet Muhammad

Hadith: Authenticated sayings of the Prophet Muhammad

Ijma: A consensus among Islamic scholars

Qiyas: Analogical reasoning

Ijtihad: Continual scholarly interpretation

There are five things or pillars that are incumbent upon every Muslim:

1) *Shahadah*: I testify that there is no God but God and Muhammad is the messenger of God

2) *Salat:* Prayer (five times a day in the direction of Mecca)

A NEW PERSPECTIVE

3) *Zakat:* Charity

4) *Sawm:* Fasting (observed during the month of Ramadan)

5) *Hajj:* Pilgrimage. (once in a lifetime on a Pilgrimage to Mecca)

The following are among the top sacred sites to all Muslims:

- The Kaaba Masjid al-Haram (Toward which Muslim should face when praying anywhere in the world)
- Masjid al Nabii (The Prophet's House)
- Masjid al Aqsa and the Dome of the Rock

The following are important to the Shi'a community:

- Karbala (the place where Imam Hussain the grandson of the prophet was martyred)
- Najaf (The first Imam of the Shi'a tradition is buried here)

From the early days in Medina, Islam was built around the notion of a religious community marked by universal faith; an affirmation in a single God and that Muhammad was His messenger. A body of Islamic law, the *Sharia,* based on the Koran and the interpretations of the Prophet's law text and sayings, was established and upheld by a religious body known as the *Ulema.* Armed which such laws and convictions, in relatively a short time, Islam was able to usher in one of the largest empires in history. The influence of Islam had spread as far in a few decades as Christianity had in as many centuries.

By 636 CE, only four years after the death of Muhammad, the Byzantines were forced to retreat from Syria and the Muslims became established in the Levant. In 641 CE, Egypt was under their control and a decade later parts of Persia. By the end of the eighth century, the Arabs had reached Spain to the west and India in the east. The early history of Islam could be broken down into crucial periods. The first is known as the four "Rightly Guided Caliphs (successors) *Al-Khulafa-ur Rashidun*" who ruled from 632- 661 CE. This is followed by the Umayyad caliphs (661-750 CE) with their capital at Damascus, the Abbasids (750–1258) with the center of their dynasty located in Baghdad, culminating with the Ottoman Empire (1299–1922) centered in Turkey.

Rightly Guided Caliphs
The first of the "Rightly Guided Caliphs" was Abu Bakr (570–634) an early follower, closest companion and father of one of Mohammad's wives. He ruled for two years

RETHINKING THE HISTORY AND MYTHS OF THE PAST

during which he instituted the collection of the Koran to be put in written form. The next caliph was Umar (Omar). He conquered Damascus in 635 and Jerusalem in 637, both from Syria in the Byzantine Empire and the Persian Empire.

It was Umar who established the basic practices of the Islamic government. Uthman (574- 656) succeeded Umar and he initiated the compilation of the text that became the Koran as revealed to the Prophet. Uthman ruled for twelve years and was assassinated. He was succeeded by Ali a blood relative of Mohammad. Ali was known for his eloquent sermons and his bravery and he is constantly revered in-text particularly among the Sufis and the Shi'ites branches. Out of the first Four Caliphs three of them were assassinated, Uthman, Umar, and Ali. In fact, "assassin" is one of the words that come to us from Arabic.

Many Westerners and non-Muslims tend to think of Islam as a monolithic religion. Islam, however, is divided into various sects with different ideologies and interpretations of the Koran. It was after the death of Mohammad, that the seeds which would ultimately splinter Islam were first planted. Abu Bakr and Umar, both companions of the Prophet from the early days in Medina, felt that they possessed the vision and the experience to follow in the footsteps of Mohammad. Some Muslims, however, believed that power should remain within the family of the Prophet. Muhammad's closest blood relative was Ali who was also married to Muhammad's daughter Fatima. Together they had two sons, Hasan and Husayn. The family of the Prophet was a constant source of opposition from the inception of the early caliphates. The selection of Ali as Caliph exposed the schism within the Muslim community regarding a legitimate successor.

Since Mohammad left no male heirs, the ascension based on blood rite was always a matter of contention. With Ali being tied to Mohammad by blood, many Muslims thought that he was the rightful heir. As a result of the ongoing friction, a civil war ensued and Ali, who the Shi'ites regard as the first Imam, was assassinated. Many Muslims thought that Ali's son, Husayn (626–680), and the grandson of the Prophet Muhammad should succeed him which led to more civil war and the murder of Husayn and his immediate family by the Umayyad caliph Yazid in 680. This was a seminal event in the history of Shi'ism and Islam because the death of Husayn took on an aura of martyrdom. The town of Karbala where Husayn was killed developed into one of the holiest shrines of Shi'ism.

Over the decades following the death of Ali and his son, Shi'ism evolved. They believed that Ali was the first Iman selected by Mohammad and that each Iman from the first to the twelfth has been selected. They also believe that Twelfth Iman went into hiding and this led to the belief in the Hidden Iman, who would someday return

A NEW PERSPECTIVE

to administer justice. Thus, Shi'ism is based on the Ali tradition and his family, and likewise, the Sunni tradition is based on the rightful rule of the Umayyad caliphate. This is the source of the friction between Shi'ite and Sunni that has lasted centuries and still rages today.

Umayyad Caliphate (661–750)
With the death of Ali and his son Husayn, the Syrian governor Muawiya becomes the fifth caliph and establishes the Umayyad caliphate. With this caliphate, Damascus became the political center while Mecca remained, as it still does today, the spiritual center of Islam. It was from this caliphate that the Dome of the Rock was built, and the Islamic Empire continued to expand from North Africa to Spain and France in the West to Sind Central Asia in the East. However, from such strife, two fashions of Islam emerged. The Shi'ites are the minority Muslim community and are based primarily in Iran and parts of Iraq. It is worthy to note that it was the Safavid Empire of Iran that established Shi'ism as the state religion in Iran led by the Ayatollah.

It was a result of conquests in northern Africa during the Umayyad caliphate that the Moorish conquest of the Iberian Peninsula was achieved in 711 CE. The face of Islam was slowly changing as more non-Arabs were converted. This caused many to question not only the power of the Umayyad caliphate but also its religious conviction which eventually led to rebellion along both ethnic and religious lines.

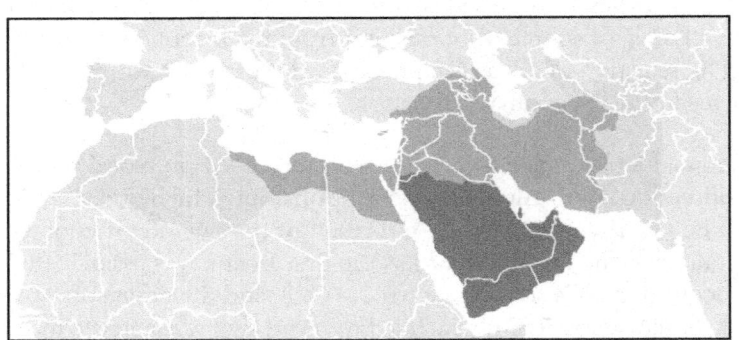

Age of the Caliphs Expansion under the Prophet Muhammad, 622–632 Expansion during the Patriarchal Caliphate, 632–661 Expansion during the Umayyad Caliphate, 661–750

Abbasid Caliphate (750–1258)
The Abbasids, taking their name from one of Muhammad's relatives and allying with Shi'ites eventually replaced the Umayyad caliphate in 750 CE. However once in power, the dominant faction of the Abbasid caliphate was Sunni and its capital moved from Damascus to Baghdad. Although this is considered as one caliphate, in reality, it was composed of several caliphates united under the banner of Islam, yet distinct in its practices and culture perhaps best exemplified by the cultures in Spain, Persia and

RETHINKING THE HISTORY AND MYTHS OF THE PAST

Turkey the latter became the Ottoman Empire which lasted until the end of World War I.

It was at the battle of the River Zab that the Abbasid era began with the defeat of the Umayyad army. The Abbasid caliphate was by far the greatest political power of the Islamic world. Often referred to as the *Golden Age of Islam*, it is as significant to world history as the Roman Empire although it is far less known. The empire stretched from Tunisia to India, leaving a vast influence that is prominent today. It was a continuation of the caliphate established by Abu Bakr after the death of the Prophet Mohammad.

It was the Abbasid Dynasty that had the greatest influence on Europe. During its long history, it would splinter into small dynasties with local control, it was from this dynasty in Moorish Spain that shined its bright light over Europe during its Dark Ages. It is not a coincidence that European nations on the Iberian Peninsula (Spain and Portugal) were the first to emerge from the shadows of the Dark Ages. Within 130 years after the death of Muhamad, the Islamic empire spread from Gibraltar to the Indus delta and had penetrated Europe and China by land and by sea.

During the Abbasid Dynasty, *The House of Wisdom* was established in Baghdad. Well before there was an Italian Renaissance, there was a Muslim Renaissance not of art but math and in science. Muslims scholars consolidated, Greek, Persian, Indian and Chinese knowledge into a cohesive package of which Europe was the chief beneficiary. Gunpowder, the compass and advanced sails all entered Europe via the Muslims. It was through the Muslims that the Greek classics were reintroduced to Western Europe. Much of the works of Aristotle, Plato, Pythagoras, Ptolemy, Euclid, Hippocrates and other prominent thinkers of Greek antiquity were all rendered in Arabic making the language the Lingua Franca of the philosophical and scientific world of Europe. As a result, words such as algebra, alcohol, alchemy, admiral, arsenal, azimuth, zenith, guitar, chemistry, syrup, zero, orange, sofa, nadir, lemon, ginger, sesame, coffee, giraffe, cotton, mask, rice, atlas, camel, and so forth are of Arabic origin. Modern Spanish contains thousands of words derived from Arabic.

In Moorish Spain, Jews, Christians, and Muslims studied together and were free to exchange ideas. Muslim learning centers in Spain were emulated in Italy. Furthermore, the Muslim Renaissance set the stage for European exploration and the establishment of universities in Europe. Muslim scientists were the masters of the sky, introduced Arabic numbers (0–9), Algebra and Trigonometry to Europe, along with advancements in Medicine, Chemistry and Physics. For example, Roger Bacon (1220–1292) was greatly influenced by Islamic scientists. His translations and commentaries led to Isaac Newton's interest to read *Al-Haytham* and to synthesize his great work on

A NEW PERSPECTIVE

Optics. Newton also used mathematics first developed by Islamic mathematicians to develop Calculus.

Mongol Invasion

The Abbasid rule ended in 1258 when the Mongols invaded parts of the Muslim world. They conquered all of Persia and Iraq. This was not a peaceful conquest with thousands of Muslims slaughtered. *The House of Wisdom* was destroyed along with its tremendous library of books. For a period, Islam was outlawed, however, true to the power of Islam the Mongols eventually converted to the faith and became known as the *Il-Khanids*. They restored the mosques, reopened schools and adopted the culture. They even extended the Muslim world into parts of India and southern Russia.

Although Arabic was the language of the Prophet and the *lingua franca* of the Islamic world, the Muslim world was a cosmopolitan mixture of people of all races, colors and ethnicities that spoken dozens of languages all united under the banner of Islam. Although often misunderstood in the West, and sometimes lurks in the shadows of Jihad; Islam is a religion that promotes peace, the arts and science.

After the invasion of the Mongols, the unitary Muslim state was dismembered and from the 13th century onward several large Muslim states competed among themselves. Among them were the Persian Empire, The Mamlukes of Syria and Egypt, the Mughals of India along with Muslim states in Africa and Southeast Asia most noted is Indonesia which further testifies to the wide geographical spread of the Islamic World before Columbus. When the Roman Empire collapsed, it fell upon the shoulders of Christianity and it also opened the door for Islam to flourish.

The Ottoman Empire (1299–1922)

The Ottoman Empire rose from the humble origins of the Turks. Osman Ghazi was born in 1258, the same year Baghdad was destroyed by the Mongols. After Baghdad fell to the Mongols, the Seljuks declared an independent Sultanate in east and central Asia Minor. Osman died in 1326, after having laid the foundation for an empire that lasted for 600 years—from the age of expansion until the end of World War I. In his honor, all future sultans of the empire were girded with the sword of Osman when they took power.

Constantinople was the heart of the Byzantine Empire and it became the capital of the Ottoman Empire when it was conquered in 1453 by the Ottoman Sultan Mehmet II and renamed Istanbul (the city of Islam). Suleiman the Magnificent completed the task of transforming the previously Byzantine city of Constantinople into Istanbul, a worthy center for a great Turkish and Islamic empire

RETHINKING THE HISTORY AND MYTHS OF THE PAST

Suleiman the Magnificent of the Ottoman Empire

The Ottoman Empire was successfully ruled by a single family for centuries. It reached its height under Suleiman the Magnificent (reigned 1520–66). It expanded to cover the Balkans and Hungary and reached the gates of Vienna. It included: Turkey, Egypt, parts of Greece, Bulgaria, Romania, Macedonia, Hungary, Palestine, Jordan, Lebanon, Syria, Arabia and much of the coastal strip of North Africa. When the Ottoman Empire finally fell, it changed the dynamics of the Middle East for a century. No longer a power in the region, European nations divided it and Israel was established.

The Muslim influence on the world, particularly in science and mathematics, is often overshadowed by the Crusades and European expansion. Fourteen Nighty-two is remembered as the year that Columbus discovered America, but it was also the year that the Moors were expelled from Europe after centuries of domination.

Without the Islamic influence, it is doubtful that the *Scientific Revolution* and the *Age of Enlightenment* would have occurred. Religion was a central part of European expansion. In this regard, and others, Christianity and Europe followed in the footsteps of Islam. In recent times, however, Islam has been viewed as a bellicose religion. Notwithstanding, history attests to the fact that Islam is no more barbaric than Christianity. Often overlooked is how Muslims greet each other:" As-*Salam Alaikum"* which means (May Allah's peace, mercy and blessing be upon you) which is responded by the greeting,*"Wa-Alaikum-as-Salaam"* ("and upon you the Peace").

A NEW PERSPECTIVE

RETHINKING THE HISTORY AND MYTHS OF THE PAST

The Nature of Our Existence: Science Confronts Religion

Cristiano Banti's 1857 painting *Galileo facing the Roman Inquisition*

The battle between religion and science has raged for centuries. In ancient times, religion was the only mechanism for explaining our existence and our place in the universe. As science emerged in the 17th century, religion found itself in direct competition with science for the truth.

The Celestial Realm

Science has revealed that we live in a cosmos adorned by trillions of stars. We revolve around a mediocre star, in a mediocre galaxy in a universe in which there are more stars than grains of sand on this earth. We are just one of the billions of species that have lived on this globe. As denizens of this blue planet, we travel through space and time around a sun that travels around a galaxy. And we wonder, are we alone? Are we the only sentient beings and the only cynosure of God's eye? Or are we one microcosm in a cosmos far beyond our imagination?

The more we learn about our universe, the smaller we become in the context of things. We, humans, stand as sentient beings in the middle of micro and macro worlds, bounded by infinity in both directions. We are just beginning to scratch the surface of the unknown. In the micro world, there are more atoms in a grain of sand, than there are known stars in the sky. Yet the atoms that comprise all things on earth have their birth in the inner sanctums of stars.

A NEW PERSPECTIVE

From the beginning, humankind has looked toward the stars as if we intuitively knew that they held the secrets of our existence. As time progressed, we moved away from worshipping upon a star toward a greater understanding of their existence. We now know that we are made of stardust and like light, molded in these celestial cauldrons that gave life to us all.

We live in the Milky Way galaxy amid billions of stars and an estimated 100 billion planets. Our galaxy is 100 light-years wide (a light-year is 5.88 trillion miles) and there are over a trillion galaxies in the known universe. There is nothing unique about our star, and it is halfway through its lifecycle. It will burn for another five billion years and die a slow death, like so many stars before it. These stars. however, did not die in vain because they gave us the chemicals of life.

Galileo with his telescope

When Galileo (1564–1642) turned his telescope to the heavens and gazed upon the moons revolving around Jupiter, humankind took a giant step into unknown territory. He confirmed what Copernicus (1473–1543) had postulated, that the earth is not the center of all things. His empirical discovery conflicted with the Ptolemaic geocentric theory in place for a thousand years and embraced by the Catholic Church as being the inerrant word of God. Science had confronted religion, and the Catholic Church felt its monopoly on the truth slipping through their hands like sand through an hourglass of time.

RETHINKING THE HISTORY AND MYTHS OF THE PAST

Galileo was made to sign a refutation of his teachings on the rotation of the earth by signing a document while on his knees before the inquisition. The facts, however, did not cease to exist because they were ignored. Over time, the Church abandoned its geocentric view of the universe and science prevailed over religion. This was a seminal moment in human history as it proved that the Church was not infallible, and that science was a legitimate search for the truth.

Standing on the shoulders of the giants that came before him and born in the same year that Galileo died, Sir Isaac Newton (1644–1727) took science to a new level. Galileo thought that the movement of the tides was proof positive that the earth revolved around the sun, but he was wrong. Newton proved that the true cause was gravity, as the moon pulled upon the earth. This is why the tides are related to the position of the moon as it revolves around the earth (full and new moons). Newton's version of a clockwork universe would lead to the *Age of Enlightenment*, in which science challenged religion in a battle for the truth.

Newton in 1702 by Godfrey Kneller

The explanation of celestial phenomena moved from the religious realm to the scientific realm to be understood by terrestrial beings without the intervention of religion or superstition that had dominated for millenniums. Standing on the shoulders of Newton, the search for the truth was followed by his scientific scions.

At the turn of the 20th century, our knowledge of space and time dramatically increased with two seminal discoveries. Albert Einstein (1879–1955) proved that space and time are relative, and that energy and mass are different sides of the same

A NEW PERSPECTIVE

coin. Edwin Hubble (1889–1953) discovered that what was once viewed as stars or nebula were in fact galaxies composed of billions of stars. And the nature of our existence, the vastness of the universe and the understanding of the cosmos began to unfold. The telescope named in his honor discovered billions of such galaxies. Since light travels at a constant speed,186,000 miles per second, we were able to determine that our universe has been in existence for at least 13 billion years. Plenty of time for other worlds to live and die and to give birth to us.

The moon no longer stood as just a reflection of the sun in the night sky, or a celestial body for wolves to howl at, but instead, as a place that a man could walk upon and take the first step in the celestial journey of humankind.

Hubble Deep Field each dot represents a galaxy light-years away

RETHINKING THE HISTORY AND MYTHS OF THE PAST

The Terrestrial Realm

In 1859, Charles Darwin released his book: *On the Origins of Species* which challenged the biblical view of Creation. The debate between science and religion continued, perhaps best exemplified by the Scopes Monkey trial that occurred around the same time that Hubble was discovering the vastness of the universe. Like Galileo, Scopes was convicted of teaching a scientific theory that conflicted with church dogma.

Charles Darwin with an ape or monkey body symbolized evolution

The capacity of Nature to create seems boundless. Over 95 percent of the species that have existed on earth, over its 4.5-billion-year lifespan, have become extinct. Yet, Nature continues to create and destroy. The dinosaurs walked the earth before the continents were formed and lasted for about 250 million years before they became extinct. Nature is not in a hurry and does not make one tree, but a series of trees, it does not make one atom, but a series of atoms or one star, but a series of stars. In recent times, we have discovered thousands of planets revolving around distant stars. For us to be the only sentient beings amid such vastness seems unlikely and improbable. To harbor such beliefs, perhaps has more to do with the hubris of humankind than it does with the search for the truth.

Science has also revealed the evolution of sentient beings on this planet. Within the cells of our bodies lies the history of our earthly existence. According to anthropological biology, humans did not evolve from monkeys, but rather shared a common ancestor. Although we share 98 percent of our DNA with chimpanzees—

A NEW PERSPECTIVE

monkeys and other primates, went down one path and humans down another. Our path has been long and arduous—from the early Australopithecines to the current day homo sapiens. An evolution that took place over millions of years.

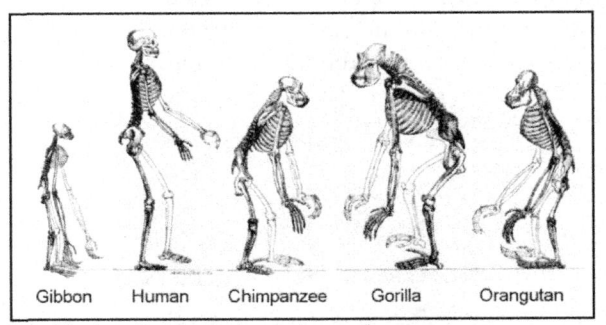

The hominoids are descendants of a common ancestor

An analogy could be drawn between the development of humankind and the development of us as individuals. Australopithecines were the first bipeds to stand erect and walk. They were, in effect, the babies of the human species. They were not carnivores, but vegetarians that existed millions of years after the extinction of the dinosaurs. *Homo hablis* followed, they made simple tools and could eat meat. In this regard, they could be considered toddlers. *Homo erectus* followed *Homo hablis*, and he was the first to leave the African continent and to use fire. In this regard, he was the wondering teenager in search of his identity.

Forensic reconstruction of an adult male *Homo erectus*. Reconstruction by W. Schnaubelt & N. Kieser (Atelier WILD LIFE ART)Homo_erectus.JPG: photographed by User:Lillyundfreya—Homo_erectus.JPG, CC BY-SA 3.0, https://commons.wikimedia.org/w/index.php?curid=9503611

RETHINKING THE HISTORY AND MYTHS OF THE PAST

Homo sapiens, our species, followed and according to our DNA record, we have been on earth for around 120,000 years. This is based on Mitochondrial DNA, and Y chromosome testing (which kept a record of the beginning of our species}. Thanks to the Human Genome Project, not only can we discern when and where our species originated, but how we migrated out of Africa to populate other parts of the world. In this regard, *Homo sapiens* are the adults. Science has proven that the diversity of races is not the result of the descendants of Noah, but rather mutations, that took place within our species.

If Nature can create such diversity on this blue dot revolving around a mediocre star, it is logical to assume that it can also create such diversity on other planets that revolve around distant stars. If our star gave birth to us, what would be the point of all the trillions of stars in the sky if some of them did not give life to planets that revolve around them? For centuries we have had a myopic view of the nature of our existence. As science continues to push the envelope, we will come to a greater understanding of the universe and our place in it.

A NEW PERSPECTIVE

RETHINKING THE HISTORY AND MYTHS OF THE PAST

Technology

A NEW PERSPECTIVE

RETHINKING THE HISTORY AND MYTHS OF THE PAST

The Dawning of the Electrical Age (Part I): The Story of Two Towns and Two Luminaries

The bright lights of Coney Island 1905

This article consists of two parts. Part I: Roselle, Thomas Edison and Electricity, and Part II: Roselle Park, David Sarnoff and the Radio

The world at the turn of the 20th century was a world without automobiles, airplanes and electricity, a world of dirt roads, horse buggies and candlelight much like the centuries before. But all of that would change. Today we live in a world of electricity in which dazzling metropolises light up the night sky. Electricity is so ubiquitous that we take it for granted. So much so that we cannot imagine a world without it. Like the light-giving fire that came before it, electricity changed the world in ways hitherto unseen. It was Edison's light bulb that was the antecedent and catalyst to myriad electrical innovations of the 20th century. It would eventually give rise to the vacuum tube, radio, television, the transistor, computers and many other inventions that help to define the century. It now reigns supreme over fire that had dominated as a source of light for millenniums.

A NEW PERSPECTIVE

But, the story of the light bulb, radio and television and their influence on the world is one of serendipity, discovery and of wonder. In it lies the stories of people and places, of Yankee ingenuity that defines America, its towns and its people. This is not only the story of two ordinary towns and two gifted individuals, but it is also the story of America and the story of an exciting century.

The allure of America has always been the pursuit of happiness. Thomas Edison and David Sarnoff were sons of immigrants and they helped to make America beautiful. Sarnoff, as much as any man, stood on the shoulders of Edison. Edison founded General Electric (GE) and David Sarnoff and RCA would emerge from its chrysalis to morph into the innovator of new mediums of communication that transformed the social landscape of the 20th century. In the early days of the electrical era, New Jersey was the Silicon Valley of its day and home of Edison's research laboratories, as well as Bell Laboratories, the Radio Corporation of America (RCA) and Princeton University.

It was also the home of two small sister cities, Roselle and Roselle Park, whose contributions to this era remain relatively unknown to the general public. They are small towns with a rich and coeval history that predates the Declaration of Independence. They were part of the oldest English settlement in New Jersey, Elizabethtown (now Union County) and dates to the time of Charles II. Although the history of these towns is older than the nation itself, the most significant contributions were made around the turn of the 20th century. Roselle gave a new light to the world and Roselle Park helped the world to hear a new voice. In these two small adjacent towns, we find the beginning of technologies that led to the modern electrical infrastructure that we cherish today. Thus, Roselle and Roselle Park not only contributed to the electrical landscape of the nation but to the development of modern culture.

Let There be Light: Roselle, Thomas Edison and Electricity

It is well known that Thomas Edison was one of the greatest inventors that ever lived. What is not well known is the contribution made by a small town in New Jersey by the name of Roselle. It was in this small town that Edison demonstrated how an entire village could be lit by electricity. Before that time, gas lighting dominated our cities and had proved to be a cost- effective but dangerous source of light. It was a time when dinner by candlelight was the norm in most homes around the world. But it was Edison's dream of making electricity so affordable that "only the rich would want to dine by candlelight."

Roselle is a community with a population of about 25,000 people and encompasses an area of about 2.6 sq. miles. It is the home of Roosevelt (Rosey) Grier, the famous football player/actor/activist, Abraham Clark, a signer of the Declaration of

RETHINKING THE HISTORY AND MYTHS OF THE PAST

Independence, and Tony Williams the lead singer of the popular 50s group, The Platters, . It is the site where one of the most renowned photos, "*The Identical Twins from Roselle, New Jersey, 1967*", was taken by Diane Arbus. Also from Roselle are Bob Sumner the former Executive Producer of Def Comedy Jam and the discoverer of many of America's top comedians: Dave Chappelle, Chris Tucker, Bernie Mac, D.L. Hughley, Martin Lawrence and more. Phil Ivey (often referred to as the Tiger Woods of poker) also resided in Roselle. It was Phil's grandfather and mentor, Leonard "Bud" Simmons, who, in 1963, sponsored in Roselle one of Malcolm X's debates on separation and integration.

Roselle is part of one of the oldest communities in America first settled by the Dutch and then the British. As in so many colonial areas, the names of the towns and cities of northern New Jersey read like a glossary of British 17th and 18th century nobility and provinces. Thus, the history of early settlement echoes a time in Britain when the New World gave birth to New York, New Jersey and Elizabethtown—places in the new world linked not only by etymology but by culture and heritage to the old world.

Thomas Alva Edison (1847–1931)

Among the Dutch settlers of northern New Jersey was a young widow of the name Edeson (Edison) who arrived at the Elizabeth port in 1730 accompanied by her three-year-old son John. Elizabethtown was very much pro-revolutionary, and John Edison was a devoted Loyalist. As a result, he was sentenced to hang in 1778. His sentence was later commuted, his property confiscated, and he was exiled to Canada. This was not unusual for this period of revolution as the Loyalist Governor of New Jersey, William Franklin, son of Ben Franklin, received similar treatment. The Edison family remained in Canada until 1842 when they settled in Milan, Ohio. On February 11,

A NEW PERSPECTIVE

1847, a new addition to the family was born on American soil. His name was Thomas Alva Edison.

Even though he was mostly self-taught at home, the young Edison showed an acute aptitude for learning. Still, it was quite by chance that he learned the fundamentals of the telegraph system. In 1863, during the Civil War, he rescued the young son of J.U. MacKenzie, the station agent at a local telegraph station from drowning. With MacKenzie's help, he embarked on a five-year period of studying, experimenting, and finally improving many aspects of the telegraph system. This early exposure to electricity provided an impetus for all his great achievements. His interests led him to Boston, New York City and finally back to Elizabeth, New Jersey, the same township from which his ancestors were expelled in disgrace.

It is also ironic, but true, that Thomas Edison's son Charles became governor of the state that exiled his ancestors in disgrace. Thus, from a family once ridiculed and deemed un-American, emerged progeny that included one of America's greatest innovators returning, like a prodigal son, to the region from which his forefathers were expelled. It was in his ancestral home, where his family first graced the North American continent, that his greatest achievements would be realized.

While living modestly in the basement of his friend and mentor, Franklin Leonard Pope, who was a resident of Elizabeth, Edison conceived and experimented with some of his earliest inventions that financed his first laboratory. Although he was later known as "The Wizard of Menlo Park", Edison had laboratories throughout the state, most notably in Newark, his first laboratory; West Orange, the home of the first movie studio, The Black Maria, and of course his legendary Menlo Park research laboratory.

Edison did not achieve his myriad accomplishments alone. For instance, the African American inventor Lewis Latimer contributed greatly to the development and longevity of the light bulb. Edison's inner circle became known as the "Edison Pioneers." One of the pioneers was Miller Fox Moore, another person with ancestral roots in New Jersey and who was also a resident of Roselle. Moore's work on Direct Current (DC) generators was an important factor in the development of the Edison Company for Isolated Lighting and the establishment of independent generating stations that served as prototypes for today's electrical utilities.

By the fall of 1882, lights powered by isolated plants were constructed in factories, stores, steamships and newspaper buildings. One of the many assignments delegated to Miller Moore was the establishment of a Village Plant System that would be capable of lighting an entire village. Edison insisted that the village be in the vicinity

RETHINKING THE HISTORY AND MYTHS OF THE PAST

of New York City and, if possible, in an area that did not previously have gas lighting. Moore's hometown of Roselle met the criteria for the Village Plant System project.

The Edison Company for Isolated Lighting began its operation to illuminate Roselle in the fall of 1882. It is important to note that in 1882 most people had never heard of electric lighting and those that did were not necessarily enthused by the idea. It did not enter the mainstream as a viable means of lighting until after the 1893 Columbia Expedition held in Chicago. To investors, however, electricity was the new shining thing and it attracted stakeholders such as J.P. Morgan and George Westinghouse eager to capitalize on this new technology.

With the financial backing of such tycoons, a completely new infrastructure, unprecedented in its construction, scope and implementation, would eventually bring not only light to homes but the power of electricity and all that it entails. Edison's lightbulb, although effective in localized settings, was not ready for large scale integration. There was a significant problem at that time with soot collecting inside electric light bulbs as filaments burned which ultimately made the light bulb turn black. This is not something you would want to happen in a village or city.

To resolve this problem, Edison placed a metal plate inside an evacuated light bulb, brought a wire from it outside the bulb, and applied voltage between the wire and the filament to attract soot particles to the plate. It worked, and the longevity of the lightbulb was significantly improved. Not only were brighter days ahead through this new technology conceived in the twilight of the 19th century; brighter days and nights were also ahead for the 20th century. Electricity transformed Roselle and then cities of the world into dazzling metropolises by delivering light amid the proverbial darkness.

The citizens of Roselle in this regard, were also pioneers, for as Edison once stated, "My greatest trouble will be to get the people to use the lights." On January 19, 1883, the bold citizens of this small town took an enormous leap into the future. Hence becoming the first town in the world to be illuminated, using a flameless device to generate light. On that day, Roselle emerged as a beacon that would guide the world to a new electrical era. The demonstration of an electrical infrastructure illuminating a complete town was so successful that in the coming years, newspapers proclaimed Roselle as the "Once Capital of the Scientific World." Thomas Edison went on to acquire 1,093 patents and he invented the phonograph, motion picture camera, and many other discoveries that required electricity. His work to improve the longevity of the light bulb used in Roselle, serendipitously led to what came to be known as the Edison Effect. Edison noticed that electrical current flowing through a light bulb's filament could make the wire so hot that electrons boiled off, sailing through the

A NEW PERSPECTIVE

vacuum inside the light bulb to a metal plate that had a positive charge. This unexpected discovery was a major step in the genesis of the modern electronic world. Yet, the practical application of this phenomenon was something that evaded Edison.

In 1904, Sir John Ambrose Fleming went to work for Marconi's company. His first assignment was to find a better way to receive radio signals. Fleming began experimenting with the Edison Effect. He discovered that radio waves passing through a vacuum tube created a varying direct current, which could be used as a valve or a switch (diode).

Sir John Ambrose Fleming

In that same year, Lee De Forest also went to work for Marconi with the same objective. Deforest studied Flemings' valve and build upon it. The valve De Forest created had something new: a grid made of nickel wire which he placed between the filament and the plate. Applying even a small amount of electrical charge to the grid disrupted the flow of electrons from the filament to the plate thus amplifying the original signal. Two years later, he developed the first vacuum tube (triode) that could be used as a valve, a switch or an amplifier.

One of the earliest applications of De Forest's vacuum tube was to amplify and modulate radio and telephone signals. The incorporation of vacuum tubes transformed electronics by adding active as well as passive elements. This was vital to the progression from a wireless telegraph system to the radio as we know it today (a device capable of transmitting sound and voice).

RETHINKING THE HISTORY AND MYTHS OF THE PAST

Lee De Forest and his vacuum tube

Vacuum tubes changed the face of electronics and were a major catalyst for future innovations. The first large scale programable computer, Electronic Numerical Integrator and Computer (ENIAC), was developed at the Moore School of Electrical Engineering at the University of Pennsylvania by John Mauchly and John Presper Eckert. The ENIAC was built between 1943 and 1945 and came online in 1946. The American military sponsored research of the ENIAC because it needed a computer for calculating artillery-firing tables. Based on the Turing machine, it used nearly 20,000 vacuum tubes and 1,500 relays to emulate ones and zeros. It weighed 30 tons and consumed nearly 200 kilowatts of power.

The ENIAC also played a role in the development of the Hydrogen bomb

The ENIAC gave birth to the Universal Automatic Computer (UNIVAC) and a host of mainframe computers based on vacuum tubes. Most importantly, the vacuum tube was the antecedent of the transistor invented at Bell Laboratories in New Jersey the following year. In the first decade of computers, more calculations had been performed by computers than all the calculations hitherto. In fact, the genesis of the

A NEW PERSPECTIVE

digital world and the burgeoning of software can be traced to the ENIAC class of computers.

But Edison's influence goes beyond his inventions. It was not necessarily the light bulb that made Edison a success, but rather his ability to see beyond it and to establish an electrical infrastructure in which the light bulb was an integral part. This infrastructure was superseded by, Nikola Tesla's AC system. Edison was a hero to Tesla and inspired him to immigrate to America in 1884. It is reported, upon meeting Edison, Tesla said: My Dear Edison, I know two great men and you are one of them. The other is this young man!" such was his reverence for the *Wizard of Menlo Park* and the confidence in his own ability. Tesla proceeded to describe the engineering work he had done, and his plans for an alternating current motor. He later was employed by Edison, however, the two disagreed over payment. Thus, began the rivalry.

Nikola Tesla: (1856-1943)

After, leaving Edison, Tesla formed Tesla Electric Lighting and Manufacturing Company in Rahway, New Jersey (also part of Union County) and was issued his first US patents. Like most great men, Edison had his flaws and was infected by paradigm paralysis that often inflicts men of conviction. It is a phenomenon of nature that like objects repel and Edison's ego would not succumb to Tesla's genius.

This should not detract from Edison's accomplishments but instead, be seen as a negative reflection of his positive attributes. Tesla's (AC) system was far superior because it could easily transmit large amounts of current over long distances generated by turbines turned by waterfalls. Although Tesla's system forms the foundation of the

RETHINKING THE HISTORY AND MYTHS OF THE PAST

electrical infrastructure that we use today, Edison's system of DC survived and is the dominant system used in batteries and digital circuits.

Edison's light bulb was just one step on the journey to modernity and the forebear of the electrical age. Roselle's contribution was vital to making Edison's dream of ubiquitous electricity and its use as a conduit for his future inventions a reality.

A NEW PERSPECTIVE

RETHINKING THE HISTORY AND MYTHS OF THE PAST

The Dawning of the Electrical Age (Part II): The Story of Two Towns and Two Luminaries

This was the world's first demonstration of the transmission of radio signals over open sea, May 13, 1897 (Wikipedia) By Cardiff Council Flat Holm Project - Cardiff Council Flat Holm Project, CC BY 3.0, https://commons.wikimedia.org/w/index.php?curid=4012156

In November of 1886, Heinrich Hertz became the first person to transmit radio (electromagnetic) waves over a very short distance. Hertz was motivated by Maxwell's equations which predicted in 1860 that such waves existed and traveled at the speed of light. Like Edison and the Edison Effect, Hertz could not think of a practical application for his discovery. Guglielmo Marconi, however, expanded Hertz's work and in 1896 was granted a patent for wireless communications. Five years later, Marconi transmitted radio waves across the Atlantic.

Wireless Communication: Roselle Park, David Sarnoff and the Radio

In the first two decades of the 1900s, Marconi's wireless radio systems used Morse code to transmit messages. The word radio is derived from the fact that signals from transmitters radiate in all directions thereby providing a broader range compared to traditional telegraph lines which were point to point. Furthermore, wireless radio systems enabled ship to ship communication at sea and could send multiple messages using the same hardware by varying the frequency of the signal.

A NEW PERSPECTIVE

With the turn of the century came new methods of transportation and communication. Just as the railroad and the telegraph emerged together in the previous century, likewise, the airplane and the radio shared a similar simultaneous development. Railroads could receive messages from telegraph lines that ran adjacent to the railway. Airplanes, however, required a different medium, one like the plane itself that could travel through the airways. Although Marconi was given credit for the invention of the radio, it is important to note that he infringed on several of Tesla's patents to transmit radio waves over long distances. Disputes and controversy over the invention of the radio loomed, but Marconi was granted the rights and awarded the Nobel Prize in 1909.

In the early 1900s, international investments were made in wireless infrastructures, which over time brought an end to hardwired telegraph lines. Marconi established a wireless telegraph station and manufacturing plant in Roselle Park, New Jersey. During colonial times, Roselle and Roselle Park were one town and part of Elizabethtown (now Union County). Roselle Park is smaller than Roselle (approximately 1.2 square miles and 13,000 people) and for decades the two towns were rivals at the annual Thanksgiving Day High School football game.

The citizens of Roselle made their contribution to the NFL through their favorite son Rosey Grier. Roselle Park made its mark by sending one of its native sons, Rick Barry, to the NBA Basketball Hall of Fame. Barry is the only player in basketball history to lead the NCAA, ABA and NBA in scoring. Rick would also have several sons to play in the NBA. Like its neighbor, Roselle, Roselle Park's history was also inextricably linked to General Electric (GE).

As fate would have it, during World War I, some transatlantic telegraph lines were cut making the Allies more dependent upon wireless communication. The United States government viewed this as a national security risk and asked General Electric to oversee wireless telegraph systems in the United States particularly the Marconi wireless telegraph systems. Moreover, the US government was not comfortable with foreign-owned companies manufacturing equipment that was vital to its national security.

Due to the nature and magnitude of this endeavor, and the post-war market potential; on December 1, 1919, GE formed a smaller company, the Radio Corporation of America (RCA) and assigned all wireless operations to this new company under the de facto leadership of David Sarnoff. The formation of this company provided growth potential for RCA and Sarnoff. Marconi's Roselle Park wireless telegraph station was later transformed into one of the first regularly broadcast radio stations in America, WDY.

RETHINKING THE HISTORY AND MYTHS OF THE PAST

This was the beginning of practical applications of vacuum tubes and the radio as we know it today. Instead of encoding the message in the carrier frequency, which was previously used to transmit Morse code, the modulated sound or voice became the message. As vacuum tubes became more efficient, powerful and miniature, the modulated signal could be transmitted further, and several tubes could be incorporated into the design. The first method used was Amplitude Modulation (AM) where sound was used to modulate the carrier frequency. Each radio station was tuned to a unique carrier frequency. At the receiving end, the carrier frequency was stripped or demodulated and what remained was the sound or voice.

Sarnoff recognized immediately the commercial potential of the radio and the broadcasting of the Jack Dempsey and George Carpentier boxing match in 1921 by RCA was a major contributing factor to the post-World War I radio boom. RCA quickly became a major player in the communication industry and a key contributor to the development of both radio and television as mediums.

Sarnoff speaking at RCA's Roselle Park station, 1921
http://www.davidsarnoff.org/gallery-radio/DS_WDY-1.html

The life of David Sarnoff is the life of the American Dream and demonstrates how America, at the turn of the 20th century, was strengthened by the huddled masses of immigrants yearning to breathe free. His life is one of those rags to riches stories of which every American should be proud. He was born in 1891 in a small Russian town, five years after Heinrich Hertz demonstrated the process of producing and detecting electromagnetic waves. He immigrated to America in 1900, one year before Marconi's

A NEW PERSPECTIVE

transatlantic wireless transmission, and he was raised in the Jewish immigrant ghetto of New York's Lower East Side.

As a schoolboy in a school for immigrants, David was told a story about a log cabin boy that grew up to become president. This story resonated and it inspired him to do great things. As he climbed up the latter, there would be two pictures in his office, one of Marconi and the other of Abraham Lincoln. Like most people of poverty, Sarnoff was driven to some extent by money, but his paramount motivation was to achieve the status of an American and a conscious determination to identify himself with his new country. He rose from office boy to chief executive of one of the largest corporations in America. He was, however, propelled as much by fate and luck as he was by ambition.

David Sarnoff (1891–1971)

Like Steve Jobs in the later years of the century, David Sarnoff was not a design engineer, or a man known for his technical prowess but rather the right man at the right time in history. Both were able to align themselves with the emerging technologies of their day and anticipated how such technologies could benefit the public. Sarnoff is quoted as saying that he "hitched his wagon to the electron instead of the proverbial star." Yet, Sarnoff's star began to rise when it was reported in April 1912, that he deciphered a relayed message from the *RMS Titanic*, once deemed to be unsinkable, had hit an iceberg and was now sinking.

RETHINKING THE HISTORY AND MYTHS OF THE PAST

The *Titanic* was the largest, fastest and most luxurious ship of its time and the pride of the British shipbuilding world. It was reported that for three days and three nights Sarnoff remained glued to Marconi's wireless station to report the status of the *Titanic*. Whether this story is true or apocryphal, it however, did much to enhance the young Sarnoff's reputation and he quickly rose through the ranks of Marconi's company. It was indeed this tragic event that launched wireless communications into the public sphere. As the head of RCA, Sarnoff ushered in several innovations in both radio and television. He was among the first to envision the radio as an entertainment medium. There were many detractors in his day, most noted was novelist H.G. Wells, (author of *The War of the Worlds*) who saw Sarnoff luminance and future products as short-lived and naïve. Yet, time would prove his critics wrong.

Edison's phonograph and the radio were a marriage made in heaven. It was Sarnoff's goal to turn the radio into a music box in which every radio station would have a phonograph to transmit music with revenue generated by advertisements. RCA went as far as to acquire Victor Records, a phonograph and record company. In addition to music, radio shows (sponsored by companies) were another feature of the radio along with real-time news reports. In fact, soap operas got their name because they were sponsored by soap companies. Sarnoff was also among the first to envision radios in automobiles and a television in every home. RCA made a fortune by selling the combination of a radio, phonograph and television all in one console. One of his monikers was the "prophet" and, in this capacity, he brought forth several ideas that help to shape the social and economic landscape of the 20th century.

Sarnoff's vision was not one radio station, but a network of radio stations and ultimately television stations centered around major US cities. The broadcasting business was big business, and RCA was getting too big for its britches. In 1926, it formed the National Broadcasting Company (NBC) and in 1943 the American Broadcasting Company (ABC). Television followed in the footsteps of radio and the establishment of radio networks was key to the emergence of television as a medium. Light, television and radio waves are part of the electromagnetic spectrum of which only a small portion is visible to the naked eye. Since electromagnetic waves radiated in all directions, the television station located in New York City also covered northern New Jersey and the one located in Philadelphia covered the southern half of the state.

In 1929, Sarnoff met Vladimir Zworykin, a fellow Russian emigrant, and this association would give birth to television as we know it today. Although many experimented with early television designs, few had the financial backing, research and network infrastructure of RCA. By the mid-1950s, television was an integral part of the social landscape. The Space Age emerged with the television and brought the

A NEW PERSPECTIVE

wonders not only of this world but of worlds beyond our own into living rooms across America.

But with success came competition. Just as Rockefeller had tried to destroy Edison's light bulb to maintain his monopoly on gas lighting, and Edison had tried to destroy Westinghouse and Tesla's Alternating Current (AC) to promote his inferior system of Direct Current (DC), David Sarnoff and RCA played hardball with its competitors. It used its power, wealth and connections with the Federal Communications Commission (FCC) to crush or diminish them. But, in Sarnoff's case, in his attempt to destroy or take credit for their products, he destroyed the people that created them. The stress placed on Philo Farnsworth to invalidate his television patents nearly drove him insane and the pressure placed on Edwin Armstrong to deny him credit for the Frequency Modulation (FM) radio drove him to commit suicide. Despite such efforts, Farnsworth was eventually given credit for the invention of the electronic television set and Armstrong's FM system, which offered superior sound quality in stereo, eventually became the dominant radio medium.

RCA made Sarnoff as much as Sarnoff made RCA. Ironically, both RCA and NBC would be acquired later by General Electric. David Sarnoff was a giant and a luminary and his contribution to the entertainment and news industries over decades was monumental. Television was the natural evolution of the radio. The social and economic impact of these two mediums cannot be overstated.

Edison and Sarnoff were visionaries with strong business acumen and a nose for future technologies. Hence, the contributions of these two individuals and small towns have been both profound and unique. They helped to shape the 20th century and henceforth the world would never be the same. Who would have imagined that the seeds planted in these small towns would later germinate into flowers whose sweet fragrances we still smell today? Their stories stand as a testimony of how serendipitous events and technology can combine to change the landscape of a century and I can't help but wonder who will be the Edisons and Sarnoffs of the 21st century and beyond. Both were essential to the history of an unprecedented technological century and they serve as exemplars of Yankee ingenuity and enterprise.

As Americans, we must always remember that the pulse of this great nation beats from the hearts of small towns like Roselle and Roselle Park. Each with its own identity, story and contribution, each linked together by cultures and traditions forged over time to become the United States of America.

RETHINKING THE HISTORY AND MYTHS OF THE PAST

Legacy
When we think of the 20th century, we think of the major events that helped to define it. Its world wars, The Space Age, The Cold War and the Civil Rights movement. We, however, seldom recognize perhaps the most defining element: the development of an electrical infrastructure which was the catalyst to many events. Radio emerged from the smoldering ashes of World War I and likewise, television and computers from the ashes of the Second World War. But it all began at the turn of the century and a series of technological achievements of which Edison and Sarnoff played major roles.

Every solution bears the seeds of another problem and the vacuum tube was no exception. Although it had many advantages, like its antecedent light bulb, it had its inherent flaws. For instance, it was prone to burnouts and vibration; it was bulky and power-consuming: initiating a space-age search for alternatives to solve such problems. Its successor, the solid-state transistor, invented at Bell Labs in New Jersey, implemented its functions in miniature using semiconductors without the inherent problems associated with vacuum tubes rendering such devices obsolete.

Similarly, transistors transformed the times and without it, The Space Age would not have been possible. Transistors also gave rise to miniature portable (transistor)radios which in turn created Japanese electronic innovations and companies such as Sony. Its portability, size and low power changed the way that people socially interacted. It was the first palm-held device that provided real-time information and entertainment to the general public. Furthermore, the transistor was an integral part of the 1950s and 1960s boom of Rock and Roll, Jazz, Rock and Soul music. Radio and television helped to bring forth a new type of revolution: not only of music but of social change bearing witness in the streets, classrooms and offices around the world of the events that shaped both decades.

The post-World War II baby boomers were ripe for the expansion and miniaturization of electronics as both television and the radio emerged as solid-state medium that carried the news of moon landings, social unrest, war and entertainment previously unseen. Such innovations also helped to shape the political landscape. For instance, it was reported that John Kennedy's 1960 presidential victory over Richard Nixon was a result of how they both appeared on TV, and the horrors of the Vietnam War were seen in living rooms across America in living color.

Moreover, throughout the century, the electronic industry continued to snowball as one invention stood on the shoulders of the other. The first electronic computer, EINAC, contained 20,000 vacuum tubes and weighed 30 tons. Today, a standard computer chip contains billions of transistors and can fit on your fingertip. Color

A NEW PERSPECTIVE

Televisions, Microwave Ovens, CD/DVD Players, Personal Computers, Cable TV and Smartphones all owe their existence to the transistor. Although the transistor remains an essential element, the Integrated Circuit (IC) has replaced it as the fundamental building block of digital circuitry.

Mark Twain is believed to have said: "History doesn't repeat itself, but it does rhyme." Just as Edison returned to his ancestral home in New Jersey, the coinventor of the transistor and 1956 Nobel Prize winner, William Shockley, left Bell Labs in New Jersey to return to his familial home in California. In 1956, he formed his own company, Shockley Semiconductor, in Mountain View, CA. Among his many skills was an eye for talent, and he recruited and nurtured the best and brightest. Most noted were: Robert Noyce and Gordon Moore, the latter the author of Moore's law.

Inventors of the transistor: John Bardeen, William Shockley and Walter Brattain at Bell Labs, 1948

This was the genesis of Silicon Valley. In fact, Silicon Valley derives its name from the Silicon used in its transistors. Because of Shockley's management style and difficult personality, several engineers (known as the traitorous eight, including Noyce and Moore) left his company to join Fairchild Semiconductor from which the Integrated Circuit (chip), coinvented by Noyce and Moore, emerged in 1959. In 1968, Noyce and Moore formed Intel which developed microprocessor chips used in several Personal Computers most noted was IBM's Personal Computer (PC). In 1980, IBM hired Bill Gates' company Microsoft to develop the Operating System (OS) for the PC. Blinded by the success of its mainframe computers, IBM neglected the market potential of the PC and allowed others to clone them and moreover allowed Gates to keep the rights to its OS. Microsoft continued to improve on its OS and the rest is history. Because of such innovations, mainframe computers, which dominated the first three decades of computing were replaced by a more distributed process centered around PCs.

RETHINKING THE HISTORY AND MYTHS OF THE PAST

As integrated circuits continued to expand in accordance with Moore's law, the bit size and speed of computers increased along with the miniaturization and sophistication of digital devices. Furthermore, assembly languages were replaced by higher-ordered software languages such as C and C++; thus, forming the spine of a new body of software-driven computers. Such devices introduced a new type of social awareness, homogeneity and access to information via the Internet. Once known for the hardware that it produced, Silicon Valley is now known as the Mecca of Social Media innovation. The ubiquitous presence of smartphones, in the dawn of this century, is a merger of wireless technologies and computers developed in the previous century. All of this started with the light bulb as if the light that emanated was a beacon, symbol and a metaphor for brighter ideas to come in the 20th century and beyond.

I am fortunate to have been born during interesting times, to be a proud native son of Roselle, to have started (and later return to end) my engineering career at General Electric and to have spent thirty years working for Fairchild. During my youth, I heard stories about my hometown being the first town in the world to have electricity and the achievements of the radio station in Roselle Park. Such stories inspired me to become an engineer. In this regard, and others, this story is an analog of my American journey.

A NEW PERSPECTIVE

RETHINKING THE HISTORY AND MYTHS OF THE PAST

Cybersecurity

A NEW PERSPECTIVE

RETHINKING THE HISTORY AND MYTHS OF THE PAST

A New Threat to Our Freedoms

The Pentagon, a symbol of our might, in the wake of the 9/11 attacks (U.S. Navy)

The shootings against Muslims in New Zealand and bombings against Christians in Sri Lanka in 2019, serve as a constant reminder that we live in a dangerous and turbulent world in which acts of terror, like the sword of Damocles, dangles over the heads of nations. Although these two attacks are interrelated and ignited by religious indifference (one was a retaliation for the other), the threat of attacks initiated by other kinds of indifference or animus looms large.

It was Benjamin Franklin who said, "Those who would give up essential liberty to purchase a little temporary safety deserve neither liberty nor safety." It appears, however, that time and technology has brought us to a juncture when we are forced to consider such trade-offs. Warfare in the 21st century is no longer limited to the conventional battlefield but to a new **distributive warfare** waged against civilians. We now face the prospect of a state of perpetual warfare that does not adhere to the standard rules of engagement but waged across many fronts, often against enemies unseen and unknown.

On the fifteenth anniversary of 9/11, I wrote President Obama a letter delineating an emerging threat to the security of our nation. September 11, 2001. is a day that will live in infamy, and like December 7, 1941, our nation was completely unprepared for such an attack. On that tragic day, we underestimated the capabilities of our enemies: they did not bomb us with their military aircraft but made bombs out of our own commercial aircraft. In the letter, I argued that the commercial technologies that will become readily available in the public sphere pose a clear and present danger to the security of our nation that may likewise catch us off guard.

A NEW PERSPECTIVE

As a former engineer in the Defense and Space industries for 35 years, I was part of the post-Moon-landing generation that brought forth technologies which ushered in the Information Age, such as the personal computer, space telescopes, cell phones, the Internet, and unmanned drones—innovations that profoundly changed our view of the cosmos and how we interact with each other on earth.

Many of these innovations were first implemented by government agencies, such as the National Aeronautics and Space Administration (NASA), the Defense Advanced Research Projects Agency (DARPA), and the National Geospatial-Intelligence Agency (NGA). Government has long assumed the mantle of R&D of the commercial world; its technologies, often invented to defend the nation against threats from distant shores or to explore new frontiers in space, which include Global Positioning Systems (GPS) and the Internet, have invariably migrated into the mainstream. Most notably, the technology developed by NASA to enable remote probes to investigate our celestial neighbors has trickled down to the commercial realm and become increasingly available and more sophisticated in its miniaturization.

But as a result of such innovations, emerging commercial technologies have the potential to implement a new type of domestic warfare hitherto unseen. Bad actors may maliciously employ the advancements in sensors in drones to covertly gather intelligence or target people and places to enact chaos and violence. Sensors suites may be further enhanced by software and incorporate low-power, lightweight mobile electronics and high capacity batteries—technologies that have been driven by innovations in laptops and smartphones.

In the near future, drones, whose costs will continue to decrease, will perform terrestrial operations, with technology conceived from celestial operations, that may also threaten our freedoms. And as drones grow greater in complexity and sophistication and become more specialized in function, they may also incorporate weapons of varying degrees of destruction. The present is nothing more than the past of the future. We must, therefore, prepare today for the unintended consequences of tomorrow.

But the future, it seems, is already here. In July 2018, the Combating Terrorism Center at West Point has reported that the Islamic State has been successfully modifying commercial drones to deploy them as vehicles for remote detonation. The Pentagon is so alarmed by such potential threats, both on land and at sea, that it has called on the collective resources of the defense industry and Silicon Valley to combat such threats, armed with a war chest of over $700 million.

RETHINKING THE HISTORY AND MYTHS OF THE PAST

These threats, so far, have been limited to the battlefield, but there is nothing to suggest that they will not be used for domestic terrorism, particularly as radical ideologies continue to be fueled by advancements in technology. Perhaps soon, the traditional suicide bomber will be completely replaced by autonomous machines whose ability to destroy and hide will be by orders of magnitude more effective than conventional means of waging war.

Furthermore, the Cold War has now moved into cyberspace. The Intelligence Agencies of the United States and the Mueller Report have concluded that Russia belligerently interfered with the 2016 elections to help to elect Donald Trump as president. Representing a paradigm shift, this interference proves that such attacks are no longer limited to misanthropic individuals or Middle Eastern foes but now include major world powers, which can use our innovations and social infrastructure to implement cost-effective ways to disrupt our democracy.

The strategic use of social media platforms, especially Facebook and Twitter, were integral to this cyber-attack, and the leaders of these companies were unaware of how far foreign entities had penetrated and abused their systems. This deliberate attack on American democracy reminds us that our social landscape and infrastructure are vulnerable. The Internet and social media platforms empower people to globally coalesce for both virtuous and malicious purposes.

In recent years, we have witnessed malicious ransomware disabling governments and institutions until the ransom is paid or a viable countermeasure is achieved. Just this month, the city of Baltimore was, in effect, held hostage and severely hindered by such an attack. Like the WannaCry attack in 2017, which crippled, among others, the National Health Service of the United Kingdom, these attacks may be driven not by ideology but simply by the motive of profit. The perpetrators of such electronic crimes often demand payment in Bitcoin or other cryptocurrencies that hinder law enforcement from following the money.

All of these examples demonstrate that the paramount danger of distributive warfare arises from its asymmetrical costs: because bad actors may employ inexpensive commercial technology pervasive in today's globalized world to undermine, exploit, and damage our freedoms at any time, countermeasures to prevent such a threat can only be more costly than the threat. It has already been demonstrated how the Internet can be used as command and control for terrorists, many of whom are savvy to its technologies. As the world becomes more cosmopolitan and dependent on the Internet and computer-controlled systems, we become more vulnerable to various kinds of attacks driven by the makings of our digital world.

A NEW PERSPECTIVE

In the next score years, autonomous technologies will dominate the American landscape. The daisy-chaining and convergence of many technologies, as witnessed during the invention of the telegraph and the photograph, of the steam locomotive and the airplane, and of radio and film can bring about monumental change. Such a synthesis in autonomous technologies can create a snowball effect that may replace the need for human involvement entirely.

To this end, we must carefully evaluate the effect of emerging technologies—artificial intelligence, 3D printing, robotics, and drones—and how they could be used to wreak havoc on our infrastructure and disseminate terror to our fellow citizens. In fact, it is not necessarily the attack but the *War of the Worlds* fear of the attack that can disrupt our daily lives, perhaps best exemplified by the Washington, DC sniper attacks of 2002. Although the only thing we have to fear is fear itself, fear is a powerful weapon and, at times, could seem formidable, foremost, and futile to resist.

What can we do to combat such threats of distributive warfare, domestic and foreign? The response must not only be tantamount to the threat but above and beyond. We must anticipate the threat and implement the infrastructure to combat surprise attacks and track those who want to do us harm. Because the threat is global, the response must also be global, in partnership with our allies around the world. But inexpensive commercial technology is a double-edged sword, and we can also maximize the use of such technologies in our own defense. It also requires, however, the ordinary citizen, in his or her own capacity, to remain vigilant, mindful, and informed. We must all be proactive and united in carrying out our patriotic duty to defend the nation.

But perhaps our response requires that we now reconsider Franklin's dilemma: should we sacrifice some of our freedoms in exchange for our security? As we build the infrastructure of the 21st century and beyond, we must keep the threats of distributive warfare in mind. To ensure that our countermeasures are effective, cyber-attack prevention and low-cost intelligence gathering should be ubiquitous in their implementation. We may, at a much broader scale, need to incorporate active verification, such as image or voice recognition, and possibly bionic identification, such as digital fingerprints and retinal scans. All of data extracted by these initiatives should be seamlessly available in real-time to the appropriate government agencies.

There is no doubt that such initiatives will evoke the specter of Big Brother. But are these initiatives worth the cost to our personal liberties? Although the Founding Fathers of America were luminaries of an enlightened age, they could not foresee the myriad ways in which technology could threaten the safety of future citizens.

RETHINKING THE HISTORY AND MYTHS OF THE PAST

Regardless, the fact remains that we are at the dawn of a Brave New World. History is not a single picture, but a mosaic of the past painted by the hands of time, and we must be aware of the pieces that form the vision of our future. We are currently living in a global age transformed by technology, and this technical tsunami cannot be abated. How best to strike a balance and avoid the new wave of terrorism is a question that warrants vigorous and immediate consideration.

The simplest solution is often the best, and it is often the one chosen by our enemies. In the biblical clash against Goliath, David did not slay Goliath with his slingshot; instead, he used it only to disable the giant before decapitating him with his own sword. Might does not always make right, and few would have predicted that the 9/11 terrorist attack would cost the United States thousands of lives, trillions of dollars and launched it into the longest war in its history.

Civilizations collapse when they do not recognize that sometimes a weakness is nothing more than a strength overplayed. For the security of our country and the safety of our nation, we Americans should not succumb to a misguided hubris or become complacent with our might but instead search beyond our strengths for the hidden weaknesses that, before long, may be exploited by those that wish to harm us.

A NEW PERSPECTIVE

RETHINKING THE HISTORY AND MYTHS OF THE PAST

Music

A NEW PERSPECTIVE

RETHINKING THE HISTORY AND MYTHS OF THE PAST

Fundamentals of Music

Anne Vallayer-Coster, *Attributes of Music*, 1770. This still life painting depicts a variety of French Baroque musical instruments

Music has been around perhaps as long as man's consciousness. However, it wasn't until Pythagoras (570–495) quantified the rules of music that the system enjoyed in the Western world was developed. Building on the foundation laid by Pythagoras, we have uncovered not only its intrinsic beauty but the mathematics that lies beneath it.

The Development of Scales

There are many legends told about the Greek philosopher, mathematician and polymath Pythagoras best known for his Pythagorean Theorem in Mathematics. Although we attribute several things to him, many scholars believe his discoveries are the product of the Pythagorean School or perhaps were known in other parts of the world. He studied in Egypt for 22 years and therefore some of the revelations attributed to him may have already been discovered. For the sake of argument and simplicity, we will tell Pythagoras' story, be it a myth or fact, because it does shed insight on the relationship of notes within a scale.

As legend has it, Pythagoras heard hammers pounding and noticed that some of the sounds were harmonious and others were not. Being a man of science and philosophy, Pythagoras set out to find the source of this phenomenon. It had long been known that some sounds produced by hammering could be consonant. It was also well known that this phenomenon could be produced by strings of various

A NEW PERSPECTIVE

lengths and thickness and with wind instruments. What Pythagoras did was to quantify the relationships that caused such phenomena.

Instead of using hammers, Pythagoras started by plucking a string of a given length, tension and thickness; then he listened to its sound as he continued to pluck. Of course, it was harmonious with itself. Next, he cut the string in half and plucked it along with the first string, the two were also harmonious. He continued, cutting the string in thirds, and the sound was also harmonious with the other strings. Next, he cut the string into fourths and not to his surprise; they all were in harmony with each other. What Pythagoras discovered were basic notes or vibrations of frequencies that were most harmonious with each other. Moreover, they were associated with each other by whole numbers.

The distance between notes is referred to as intervals, and for that matter, when we speak to each other we speak in intervals. Sounds that share the same interval relationship are harmonious to each other and that is why some words and phrases rhyme. The plucking of the first string created what is called unison and it is also referred to as the tonic, the second string the octave, the third string the dominant. By cutting strings into these various whole number proportions, what Pythagoras did was to increase the vibrations of the strings in corresponding proportions. That is to say, the string with half the length vibrates twice as fast, a third the length three times as fast and so forth.

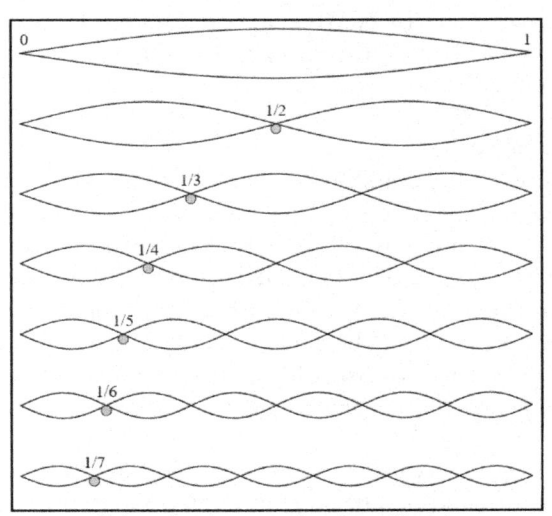

String vibrations as a function of length

RETHINKING THE HISTORY AND MYTHS OF THE PAST

The formula for strings could be expressed (given a constant length) as: $T = mv^2$ where T is the tension, m the mass of the string and v the velocity of the sound traveling through the air.

Although he had his eureka moment, Pythagoras was by no means finished. After all, you could make some music with these basic notes, and to be honest, people around the world had been making music with them for centuries if not millenniums before Pythagoras. However, making music wasn't the goal, identifying musical relationships was. In music, it is ultimately the relationships of notes (frequencies) to each other that counts and what Pythagoras had discovered were those notes that have the strongest relationship with each other.

What Pythagoras did next is perhaps the most ingenious part. He made a string with a thickness that gave the sound of the previous string that was divided into one third. He had noticed that the string that was divided in half was essentially the same sound only higher in pitch. However, the string that was divided into one-third was unique. This is perhaps the most essential aspect of the dominant tone; it is the simplest way to generate new tones. He continued by dividing this new string into one third. He plucked it and a new sound was heard that was also harmonious with the other sounds. This process continued until he found a relationship that was not harmonious, and he stopped. What he had was a scale, a collection of eight notes all harmonious with each other. This became the C major scale which corresponds to the white keys on the piano. In effect, he divided an octave by using harmonious fifths as the yardstick of music.

The following is the scale: **C D E F G A B C**

The ratios are as follows:

C 1:1, **D** 9:8, **E** 5:4, **F** 4:3, **G** 3:2, **A** 5:3, **B** 15:8, **C** 2:1

It is also known as the *diatonic scale*. The last C is an octave above the first one. Now it is important to note, that plucking a string with one-half the length of the original string was also significant because it defined the range of notes that could be contained without repeating a fundamental tone.

With this formula in place, additional octaves were later developed with the keys on the piano essentially representing the range of notes of most instruments from about 30 Hz to 4100 Hz, about eight octaves. Scientists would refer to this as bandwidth. However, notes have additional harmonics associated with them, and since our hearing range extends to 20,000 Hz, we can hear some of these harmonics.

A NEW PERSPECTIVE

The instruments that we are all familiar with today have a specific range and instruments are distinguished from each other by their range and their harmonic content. By harmonic content, I mean, although two instruments my play the exact note, they vary in how that note propagates through the air, thus a Middle C, 261 Hz, on the piano and one on the guitar will vibrate at the same fundamental frequency, but each will have different combinations(harmonics) of other frequencies that gives it its *timbre*. This is why one instrument sounds different from another.

Experimentation with the eight notes in the diatonic scale gave birth to modes each assigned a Greek name. Instead of starting on the tonic, it started on another note within the key. For instance, C Dorian would start on D and end on D, etc. The modes for the key of C are as follows. Ionian, Dorian, Phrygian, Lydian, Mixolydian, Aeolian and Locrian. During the Middle Ages, Church music was heavily dependent on modes. However, in the late Middle Ages and early Renaissance, musicians, composers, and instrument makers discovered that although interesting, Pythagoras did not go far enough in his exploration of scales. Even though the note F# that was produced by Pythagoras' successive adding of perfect fifths was not harmonious with the unison or toni, it was harmonious with its fifth note G. As a result, of their experimentation, another scale based on G was born which substituted F# for F.

G A B C D E F# G

By repeating the process of adding fifths, other notes and scales were developed leading to our current system known as the *chromatic scale*. The additional notes and scales were designated as sharps, # and flats, b. A sharp raises the tone a half step and a flat lowers a tone a half step, thus Db and C# are the same note. The chromatic scale is as follows:

C Db/C# D Eb/D# E F Gb/F# G Ab/G# A Bb/A# B

Instead of having one diatonic scale, there were now twelve. This was the second great epiphany in music theory although, like Pythagoras, no one knew the source of the phenomena.

The additional five notes correspond to the black keys on the piano. It is most ironic that the fifth turned out to be the perfect slice of the musical pie because, unlike the octave, it produced a harmonic frequency that was not generated by C. The chromatic scale is divided into semi-tones and the relationship to each note is equal to the twelfth root of two or approximately 1.06. Hence C# is 1.06 times C. The following is the chromatic scale as illustrated on the piano:

RETHINKING THE HISTORY AND MYTHS OF THE PAST

By Tobias R.—Metoc—Own work, CC BY-SA 2.5,
https://commons.wikimedia.org/w/index.php?curid=1256764

Note that the black keys on the piano, the sharps and the flats, form a pentatonic scale (scale of five notes). Therefore, it could be said that the chromatic scale is a combination of two scales, the diatonic (white keys) and the pentatonic (black keys). Only eight notes are diatonic to a key. For C, it would be the white keys on the piano.

The Pentatonic scale is any scale consisting of five notes an appears in several cultures around the world. One of the most popular pentatonic scales is the Blues Scale consisting of I, IIIb, IV, V, and VIIb notes. This scale is a powerful improvisation tool and is often used in Rock, R& B and Jazz.

Chords
In addition to modes and key signatures, chords, or the use of several notes played at the same time, were developed and could be played together on polyphonic instruments such as the piano or the guitar. These chords were generally built on triads and were diatonic to a key. For example, take the C diatonic scale

C D E F G A B C

A C Major triad would consist of notes: 1, 3, 5 or CEG. Since these three notes are also diatonic to the G and F keys, the chord is also diatonic to all three keys.

Each chord could be extended to include 7th, 9th, etc. Jazz musicians normally play chords in their higher extensions (at least a 7th chord). This allows them to substitute chords while maintaining the same or similar tonality. The Jazz saxophonist John Coltrane developed Coltrane Changes (substitutions) which, in its simple form, a chord a third above or a third below could be substituted for the tonic, e.g., Em7 (iii)or Am7 (vi)for Cmaj7 (I) and keep the tonality because three out of the four notes are common.

Chords that are diatonic to the keys are normally given the Roman Numeral designation for example: In the major scale, the I chord is called the tonic, the ii chord is minor and is called the subtonic, the iii chord is also minor and is called the

A NEW PERSPECTIVE

mediant, the IV is major and is called the subdominant, the V chord is also Major and is called the dominant the vi chord is minor and is called the submediant and the vii chord is diminished and is called the subtonic. Below are the chords for C Major and C Minor keys. Although keys may share common Minor and Major chords, the V7 is unique to a key and in this regard defines the key.

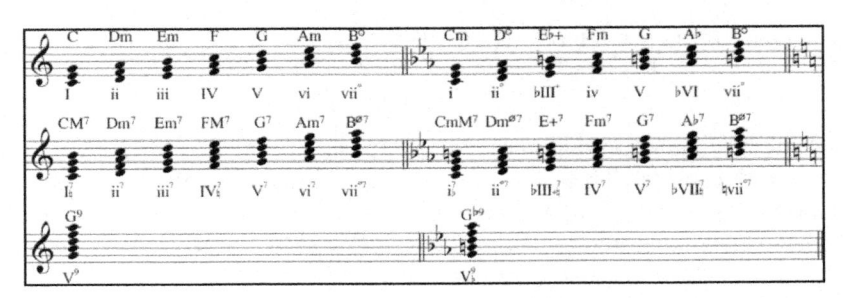

Bernhard Ziehn's 1907 list of, "diatonic triads", diatonic seventh-chords," and two examples of, "diatonic ninth-chords," the "large" and "small" ninth chords; all from the C major or the C harmonic minor scale

A Chord Progression is a series of chords played in a sequence which usually establishes the harmonic content of a musical piece. Melodies are normally played atop of a harmony which gives the music a sense of completeness. A popular chord progression called: a turnaround consisting of ii, V7, I7 chords. By using Roman numerals, musicians can outline chord progressions to be played in any key. Furthermore, there is a relationship between the modes of a key and the chords that are diatonic to a key. For example, in a Major key, a Dorian scale could be improvised over the Dm7 (ii) chord and likewise a Mixolydian scale over G7 or the V cord and so forth.

Modulation
A Modulation is a change in key. Modulations are used to create movement. Some argue that the first rule of music is to maintain the key, and the second rule is to break the key. To this end, there are four types of modulations: Direct, Prepared, Pivot Chord and Transitional. In *Direct Modulation*, the key changes from chord to chord without preparation. In *Prepared Modulation*, however, normally a series of cords (cadence) is played between keys. In *Pivot Chord Modulation*, a series of chords that are diatonic to both keys are played as part of the transition. And finally, a *Transitional Modulation* occurs when following a cycle of chromatic ii-V's or a sequence of dominants, with the music winding up in another key.

The Cycle of Fifths
With the final musical structure in place, relationships between the eight notes in a diatonic scale and the twelve notes in the chromatic scale were developed with each

RETHINKING THE HISTORY AND MYTHS OF THE PAST

note having a musical key associated with it. Each one of the notes in the diatonic scale is representative of partials or overtones of the key signature. As mentioned previously, the major tones in any diatonic collection are the tonic, the octave, the dominant and the subdominant. This is also true of the keys. That is to say, that the key a fifth above (dominant) and a fifth below (subdominant) are harmonically closer to the tonic and their respective scales differ by only one note.

For example, the musical keys closest to the key of C, are the key of F (subdominant) and the key of G(dominant). These relationships are the most aesthetically pleasing to the ear, and it is as if they are ingrained into the human psychic. There are countless songs written around this basic relationship and it is common in the music of all cultures. They are as common to us as the primary color, which by the way are frequencies as well with each color assigned to a specific frequency (wavelength). The V7 chord is the second power chord in the key and tends to pull toward the I chord.

The Cycle of Fifths forms the roadmap for the harmonic structure of music. It is like a clock with note C located at twelve o'clock with its most dissonant note or scale opposite it at six o'clock. This is true of any key. The following chart illustrates the Cycle of Fifths. The outer circle denotes the number of sharps or flats in each key, the next outer circle denotes the Major key and the inner circle represents its Relative Minor key which has the same key signature but its starting point is shifted relative to its Major key.

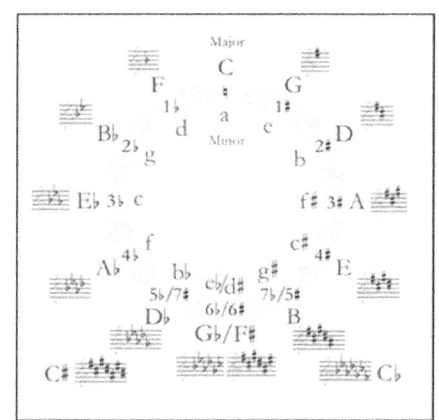

The Cycle of Fifths By Just plain Bill—Own work, CC BY-SA 3.0, https://commons.wikimedia.org/w/index.php?curid=4463183

For instance, for the Major key of C, instead of starting on C, you would start on A which would yield the A Minor scale. Therefore, by adding five additional notes to the original scale, we progressed from one Major key and one Minor key to twelve Major

A NEW PERSPECTIVE

keys and twelve Minor keys. The Major and Minor keys are like night and day. Typically, the Major keys have a happier sound and the Minor keys a sadder sound. Moreover, as Nature would have it, the musical cycle was finally complete. As seen from the chart, keys and scales that are harmonically close to each other are adjacent in the clockwise and counterclockwise directions

The beauty of the Cycle of Fifths lies in its simplicity and its symmetry. It is important to note, that harmony is maintained not by the individual notes or scales, but by the relationships of notes and scales to each other. This dictates which notes or keys are valid and the migration paths (modulation) from one key to the other. Each note added to form a successive key is also a fifth apart from each other, e.g., C to G, G to D, etc. The standard ii-V7-I chord progression is so powerful because it moves counterclockwise in the Cycle of Fifths. The subdominant of any key and the dominant are in many ways the mirror image of each other, one is a fifth above the tonic and the other is a fifth below the tonic. Moreover, the tonic is the fifth or dominant of the subdominant. In terms of vibrations or frequencies, the ratio is *3/2* in the clockwise or *4/3* in the counterclockwise direction of the Cycle of Fifths.

It is also important to note that the overall ratio between the diatonic scale and the chromatic scale in terms of the number of notes in each scale is *12/8* or *3/2*. Thus, the ratio of *3/2* seems to be integral to the rules of harmony, and as noted previously was the first ratio that Pythagoras observed as truly being different. The rules of harmony must adhere to the relationships delineated by the Cycle of Fifths and from such relationships, a musical hierarchy is developed—from notes to chords, to chord progressions to songs and scores. As the history of music attests, the number of musical permutations from these basic building blocks seems to be inexhaustible.

Music and Mathematics
Gottfried Leibniz, the co-inventor of Calculus once said: *Music is the pleasure the human mind experiences from counting without being aware that it is counting.* The relationship between music and mathematics has long been noted. Some have claimed that listening to music helps with cognition, a phenomenon known as the *Mozart Effect*. Notwithstanding, there appears to be a relationship between the cognitive skills required for music and mathematics. Physicist Dr. Stephon Alexander outlines such relationships in his book entitled: *The Jazz of Physics: The Secret Link Between Music and the Structure of the Universe*.

In addition to cognition, music is directly related to mathematics as illustrated by the following series. The Fibonacci series is a series of numbers starting with consecutive ones and adding them together to get 2, then add 2 to 1 (the previous number) to get 3, then 2 to 3 to get 5, then 3 to 5 to get 8 and so on. The first 25 numbers of the

RETHINKING THE HISTORY AND MYTHS OF THE PAST

Fibonacci series are: 1, **1, 2, 3, 5, 8, 13**, 21, 34, 55, 89, 144, 233, 377, 610, 987, 1597, 2584, 4184, 6765, with each new term being the sum of the previous two terms. From the series, Fibonacci boxes can be drawn, e.g., 1x2, 2x3, 3x 5, 5x8, 8x13.

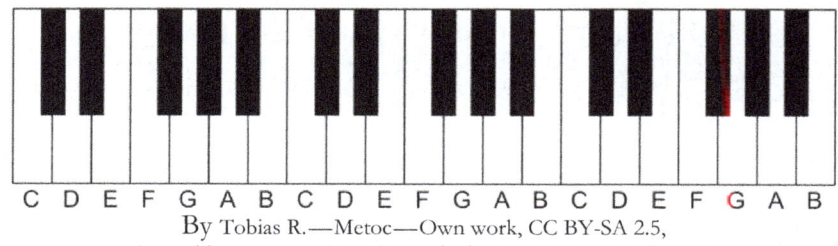

By Tobias R.—Metoc—Own work, CC BY-SA 2.5,
https://commons.wikimedia.org/w/index.php?curid=1256764

A careful examination of the piano keyboard reveals a relationship with the Fibonacci series. First, a black key is always between two white keys, ratio 1 to 2 Fibonacci ratios. The first group has two black keys and three white keys, 2 to 3, which are Fibonacci ratios, the second group has 3 black keys and 5, 3x5, white keys, also Fibonacci ratios, in the third group, there are 5 black keys and 8 white keys 5x8 which are Fibonacci ratios and finally in the total set; there are 8 white keys and 13, total keys 8x13, which are also Fibonacci ratios.

In addition to the Fibonacci series, the Fourier series explains why instruments sound differently when playing the same fundamental note. The theory states that any periodic waveform could be deconstructed into a series of sine waves. In this regard, each instrument has its signature, differing in amplitude and relevant harmonic frequencies (overtones). Within the vibration of the bass guitar string, there are multiple vibrations at different frequencies as shown below. Pythagoras accounted for the initial or fundamental vibration of the string, but he did not account for the harmonics that were produced by the fundamental frequency. The harmonic series is defined as the sum of: $1 + 1/2 + 1/3 + 1/4 + 1/5 + 1/6$ … and has been proven by several mathematical proofs to continue to infinity.

A NEW PERSPECTIVE

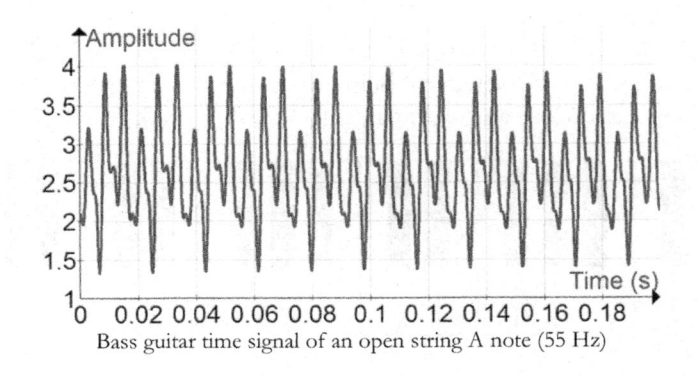

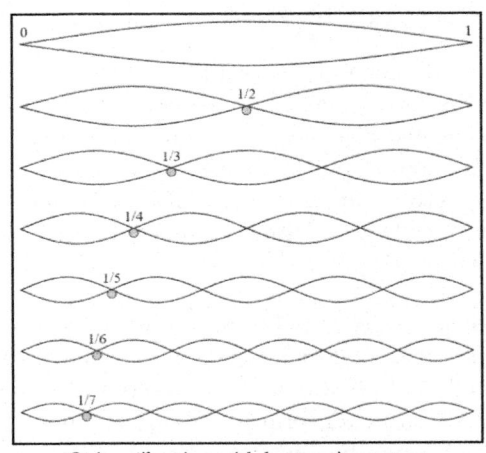

Bass guitar time signal of an open string A note (55 Hz)

String vibration with harmonic content

These frequencies vary with amplitude in accordance with the following formula.

$$s_N(x) = \frac{a_0}{2} + \sum_{n=1}^{N} \left(a_n \cos\left(\frac{2\pi n x}{P}\right) + b_n \sin\left(\frac{2\pi n x}{P}\right) \right).$$

Fourier series

Some sounds have odd harmonics, some have even, and some have both (that is why we have sine and cosine terms in the equation). A true sine wave, however, does not have any harmonics (e.g., the sound produced by a tuning fork). What the Fourier series does is explain how the ear processes sound and by doing so connects all sounds, including music to the mathematics that produced it. It breaks down sounds into their sinusoidal components. This discovery gave birth to synthesized instruments that could emulate the sounds of various instruments or create new

RETHINKING THE HISTORY AND MYTHS OF THE PAST

sounds hitherto unheard by varying the harmonic content of the fundamental frequency.

Throughout nature, we repeatedly find that these two series. Fibonacci named after the Italian mathematician, Leonardo Pisano Fibonacci (1170–1240 or 1250), who brought Arabic Numbers (0–9) to Europe and the French scientist Joseph Fourier (1768–1830), tend to define the rhythm of Nature's song. Both men developed their series without music in mind. In this regard, music is telling us more than meets the ear. It is singing the song of Mathematics that our brains readily comprehend and makes us want to vibrate or dance with it.

Pythagoras proposed that there is a rhythm or harmony to the universe which he denoted as the *harmony of the spheres*. Perhaps, in this regard, Pythagoras was right. We now know that baryonic matter (the stuff that stars and life) is composed of, can be deconstructed into a series of vibrating waves or strings at the subatomic level. Maybe we do live in a *clockwork universe* where everything is composed of notes played in a symphony conducted by the mathematical principles of the cosmos.

A NEW PERSPECTIVE

RETHINKING THE HISTORY AND MYTHS OF THE PAST

Roots: The Impact of Black Music on America and the World

The Old Plantation, ca. 1785–1795, the earliest known American painting to picture a banjo-like instrument

The essence of music is to reflect the times and by doing so, recreate the times.

Long before Rap and Hip-hop dominated the music culture, Black Music had a profound influence on the culture of the United States and the world. From the turn of the 20th century to modern times, African American music has been the heartbeat of America and emulated around the world. The roots of this uniquely American music lay in those rhythms emanating from the same continent that gave birth to humankind. It was from the shores of Africa that slaves were imported to the Americas in droves, bringing with them the core of the music that would later engulf the world.

Stripped of their humanity and burden with shackled labor driven by the ominous sting of the whip, slaves, in the form of their music, held on to the only piece of their homeland that they could truly embrace. It was music borne of their struggles, of their experiences in a foreign land that professed liberty and justice for all, yet treated them like livestock, unworthy of the amenities of humanity in a nation under God. Music was a release from the toils and burdens of slavery. Slaves were forbidden to use

A NEW PERSPECTIVE

drums because slave masters believed that drums could be used to send messages to other plantations. Yet in this trouble milieu, they found a way to save their souls through the magic of their instruments. Some, like the banjo, were fashioned by their hands, others like the fiddle were provided by their masters. They sang not out of happiness or merriment, but out of a desire to be free. Although their hands and feet were often shackled; their souls remained unchained.

One of the earliest expressions of Black Music was the cakewalk. It was a dance performed as a contest in which music was played while slaves did a cakewalk to the beat, often making fun of old master without his knowledge. The winner won a cake or took the cake, which is the source of the idiom cakewalk used today. In the late 1800s, artists such as Ernest Hogan and Bob Cole brought this music to off-Broadway.

The rhythms and lyrics of Black Music could be found throughout America. For instance, *Dixie,* the battle song of the South, was borne from the 1859 minstrel song performed by D.D. Emmett who imitated Black Music in blackface during his minstrel act. It was so popular in the South that it was played at Confederate President Jefferson Davis's inauguration in February 1861 and it later became synonymous with the South itself. (Dixieland).

Bert Williams (Library of Congress)

Perhaps one of the greatest black artists of the minstrel era was Burt Williams (1874–1922), who was not only known for his musical compositions but also for his ability

RETHINKING THE HISTORY AND MYTHS OF THE PAST

to entertain on stage. Unfortunately, to appease white audiences, talented musicians like Williams often dressed in blackface to promote the image of the servile Negro. He was the mentor and friend of W.C. Fields.

The 1893 Columbian Expedition held in Chicago to celebrate the 400th anniversary of Columbus' landing was a display of the new America and a presage of myriad innovations: electricity, the telephone, the microphone, the phonograph, motion pictures, automobiles, airplanes, etc. that changed, not only America but the world. It also gave birth to a new form of music that would define the turn of the 20th century. The invention of the phonograph by Thomas Edison provided a new conduit for black musicians to display their craft. Before the popularity and convenience of records, sheet music, often played in the homes of white America by white women, was the principal source of revenue.

Scott Joplin, 1903

The bourgeoning of America was reflected in its music. The Statue of Liberty, inspired by the abolition of American slavery and gifted to America in 1886, now stood as an emblemed of freedom for European immigrants. America became a melting pot for people of European descent. Yet African Americans remained in a separate cauldron heated by racism, bigotry and discrimination. Ragtime emerged and would dominate the first fifteen years of the 20th century. At its core were the syncopated techniques rooted in African music. This method was known as "ragging a tune" in which any tune could be improvised while maintaining its harmonic structure. Just like there were cakewalk contests, there were ragtime contests in which musicians ragged over a standard composition.

A NEW PERSPECTIVE

Scott Joplin's (1868–1917) is often referred to as the father of ragtime. Maple Leaf Rag (1899), The Entertainer (1902) and *Elite Syncopation* (1902) are among his most popular songs and prime examples of syncopation that defined the music. The 1973 movie, *The Sting*, featured his music and stands as a testimony of its enduring nature and ability to capture the temperament of the times. Joplin's music also influenced white composers such as Irving Berlin (frequently referred to as the man who was American music). Berlin's first major international hit was *Alexander's Ragtime Band* in 1911, although *Piano Man* (1910) was also popular.

Ragtime was followed by a flurry of the Blues. W.C. Handy was among the first to popularize this music with the introduction of Memphis Blues (1912) and St Louis Blues (1914). This music primarily consisted of a 12-bar structure featuring three cords (I, IV, V) and incorporated call and response techniques rooted in the slave songs sung on plantations. The Blues also incorporated the use of "blue notes" and the blues scale (I, IIIb, IV, V, VIIb) and is often used as the principal source of improvisation. The genius of the Blues is rooted in its simplicity and its ability to transform raw emotion into a coherent sound.

Billie Holiday at the Downbeat Club in New York City

Handy was followed by a string of female vocalists most noted were Ma Rainey, Bessie Smith, Ethel Waters and Billie Holiday "Lady Day" whose life was chronicled in the hit movie *Lady Sings the Blues*. The racy lyrics of these songs were embraced by the youth of the day, which helped to change the social landscape of succeeding generations. Although the walls of segregation were still in place, it was the allure of Black Music that helped to bring the walls tumbling down. Male singers such as Charlie Jackson and Huddie Letbetter (Leadbelly} help to propagate the Blues while setting the foundations of Country Music.

RETHINKING THE HISTORY AND MYTHS OF THE PAST

Leadbelly is alleged to have sung his way out of prison

The Blues was further enhanced by Muddy Waters, John Lee Hooker, B.B. King and others. Blues and Gospel Music are two sides of the same coin. Some have argued that Gospel Music is a saintly version of the Blues: singing and praying at the same time. Perhaps best portrayed by the music of Mahalia Jackson. The sound of the Blues never truly went away, but rather was integrated into other styles of music. For generations to come, the Blues was the undercurrent of the musical river that flowed across America and eventually poured into the oceans of the world.

Jazz (often referred to as America's original art form) was the culmination and fusion of previous African American music. So much so that it is hard to discern the lines between early Jazz, Ragtime and the Blues. Although Jelly Roll Morton, is the self-proclaimed father of Jazz, the origin is the product of its times and not a single individual. Some of the earliest Jazz musicians, including Morton were former ragtimers that helped to transform the music. Among some of the earliest Jazz musicians were: Eubie Blake, King Oliver, and Louis Armstrong; the latter was the first to receive national recognition and fame and did much to form the foundation of Jazz. The key to Jazz is real-time syncopated improvisation of melodies over a harmonic structure. This musical artform was ripe for the post-World War I "Roaring Twenties" often referred to as the *Jazz Age*: the latter a moniker given to the decade by F. Scott Fitzgerald.

Many argue that the roots of Jazz emanated from the funeral marches of New Orleans and the Dixieland bands. On the way to the gravesite, a slow somber and melancholy tune was heard. However, on the way back, a more joyous and uplifting song was played as if to raise the soul of the deceased to the gates of heaven where the saints could come marching in. The essence of Dixieland Jazz was its syncopated

A NEW PERSPECTIVE

polyrhythmic sound often including several melodies simultaneously. Since this music was in existence before the microphone, it often included instruments such as horns and the banjo that could be heard clearly without amplification.

Young Louis Armstrong

The invention of the microphone in the mid-twenties changed the face of Jazz and music forever; because it allowed the inclusion of instruments such as the guitar and enabled vocalists to be heard over the band. It was also during the 20s that white musicians, like Frank Sinatra, Bing Crosby, Al Jolson, and others began to emulate black Jazz musicians. The 20s was also the beginning of the Harlem Renaissance, a rebirth and merger of black literature, music, and fashion located in Harlem, NY. It was the Who's Who of black folk and a place where they could celebrate, mingle and be proud of their African heritage. It featured white and black patrons, who for a moment, could be kindred spirits in the post-World War I age of prohibition and organized crime.

The 1930s introduced Swing Jazz; a form of Jazz that abandoned the polyphonic lines in favor of a homophonic mainstream swing. One of the early giants of this art form was Fletcher Henderson. Along with Duke Ellington, Cab Callaway, Count Basie, and others, he helped to define the Swing and Big Band era which dominated the 1930s and 40s. Ellington and Count Basie were Jazz icons and their contributions to American music over several decades cannot be overstated. Their bands were more than orchestras, but instead academies in which young Jazz musicians could learn and further enhance the artform.

RETHINKING THE HISTORY AND MYTHS OF THE PAST

Duke Ellington at the Hurricane Club 1943

This era also saw the increase of white musicians and singers such as Benny Goodman, Tommy and Jimmy Dorsey, Bing Crosby, Glen Miller and others that made white audiences embrace Jazz as their own. Unlike the Roaring Twenties, the 30s was the decade of the depression, and the music of this era was full of hope. Nat King Cole was one of the popular black singers of the late-30s and the World War II years. From the waning of the depression and through the waxing of another world war; Swing and the Big Band sound was the beacon of hope amid a sea of despair. But it was not the only beacon. This era also produced the Boogie Woogie happy sound which had its roots in the African American community as far back as the 20s. In fact, *The Boogie Woogie Bugle Boy,* by the Andrew Sisters, was an iconic hit during World War II. Boogie Woogie was essentially the piano Blues with a repeated baseline in the left hand and varying melodies in the right.

The post-World War II era saw the emergence of Rock and Roll and Bebop Jazz. After two decades of stress, the music of the 50s, once again led by African American musicians, migrated toward a free and open style; and the leitmotif of white musicians imitating black artists continued. Between the two world wars, records and radio were the mediums of musical expression. The 50s, however, gave rise to a new medium called television; and by the end of the decade, it was a staple in most American homes.

A NEW PERSPECTIVE

Former Big Band singers such as Frank Sinatra, Doris Day and others emerged from the shadows of the Big Band as television raised the singer above the band. Musicians were no longer relegated to live shows, radio and records, which ushered in a new era of stardom hitherto unseen. Doris Day was pretty, and Sinatra was handsome; such features were enhanced by the magic of television.

Undeterred by what many viewed as the annexation and commercialization of their music by white singers and musicians, black artists created new forms of music that once again, became the signature of the decade. The chief architects of Bebop Jazz were Dizzy Gillespie on trumpet, Charlie Parker on saxophone, Thelonious Monk on piano, Max Roach and Kenny Clarke on drums and Charles Mingus on bass. This style of jazz was a referendum on Swing and the Big Band sound.

Charlie Parker, with Dizzy and a young Miles in the background

It was common for Beboppers to improvise over the harmony of popular songs, thus giving the song a new life and sometimes a new name. Although the principal timekeeping remained the responsibility of the drummer, more and more of this responsibility was given to the bass player, an evolution that continued in other Jazz forms. Also popular in the late-fifties and early sixties was the smooth guitar playing of West Montgomery and Grant Green. Both were influenced by the playing style of Charlie Cristian one of the first Jazz guitarists.

RETHINKING THE HISTORY AND MYTHS OF THE PAST

Cool Jazz was introduced in the-50s by, Miles Davis: the premier disciple of Gillespie and Parker. Although Davis was a gifted musician, he was a much better teacher who recognized talent and helped musicians develop their musical voice. Chief among them were: saxophonists John Coltrane and Wayne Shorter, pianists Herbie Hancock, Chick Chorea, Joe Zawinul, guitarist John McLaughlin and bassist Ron Carter. Many became leaders of Jazz Fusion bands. Unlike Bebop and Swing, Cool Jazz was so cool and quiet that you could snap to it, but you couldn't clap to it.

Even though Jazz was popular in the United States, many Jazz musicians such as Miles, found Europe, particularly France, more appreciative of their music. The most innovative of Miles' protégés was John Coltrane. He is not only renowned for his music but in some circles worshiped as a saint. In fact, he is the patron saint of John Coltrane Orthodox Church in San Francisco. In the late 50s, Coltrane had a spiritual epiphany the helped him to kick drugs and this spiritual experience was reflected in his music. He is consistently considered the quintessential Jazz saxophonist, often imitated but never duplicated

The Boogie Woogie sound of the 40s was extended to form the foundation of the Rock and Roll craze of the 50s and once again it started with America's youth. In the post-World War II years, America emerged as the undisputed leader of the free world and the standard-bearer of democracy around the world. With the threat of Armageddon looming over the world in the form of Nuclear War and the more immediate threat of the Soviet Union in the form of the Cold War, the 50s was a transitional decade and a prelude to "the race for space." America was not only seen as a military power, but it was also viewed as a new cultural center and the musical Mecca of the world.

Rock and Rollers were perhaps the biggest beneficiaries of television. It provided a forum for showmanship and was seen and heard simultaneously in cities and small towns across America. African American musicians such as Chuck Berry, Little Richard, Fats Domino and Bo Diddley were the trendsetters of this new genre. The 50s saw the incorporation, many argue the imitation, of this style of music by white musicians. Record companies quickly realized that more money could be made by having white artists perform black songs.

A NEW PERSPECTIVE

Chuck Berry (1926 -2017)

Elvis Presley became the dominant figure of this style of music, not because he was the best or the most innovative, but because white youth could identify with him. Young white girls could think of Elvis and other white singers as being cute or sexy, but they could not think of any black male singer in this way. During the 50s, as in the decades before, interracial marriages were not only deemed taboo, but against the law in some states.

The introduction of televisions shows such as American Bandstand, hosted by the legendary Dick Clark and the Ed Sullivan Show, launched Rock and Roll into the public sphere. Such changes were not welcomed by all, as the merger of Black Music and whites dancing alongside blacks disturbed many during an era when segregation and "separate but equal" laws were being challenged in the highest court in the land. Many whites, particularly in the South, viewed Rock and Roll as the corruption of the white youth and the smearing of the color line long held between the two races.

Other technological inventions of the late 40s also contributed to the advancement of Rock and Roll in the 50s. The electric guitar was further enhanced by Leo Fender and Less Paul. Additionally, Columbia Records released the first 12-inch LP which allowed musicians to experiment. The 45 rpm smaller record provided enough space for a three-minute song to be recorded on one side and another on the flip side. These innovations set the stage for the music of the 60s and beyond.

RETHINKING THE HISTORY AND MYTHS OF THE PAST

Also popular during the 50s were Doo-wop groups such as The Platters, The Drifters and others which had a softer and more romantic sound. In the late-fifties, singers such as Ray Charles and Sam Cooke combined Blues, Gospel and Jazz into a soulful sound that was a preface to the Soul Music of the 60s. Blind since the age of seven, Charles was not only a great singer but a talented musician. Sam Cooke's career was short but fruitful. His Gospel roots could clearly be heard in his soulful singing. So much so that he was often called "The King of Soul."

Ray Charles friend and mentor of Quincy Jones

The 60s was a decade of rebellion, Civil Rights and civil discourse often reflected in its music and style of dress. By the mid-sixties, the clean-cut look of the 50s was superseded by long hair, bell-bottom pants and miniskirts. Gone, was the straight processed hair of Black artists—abandoned in favor of the Afro which reflected their affinity with Africa, and moreover, with themselves. They rejected the term Negro, in favor of black or Afro-American. Black people rebelled against injustice at home and white people rebelled against the Vietnam War abroad.

The Baby Boomers had come of age and with it came a disdain for the umbrella of war from which they were conceived. As in previous decades, African American musicians and vocalists were the pacesetters: from the soulful sounds of Motown and the gospel-like songs of Aretha Franklin that demanded respect—to the austere electric Rock of Jimi Hendrix. Although centered in Detroit, MI, Motown was more

A NEW PERSPECTIVE

than a city; it was the voice of America. As blacks migrated from the South to the *Motor City,* they forged the sound of a nation. Motown helped to transform the Rock and Roll and Doo-wop sound of the 50s into Soul Music of the 60s. Aretha's style of singing was so soulful and so powerful that it made you feel like saying "Hallelujah" after hearing her sing.

Hendrix got his start with the Isley Brothers and also played in Little Richard's band. Known for his unique playing style and on-stage theatrics, such as playing the guitar with his teeth and setting it on fire. He was instrumental in transforming Rock and Roll into Rock. During his lifetime he was idolized by other Rock guitarists. Although other black musicians had crossed over to white audiences, Hendrix was a black star in a genre comprised primarily of whites and included white members in his band.

Jimi Hendrix (1942–1970)

The British Invasion of The Beatles, The Rolling Stones, Eric Clapton, and others was also stimulated by African American music. The Blues was a gift to them, and it returned to America in different draping. In fact, The Rolling Stones took their name from a Muddy Watters song. Yet, most white Americans saw this music as something different and of foreign origin. The 1969 Woodstock concert was a seminal moment as black and white artists united under the banner of Peace, Love and Music. Woodstock was the culmination and the reflection of a turbulent decade—plagued by assassinations of American leaders, America's confrontation with its hypocritical past and the direction of its future. It was, however, the popularity of this concert that

RETHINKING THE HISTORY AND MYTHS OF THE PAST

convinced Miles Davis to develop an electric Jazz band which gave birth to Jazz Fusion, Jazz Funk and Smooth Jazz.

Moreover, Marvin Gaye's What's Going On and *Mercy Mercy Me* along with Stevie Wonder's Music of my Mind and Superstition were both a reformation on the Motown sound of Smoky Robinson, The Supremes, The Temptations and others of the 60s and a window into the music and mindset of the 70s. Furthermore, in the late 60s, James Brown, Sly in the Family Stones and others helped to lay the foundations of what would become the Funk of the 70s. In the early 70s, the music of Isaac Hayes, Barry White, Curtis Mayfield and Gill Scott-Heron included rap, although it was not called it at the time.

Isaac Hayes 1973

In the 70s, Funk, Disco and Jazz Fusion conquered the airways and would give birth to Rap and Hip-hop music. The music of Earth, Wind and Fire, Parliament, The Ohio Players, Kool and the Gang, The O'Jays, and Donna Summer helped to define a new decade of Soul Music. Donna Summer (the Queen of Disco) dominated the Disco era, so much so that it is difficult to think of the era without thinking of her. Frequently referred to as *Old School*, the music of this decade had a profound impact on Rap and Hip-hop music which sampled its funky music to produce a new genre that has lasted decades. During an era, in which the CD became the widespread music media, young rappers went in search of LPs "to scratch"; thus, overlaying raps atop of sampled 70s beats.

A NEW PERSPECTIVE

Donna Summer in a recording studio, 1977

In the 80s, the music and showmanship of Michael Jackson, reminiscent of the 50s Rock and Rollers, helped to define the music video and further heightened the Rap and Hip-hop culture. Jackson's music was produced by Quincy Jones, a thirty-year composer of Jazz and Pop. Their collaboration began in 1979 with the hit album *Off the Wall*. A child protégé of the Motown era, "The King of Pop", as Jackson was so often called, was a megastar, treated like royalty and admired around the world. It was not necessarily the music of Michael Jackson that the new generation of rappers gravitated toward, but rather his showmanship.

The sampled music of 70s groups such as Chic's *Good Time* (1979) and contemporary sounds such as Herbie Hancock's *Rockit* (1983), which featured synthesizers and drum machines to produce unique sounds without a band, became the core of the early Rap and Hip-hop sound. Breakdancing, a new and innovative style of dancing that was frequently driven by Rap and Hip-hop, was also a product of the 80s. Such techniques set the stage for N.W.A, Dr. Dre, 2Pac, Biggie, and others that would emerge in the 90s as part of the Gangsta Rap craze. Although previous styles often included racy lyrics in their song, the use of profanity, the N word and the degradation of women in the form of the B word, along with the glorification of violence, was viewed by many as a bridge too far. As in other genres, these rappers became the mentors and models of a new generation of rappers, including: Jay-Z, Kanye West, 50 Cent, and others.

RETHINKING THE HISTORY AND MYTHS OF THE PAST

Hence, the current dominance of Rap and Hip-hop is just one link in a long chain of music—from the slave plantations of the South, to the modern-day. From the syncopated rhythms of Joplin to the synthesized melodies of Dr. Dre, Black Music has defined "what is hip", before it hopped over to other forms of music and it has been a constant ambassador of American culture. Although the allure of freedom has always been the linchpin of America, it is somewhat ironic that it was the music of those held in bondage for centuries that helped to convey and display this message.

The embedded links represent a discography and history of 20th century African American music (Ebook only).

A NEW PERSPECTIVE

RETHINKING THE HISTORY AND MYTHS OF THE PAST

Black History

A NEW PERSPECTIVE

RETHINKING THE HISTORY AND MYTHS OF THE PAST

Origins of the African Slave Trade

The Arab Slave Trade

The annals of antiquity are full of stories about slavery as if it was a natural condition of humankind. Notwithstanding, when we think of slavery today, we often think of the African slave trade. However, slavery at its core is not about race, it's about indifference. The African slave trade is just one chapter in a book of Man's inhumanity toward Man. A book that proves the adage that (*Homō homini lupus*) man is the wolf of man.

Arab Slave Trade

Much attention has been drawn to the Trans-Atlantic slave trade but not much has been given to the Arab slave trade that preceded it. As far as blacks were concerned, Islam was a double-edged sword. In many ways, blacks of North Africa were the benefactors and beneficiaries of Islam. The Moors would be placed in this group. However, many blacks suffered under Islam particularly those that did not convert. Islam prohibits the enslavement of free Muslims regardless of race and special exceptions were sometimes made for *The People of the Book* (Jews and Christians).

The denizens of Africa; however, were generally not considered *People of the Book*. Even though Islam is a religion comprised of many different racial and ethnic groups, it is evident from the writings of Al Jahiz (776–868) and other contemporary black scholars that racial discrimination and stereotypes existed in the Islamic world from its

A NEW PERSPECTIVE

inception. Jahiz, a renowned scholar, went as far as to respond to discrimination in his book entitled: *The Superiority in Glory of the Black Race over the White*.

The Arab slave trade was established centuries in Africa before the Portuguese arrived in the 15th century. In this regard, Europeans, once again, followed in the footsteps of Islam and the Arabs. It is safe to say that the change in attitudes toward blacks within Islam began with the expansion of their empire. Before the Islamic expansion, slaves on the African continent, for the most part, were prisoners of war and localized without any racial connotation attached. However, as more and more slaves entered Arabia from Africa, a color connotation was attached. Blacks were transported from West Africa across the Sahara and along the Nile River from East Africa to Arabia. Many of the slaves had to walk across the burning sands of the Sahara, thus, leaving a trail of skeletons along the way.

Arab slave-trading caravan transporting black African slaves across the Sahara

Unlike white slaves from Europe and Semitic slaves from the Middle East, black skin was a Scarlet Letter within some circles of Islam, and many began to use race as a social status. Some went as far as to use the biblical narrative of the curse of Ham to justify the enslavement of black people. Furthermore, it was much easier for white and Semitic slaves to blend into the population and this provided a means for many of them to escape the stigma of slavery. This is somewhat illustrated in the word used for blacks in Arabia today. White slaves were normally called *mamluk* while black slaves were called *abd*, and over time, the word *abd* ceased to be used to refer to black slaves and was applied to black people.

RETHINKING THE HISTORY AND MYTHS OF THE PAST

In the Islamic world, if the mother was a slave then that status would transfer to the child. Arab fathers, however, had the option to free the sons of their slave concubines and many sons of mixed relationships achieved high social standings. The practice of castrating black male slaves virtually assured that the black slave population was limited.

The Arab slave trade continued for centuries even during the late Victorian era when it was illegal in Europe and the Americas. For example, as recent as 1878, the holy cities of Mecca and Medina were major slave-trading hubs. In all fairness, after the abolition of slavery in Europe and the Americas, Europeans, in some cases, tried to stop or impede the Arab slave trade.

Origin of the Trans-Atlantic Slave Trade
The Trans-Atlantic slave trade did not start as a quest to enslave Africans, but rather, as an attempt to explore the African continent and to find a route to India and the spice market. When the Muslims conquered Constantinople in 1453, it changed the dynamics of Eastern trade and the need to find alternative routes became paramount. This was the source of Columbus' voyage in 1492. As in the case of the Arab slave trade, the enslavement of Africans was a product of expansion.

Prince Henry the Navigator

It was the contact with the Moors on the Iberian Peninsula that gave the Portuguese and Spanish a new type of ship, the caravel, capable of making it windward without the use of oars. From 1415 until his death in 1460, Prince Henry the Navigator collected the latest information on sailing techniques and geography, advocated a new Crusade against the Muslims and pushed for exploration. The Portuguese always believed that the quickest route to India was around the horn of Africa. Columbus'

A NEW PERSPECTIVE

voyage to the New World discovered new lands, flora and fauna hitherto unknown and initiated a race between Spain and Portugal.

In 1494, Pope Alexander VI initiated the *Treaty of Tordesillas* which divided the lands explored by Spain and Portugal, granting Brazil and Africa to Portugal. This was the opening salvo to African slavery. As more and more European nations began to explore, they followed the paragon established by Spain and Portugal and approved by the Catholic Church. In the pre-Columbian world, the myth of Prester John, who was believed to reside in Africa, captivated the imagination of Henry the Navigator. It was, however, the capture of the Moorish city of Ceuta in 1415 that started Portugal on its quests for spices and their Christian hero Prester John. Rumors of gold, perhaps driven by the legend of Mansa Musa's pilgrimage (1324), was also a catalyst for European expansion into Africa. Mansa Musa brought so much gold with him that he suppressed the gold market in the Middle East for 12 years. This gave Europeans the impression that Africa was a land full of gold.

Mansa Musa sitting on a throne and holding a gold coin

For centuries finding Prester John's kingdom was one of the causes that united Europeans and he was important to the overall psychology of the Crusades. Letters supposedly written by him were received in Europe with delight and zeal. In their darkest hours, it was the legend of this black hero that gave light to the European continent besieged by fear of conquest. Prester John was indeed their Pygmalion, their ray of sunshine during those days when the Islamic cloud lurked over Europe. To them, he was real and not a figment of their imagination.

So strong was their conviction to Prester John, that the Portuguese explored the African continent in search of his kingdom. Vasco da Gama on his trip to India in 1497 carried a letter for Prester John. However, in the quest for their hero, the Europeans, and the Portuguese in particular, was presented with an interesting racial dilemma. Their expeditions to Africa exposed them to a variety of blacks at a time

RETHINKING THE HISTORY AND MYTHS OF THE PAST

when there was a growing demand for labor to work the fields of the New World. This virtual limitless supply of labor soon became their black gold.

The availability of black slaves for sale was a fortuitous and unexpected consequence of their search for Prester John and the desire for gold. Over time, their quest for gold and slaves superseded all other desires, and their dreams of finding the kingdom of Prester John were replaced by delusions of grandeur. When the Portuguese established plantations in Brazil, they began to ship slaves directly from Africa to the New World. This, unfortunately, became the paradigm of the future as additional land discoveries by European nations led to the importation of slaves into those regions. The once Gold Coast of Africa was transformed into the Slave Coast.

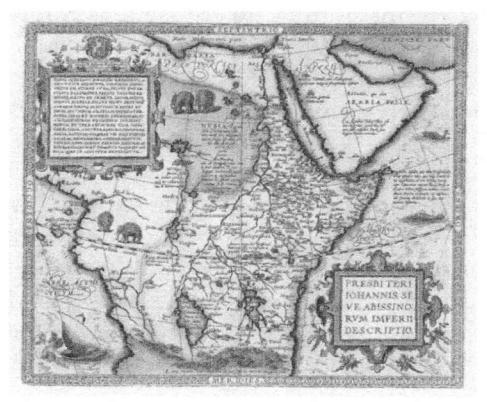

A map of Prester John's kingdom as Ethiopia

Ronald Sanders in his book the *Lost Tribes and Promised Lands* explains this phenomenon.

The assault on the blacks now being begun by Portugal and Spain was in a sense, just a part of the burgeoning vengefulness upon the entire legacy of those civilizations that had once overrun the peninsula from the south and ultimately the east, but in another, the outcome of the attitudes inherited from it. Whatever had been feared or loathed in medieval Spain by the Christians and Muslims alike had come from the deep south. The southern thrust that the Portuguese were now undertaking was the beginning of a voyage into terrifying dark recesses of the Iberian collective unconscious. The farther south their ships took them in the search of an eastward passage, the more the benign black image of Prestor John became obscured under the frightening and then contemptible ones of the Moor at Ceuta and the Guinea slave. [Lost Tribes and Promised Land, p.59]

Basil Davidson in his book entitled: *The Lost Cities of Africa* delineated a similar view:

If early Portuguese thought of Africa as the land of Prester John, of the gold of Ophir and the Queen of Sheba, marvelous and splendid rich beyond dreams, those afterward would return to another extreme. Africa

A NEW PERSPECTIVE

would become by reputation altogether a land of savage torment, moral and mental darkness, childlike or perverse. [Basil Davidson: The Lost Cities of Africa, p.201]

The influence of Prester John's legend on the maritime efforts of Europeans particularly the Portuguese should not be underestimated. What often started out as a game of enterprise and friendship between Africans and Europeans quickly transformed into a game of survival. It is most unfortunate that over time slavery became an ingrained part of the African landscape.

A perfect example of this phenomenon was Nzinga Mbemba who wholeheartedly embraced Christianity. He was a very articulate man that became King Alfonso I of the Congo in 1506. With the aid of Portuguese firearms, he expanded his kingdom and provided 3,000 slaves to the Portuguese each year as part of his conquest. In return, he received goods from Portugal and members of his court were educated by the Portuguese and showered with gifts. He and his court dressed like Europeans and acted like them too. There were nuns there to teach them the Bible and life was good.

By 1526, however, Alfonso's subjects were being enslaved and even some of his noblemen and relatives. He complained to the king of Portugal who he thought was a good friend addressing him as "brother monarch". He wrote the following regarding the condition of his kingdom: and so great, Sir is the corruption and licentiousness that our country is being completely depopulated.... it is our will that in these kingdoms there should not be any trade of slaves nor outlet for them. To which the king of Portugal replied: your kingdom has nothing else to offer and if he wanted to continue receiving goods and services from Portugal than he must continue to supply slaves. Slavery, and all it entailed, not only corrupted the body and soul of Africa, it corrupted the body and soul of humanity. It is estimated that 12 million African slaves were shipped across the Atlantic Ocean.

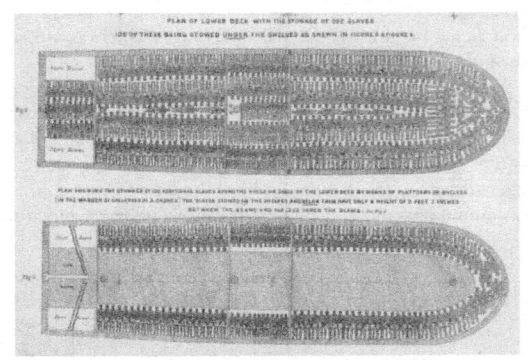

Stowage of a British slave ship (1788)

RETHINKING THE HISTORY AND MYTHS OF THE PAST

Differences Between the Two Slave Trades

The Arab slave trade, although also a stain on humanity, was not as universally brutal as the Trans-Atlantic slave trade for a variety of reasons. For the most part, the Arabs took more women than men and the Europeans took more men than women in inverse proportions (two-thirds of the trans-Atlantic slaves were men, and two-thirds of the Arab slaves were women). The women were used as domestics or concubines, and the male slaves were often used as bodyguards and servants. However, there is documentation of black slaves working in the Saharan salt mines in harsh and inhumane conditions. Although the Arab slave trade lasted far longer than the European slave trade, there are not as many people of African descent in Arabia as there are in the Western Hemisphere.

There was, however, a distinct difference between the Arab and the Trans-Atlantic slave trades. Slaves in America were treated as livestock, and after the slave trade was ended by Thomas Jefferson in 1807, the demand for domestic slaves increased as a result of cotton and an expanding America. Moreover, Americans drew a sharp line of demarcation based solely on race, to the extent that if you were not 15/16 white you were still a slave. The line was drawn so sharply that even if 15/16 was comprised of descendants of the master as in the case of Thomas Jefferson's and Sally Hemings' progeny, it could not be knowingly crossed. This line did not exist among the Arabs. For example, Umar, the most powerful and influential caliph and companion of the prophet Mohammad was the grandson of a black mother, something unimaginable in ante-bellum or post-bellum America until the election of Barack Obama as president in 2008. In some cases, within the Arab world, the color of the skin did not matter, particularly if you were someone like Mansa Musa that had something to offer. Moreover, Muslims often point to Bilal ibn Ribah (Bilal) a revered black companion of the Prophet Muhammad and the first Muezzin, to illustrate the non-racial aspect of Islam.

Conclusion

The Sahara Desert was a barrier, and this geographically isolated many of the African tribes from advancements, such as guns, ships, etc. that were developed outside of Africa. This placed Africans on the continent at a severe disadvantage. Arabs and Europeans stood on the shoulders of antiquity and were the beneficiaries of fallen empires such as Egypt, Persia, Greece and Rome that came before them. Furthermore, the Muslim expansion set the stage for European exploration by introducing, the compass, and gunpowder from the Far East and by laying the foundations of the Scientific Revolution that further enhanced European dominance around the globe.

A NEW PERSPECTIVE

In a nutshell, it could be said that the exploitation of black people in Africa was a cancer that spread from the Islamic world into the European world. This was driven by the demands for labor in the New World. There were, African tribes that collaborated with the Arabs and Europeans, not so much as to provide slaves from their tribe, but prisoners of war from their internal conflicts. Africa and its inhabitants were trapped between the global expansion of Europe and the Arab expansion that preceded it. What is often overlooked is how much slavery was ingrained into the economies and politics of Europe and America.

RETHINKING THE HISTORY AND MYTHS OF THE PAST

Haiti and the Louisiana Purchase

Bureau of Engraving and Printing—U.S. Post Office

Some Americans may look at Haiti today, burden by its poverty, plagued by a string of corrupt leaders and natural disasters and say: What does it have to do with America? Yet past events on this Caribbean island had a profound impact on the continental expansion of the United States.

The Slave Revolt in Haiti

Saint Domingue (now Haiti) was one of the richest and cruelest colonies in the Western Hemisphere. More than one-third of its slaves died within a few years of their arrival. By 1791, it had accounted for two-thirds of the French overseas trade. To put things in the proper perspective, Saint Dominque's trade was greater than the entire United States and all of Britain's rich Caribbean colonies combined. Saint Domingue was comprised of about a half-million slaves all under the thumb of French tyranny. They also had a substantial mulatto (*gens de couluer*) population of 55,000 blacks which was equal to the white population on the French part of the island shared with the Spanish Dominican Republic, the site of Columbus's landing in 1492.

When we speak of colonial revolutions, we often think of the American and French Revolutions and those of Latin America. Yet, this era also gave birth to the most successful slave rebellion in all of history. For the most part, slave rebellions were

A NEW PERSPECTIVE

unsuccessful in achieving their objectives. Notwithstanding, in August of 1791, two years after the French Revolution, the slaves of Saint Domingue began to revolt. The initial demand, in 1790, was that mulattos and free black men be given the same rights and privileges of Frenchmen. They had found allies in a group known as *Les Amis des Noir* or Friends of the Blacks. They were supported by prominent Frenchmen such as Brissot, the Rolands and Robespierre. This led to the unsuccessful first revolt, which consisted primarily of mulattos under the leadership of Oge' who was later captured and executed.

Under the leadership of Toussaint Louverture, the revolt continued. Determined to seek freedom for his people, he aligned with Spanish forces, and later fought for France against Spain and Great Britain. Negotiations with Spain and Great Britain ceded Saint Domingue to France. Events on the island, as well as events in Europe, eventually led to the emancipation of slaves in 1794. France decided that in order to keep control of the island, it must free its slaves. This was not, however, a declaration of independence, but rather a proclamation of emancipation.

Toussaint Louverture (1743–1803)

After the slaves were freed, the island was granted some degree of autonomy under Louverture's leadership. He was the son of an African slave and he could speak his father's native language, along with the Haitian patois as well as French. As a child, he was an avid reader and was inspired by the works of Rousseau and other Frenchmen. He truly believed that *Liberté, Egalité, Fraternité* had come not only to white Frenchmen but all Frenchmen. He initiated several reforms to stabilize the economy and to keep the peace between the different ethnic groups on the island. Such conditions proved

RETHINKING THE HISTORY AND MYTHS OF THE PAST

to be too great because problems on the island and the burgeoning war on the European continent between France and Great Britain hindered his efforts.

Freeing the slaves hurt the pockets of the landed gentry both home and abroad. When Napoleon came to power, he was persuaded by the rich plantation owners to reinstate slavery in May of 1802. This was soon followed by a flurry of racial laws. The most disgraceful was the dismissal of many black officers from the army. This measure affected twelve generals and several officers. Interracial marriages were now outlawed, and persons of African descent were denied the right to reside in some parts of France. Jean-Baptiste Belly, the once hero and icon of black abolitionists, was thrown into prison. This infuriated the blacks of San Dominique both mulatto and slave and they united in a full-scale revolution.

Thus, betrayal was the catalyst of the Haitian slave revolt that eventually led to its independence. Toussaint Louverture decided that if freedom was not given to him then he would take it. He had previously put together an army of 14,000 disciplined slaves to repel and defeat the British and the Spanish in the name of France. Now that army demanded that France honor its initial agreement to abolish slavery. Hence, the bloodbath on this French island was reinitiated with the same vigor that spun the revolution in France. If the saying an eye for an eye and a tooth for a tooth was ever applicable, it was in Saint Dominque. For instance, when the French captured and executed 500 blacks, Jean Jacques Dessalines retaliated by executing 1,000 whites.

If there was a failing in Toussaint Louverture, it was that he really wanted to be a Frenchman. He was a Francophile and a Catholic at heart. He and others were referred to as the black Jacobins and they believed in the ideals of the French Revolution. After all, they were ideals which he fought for with vigor under the French flag. In his memoirs, he wrote about how many men he killed for France and the wounds on his body endured for France. This is perhaps why he accepted the terms of surrender, to have his day in court and to be tried as a French general. He wanted to put France on trial for its betrayal to the cause of liberty. This was part of the agreement of his surrender. Of course, this never happened, and he died while in prison.

Napoleon later wrote while in exile that it was a mistake to try and take Saint Dominque by force, and he should have negotiated with Toussaint as a Frenchmen. Moreover, he knew it was an error at the time but yielded to the pressure of rich Frenchmen. Furthermore, Napoleon had firsthand knowledge of the prowess of black men on the battlefield as one of his best generals, Thomas Alexander Dumas, (father of Alexander Dumas author of: *The Three Musketeers* and *The Count of Monte Cristo*) was of Haitian descent. The irony of it all is that the French did not feel that blacks were

A NEW PERSPECTIVE

born with the same yearning for freedom as white people. They also underestimated the intellect and the fortitude of Saint Domingue's black population. They quickly found that the capture of Toussaint did not stop the revolution. Now the slaves wanted more than emancipation; they wanted independence from France.

Under the leadership of Toussaint's generals, Jean Jacques Dessalines and Henri Christophe (the latter along with Jean Baptiste Belly are believed by some to have fought in the American Revolution). It is believed that Dessalines was born in West Africa and came to the island as a slave. Because of the inspiration and genius of Toussaint Louverture and the desire for freedom espoused by its slave population, Haiti became the first black republic. Dessalines became the first "Emperor" Jacques I. It is most unfortunate that the only successful slave revolt proved to be a Pyrrhic victory as Haiti felt the wrath of the world for its success against the French.

The Louisiana Purchase
It was France that came to the aid of the thirteen colonies during the American Revolutionary War. Yet, thirteen years after the American Declaration of Independence, France was embroiled in revolution. The French Revolution not only brought, *Liberty, Equality and Fraternity* to France but it also brought war and destabilization to the European continent. France would push across the continent and deep into Russia. Napoleon would leave his indelible thumbprint on Europe for a century. His army became the martial force to emulate and France would scribe its annals into the history of Europe. Although his thumbprint was on Europe, his hand reached across the Atlantic.

The French originally occupied the Louisiana Territory. Notwithstanding, in 1762, it was given to Charles III of Spain by Louis XV as payment for debts incurred during the French and Indian War (also known as the Seven Year War). During the Spanish occupation of the territory, the United States had a very amicable relationship with Spain. When Napoleon's army overran Spain, it changed the dynamics in the United States. Jefferson, who was president at the time, did not know what Napoleon's next move would be.

If Napoleon had any signature to his actions, it was that he only honored the last treaty that he concocted and signed. Of relevant importance were the control of the Mississippi River and its gateway the port of New Orleans. Thus, began the chess game between Jefferson and Napoleon. Jefferson was aided by two future presidents in this endeavor, James Madison and James Monroe. He believed that Napoleon would either change the rules of the game or perhaps invade the United States. More importantly, America was unprepared for war. It only had a small army and practically

RETHINKING THE HISTORY AND MYTHS OF THE PAST

no Navy. Napoleon and France, therefore, represented a clear and present danger to the security and future of the United States.

Napoleon Bonaparte (1769–1821)

Although the war between Great Britain and France was primarily waged on the European continent, both were colonial powers with interests and land in North America. This placed Jefferson and the United States between two powers and made its position of neutrality difficult. Jefferson had lived in France before the French Revolution. He, therefore, had some idea of the events that led to that revolt and the spirit of the French people. Many of those faces that laid face down at the guillotine were aristocrats and scholars that he once befriended. Yet, he was very suspicious of Napoleon and the new regime and his suspicions were warranted.

It was Napoleon's plan to send a fleet to attack the United States and that fleet would be launched from Haiti. Without a secure Haiti, an invasion of the United States or a defense of the Louisianan (French) territory would not be possible. When the United States gained its independence from England, it was nothing more than a strip of states along the Atlantic seacoast. But there was always the frontier and as time went on, more and more Americans began to push west. America always had its eyes on land east of the Mississippi and by the early 1800s, it had become more and more dependent on this majestic river.

Because of the events unfolding in Haiti, one of Napoleon's key strategic options was taken away. The Haitian revolt not only hurt Napoleon tactically, but it also hurt him economically. It could not have occurred at a worse time for Napoleon and a better time for the United States. As the saying goes: "God protects fools, drunks and the

A NEW PERSPECTIVE

United States" and at least in this case, the latter was definitely true. Thus, Jefferson's dilemma was to support the Haitian slave revolt that threatened the core of America's slave institution or to risk America's sovereignty by letting the French forces coalesce on the island. Previous administrations had taken different sides of the revolt in Haiti. The Washington administration supported the slave-owners, and the Adams administration bargained with Toussaint and the rebels. But neither had the threat of invasion at their doorsteps.

Jefferson decided to let the events unfold, and the French army was decimated by the Haitian forces and disease. This and the events developing on the European continent eventually led Napoleon to sell the Louisiana territory to the United States for 15 million dollars which resulted in the doubling of the American landscape. This "grand bargain" was perhaps the greatest single step in the expansion of the United States from a group of colonies along the Atlantic Ocean to its current nation from sea to shining sea.

The Louisiana Purchase paved the way for the creation of a new America, adding thirteen new states. It stretched from the Mississippi River to the Rocky Mountains. The acquisition, however, did not come without its set of problems. Rather than resolve the slave question in the United States, it only intensified it. Over the coming decades, it opened debates and compromises regarding the expansion of slavery into the new territories. Although the Louisiana Purchase was prosperous for Americans of European descent, it unfortunately, led to the growth of a repressive system that the Haitians fought to eliminate as well as the expulsion of Native Americans. While the foreign slave trade was ended under Jefferson's administration, the domestic slave trade continued. Moreover, the elimination of the foreign slave trade helped states like Jefferson's Virginia. Tobacco had long depleted the soil of Virginia and the selling of slaves to the Deep South and the west became the new crop of Virginia. Jefferson himself sold 85 slaves.

Fear of Slave Revolts in America
The Haitian revolt was the nightmare of every slave-master, and as a result, sent shockwaves through the American colonies. How did such an event happen? Could the revolt spread to the United States? These questions lurked in the minds of colonial slaveholders. The newspapers in America were full of stories regarding massacres of white people some were true others were fabricated to arouse fear among the Southern population.

Whereas it was beneficial to the United States in the long term, the uprising in Haiti was not well received in the South as fear of slave revolts permeated Southern society. Rightfully so, because it served as inspiration for slave uprisings in America, most

RETHINKING THE HISTORY AND MYTHS OF THE PAST

noted were the Nate Turner rebellion in 1831 and John Brown's raid in 1859. In fact, the martial buildup in the South along with the establishment of military institutions such as the Virginia Military Institute (VMI), founded in 1839, and the Citadel in South Carolina, founded in 1842, were direct results of such fears. There was also an increase in white refugees from Haiti arriving in port cities such as Philadelphia, Pennsylvania and Charleston, South Carolina.

South Carolina was extremely sympathetic to the influx of white planters replete with their horror stories of masters being massacred by their slaves. It was a state that had more slaves than it had white people therefore it was always sensitive to slave rebellions. This paranoia continued up until the Civil War as the first shots of this bloody fratricidal war were fired in this state. On the other hand, New Orleans, a city with a French heritage, became a haven for Haitian immigration. Many of which were free people of color. The black population of New Orleans increased in the early 19th century from a wave of Haitian immigrants. These immigrants, of diverse backgrounds, helped to shape the culture of Louisiana for generations.

Haiti's independence posed a new problem for the world. Many believed it was the harbinger of things to come and a symbol of the dangers of slave revolts. As a result, Haiti was ostracized by the world and was perceived as a pariah and not a vanguard. What the French could not achieve on the battlefield, they achieved through harsh diplomacy. France did not fully recognize it until 1838 (although conditional recognition was granted in 1825 only after it agreed to pay compensation for France's losses). The United States did not recognize Haiti until 1862; a time when America was trying to find a home for free black people as part of Lincoln's plan of gradual emancipation.

So when Americans travel from east to west: from Missouri to Colorado and from north to south from: Louisiana to Montana, or when Haitians are in need because of natural disasters, they may want to reflect on how Haiti helped to make such a grand bargain possible.

A NEW PERSPECTIVE

RETHINKING THE HISTORY AND MYTHS OF THE PAST

Black Literary Giants: Dumas and Pushkin

Pushkin exam at lyceum, given to those that espouse
excellence in the Russian language

Before [Richard Wright](#) and [James Baldwin](#), [Zora Neale Hurston](#) and [Toni Morrison](#) and other African American writers of the 20th century, there were black writers of distinction of which any race would be proud. Chief among them were Alexander Dumas (1802-1870) and Alexander Pushkin (1799–1837). Both men were the progeny of black generals that displayed extraordinary prowess and ingenuity on the battlefield. General Thomas-Alexander Dumas (1762–1806) served under Napoleon and Abraham Hannibal (1670–1761) served under Peter the Great.

Thomas Alexander Dumas

Thomas Alexander Dumas was the father of Alexander Dumas and the son of a black woman, Marie Louise Labouret, and Thomas-Alexandre Davy de la Pailleterie, a French aristocrat. He was born in Saint-Domingue (Haiti) in 1762. The Dumas family name was adopted from Alexandre's grandmother, an enslaved Haitian woman named Marie-Césette Dumas. He received his first officer's commission at the head of a group of fellow black swordsmen: revolutionaries called the Legion of Blacks, or *la Légion Noire*. He had a Herculean physique and he was legendary among French soldiers. He was reported to be the best looking and strongest man in the French army. The women of France loved him, and he had several affairs.

General Dumas was one of Napoleon's greatest warriors and in Egypt, he was one of the first men off the ship. He was known as "the black devil" and his military prowess and swordsmanship were legendary. He was by all accounts the Othello of his day.

A NEW PERSPECTIVE

Quite often he would take on more than one man at a time. As Napoleon rose through the ranks so did Dumas and he was the commander of the cavalry. He commanded tens of thousands in the field. It was during the Egyptian campaign that Dumas's and Napoleon's friendship fractured. Some have speculated that it was because he refused to accept a command from Napoleon to put down the revolt in his mother's native land of Haiti. Others have stated that the disagreement stems from a dispute over tactics while in Egypt. Nonetheless, he was sent back to France before the Egyptian campaign was over. This was not an easy task as the British had a formidable blockade that made travel by sea difficult.

General Thomas-Alexandre Dumas, father of Alexandre Dumas

The perils of his journey back home are reminiscent of the legendary Odysseus' voyage back from Troy and Richard the Lionhearted's trip back from the Middle East during the Crusades. His ship was shipwrecked, and Dumas was captured as a prisoner of war. He was held prisoner in a dungeon at the Taranto fortress. When he was finally released from prison, he returned to France. The France that he returned to, however, was not the France that he left. During the French Revolution, rights and privileges were given to people of color. Now they were being revoked.

He had been the hero of the day at Maulde, at Mon Cenis, at the Siege of Mantua, the bridge of Brixen and at Cairo. He had suffered in the dungeons, and by all accounts, he was a soldier's soldier. Yet, he was denied entry to the Legion of Honor. Like Toussaint L'Ouverture, he thought *Liberty, Fraternity and Equality* had come to all Frenchmen, but he soon found, in the words written later by his own son: *"remember that what has once been done may be done again."*

Slavery in the colonies and overt discrimination were back in France which essentially restored France to its pre-revolutionary state. Additionally, Napoleon outlawed marriages between people of different races. He also passed laws forbidding all

RETHINKING THE HISTORY AND MYTHS OF THE PAST

soldiers of color who had been discharged or retired from living in Paris and the surrounding areas. Dumas needed a special request to live in his old home. After his death, Alexander Dumas and his mother were put out on the streets.

For years, a friendship between Dumas and Napoleon endured and when Dumas left for Egypt, it was assumed by both that if he had a son, Napoleon and Josephine would be the godparents. The honeymoon between France and its black population was over. Perhaps driven by the politics of the day and the events in Haiti. Such underlining politics may have also been the source of friction between Dumas and Napoleon. During his two years in prison, his health continued to decline. At the time of his son's birth, Thomas was poor, and he died when Alexander was four years old. All of this, however, became kindle for the fire that burned in the heart of his son who became one of France's most celebrated literary giants.

In February 1906; the French finally honored this outstanding general with a statue of him erected in Paris for the one-hundredth anniversary of his death. It was removed by the Germans just before Hitler's visit to "occupied" Paris. One must wonder: what would have become of the legend of General Dumas, if not for the literary genius of his son? Although his African ancestry is not well known to people outside of France, he was proud of it and spoke of it in his writings.

Alexander Dumas
Alexander Dumas was born on July 24, 1802, in Villers-Cotterêts, Aisne, France. Although poor, the young Dumas was full of curiosity; and read everything he could get his hands on. In 1822, he moved to Paris and worked in the household of the future King Louis-Philippe. It was here that he began to write. He became a successful playwright and then a historical novelist with sections of his writings appearing in newspapers. Among his most seminal works are: *The Three Musketeers* and *The Count of Monte Cristo.*

Even though Alexander's memory of his father is sparse at best, his mother told him stories about the bravery of his father and his relationship with Napoleon. If ever there was a case of the son resurrecting the legacy of the father, this would be the one. Most scholars believe that Dumas drew from the experiences of his father in creating his memorable and realistic characters, most noted in *The Three Musketeers, The Count of Monte Cristo,* and *The Man Behind the Iron Mask.* His works have been translated into more than 100 languages and adapted for numerous films. Although famous for his novel, Alexander Dumas was prolific in several genres: Fiction, Non-fiction and Drama.

A NEW PERSPECTIVE

In his book: *The Black Count: Glory, Revolution, Betrayal, and the Real Count of Monte Cristo*, a biography of Thomas Alexander Dumas, Tom Reiss points out how the life of the famous French black general served as a paragon for Dumas' novels. For example, in the Count of Monte Christo, he wrote: "The difference between treason and patriotism is only a matter of dates." A statement reminiscent of the way that his father was treated by Napoleon. During his lifetime, Alexander Dumas, despite his fame, could not escape the scorn of racism. In response to a man who once insulted him about his African ancestry, Dumas replied: My father was a mulatto, my grandfather was a Negro, and my great-grandfather a monkey. You see, Sir, my family starts where yours ends.

Alexandre Dumas

Buried in the place where he had been born, Alexander Dumas remained in the cemetery at Villers-Cotterêts until November 30, 2002. Under orders of the French President, Jacques Chirac, his body was exhumed and in a televised ceremony, his new coffin, draped in a blue velvet cloth and flanked by four Republican Guards costumed as the Musketeers—Athos, Porthos, Aramis, and D'Artagnan—was transported in a solemn procession to the Panthéon of Paris: the great mausoleum where French luminaries such as Victor Hugo and Emile Zola are interred. Jacques Chirac stated at Dumas' honorary ceremony:

With you, we were D'Artagnan, Monte Cristo, or Balsamo, riding along the roads of France, touring battlefields, visiting palaces and castles—with you, we dream.

RETHINKING THE HISTORY AND MYTHS OF THE PAST

So, when we think of *The Count of Monte Cristo* or *The Three Musketeers*, we should not only think of the son, but of the father that posthumously inspired his son to write such masterpieces. Alexander's son and namesake was also a French literary figure. He is referred to as Alexander Dumas *fils* (the younger).

Abraham Hannibal

It could be argued that Abraham Hannibal (Abram Petrovich Gannibal) was a precursor to General Dumas. He died a year before Thomas Dumas was born and had studied in France. His origins and date of birth is somewhat obscure. Some argue that he was the son of an Ethiopian prince; and when he was a few years old, his father waged war with the invading Turks. As a result, Abraham was taken hostage as a young boy and sent to Constantinople (Istanbul). Others contend that he was not the son of an Ethiopian prince, but rather, sold to Turkish slave traders in Cameroon. He adopted the name Hannibal from the legendary Carthaginian general that challenged Rome.

Abraham Hannibal By Ludushka—Own work, CC BY-SA 3.0, https://commons.wikimedia.org/w/index.php?curid=19010606

Notwithstanding, it was not unusual to have little blackamoors (as they were called) prevalent at European courts and Peter the Great wanted one. At the age of eight or so, Abraham was sent to the court of Russia. Peter the Great immediately took a liking to him, so much as to give the boy the name Peter and to be his godfather. His godmother was Peter's wife, Christina, the Queen of Poland. Although Abraham never fully embraced the name of the emperor, in many ways he was treated like Peter the Great's son. He was sent to France to be educated. While in France, he studied

A NEW PERSPECTIVE

Engineering and Mathematics and joined the French Army. His scholastic prowess was apparent and in 1723 he returned to Russia and brought with him over a hundred books.

After Peter the Great died, Abraham was ostracized and sent to Siberia and then to the Chinese front. However, when Empress Ivanovna came to the throne, he returned, and his star began to rise. He became a Major General in the Russian army and was universally renowned for his technical skill. In 1746 Empress Elizabeth Petrovna gave him a large estate. He was the father of eleven children, and he died a wealthy and prominent man. His great-grandson, Alexander Pushkin, became a seminal figure in Russia and was one of its greatest literary figures. Pushkin honored his great-grandfather in an unfinished novel entitled: *Arap Petra Velikogo* (The *Negro of Peter the Great*).

Alexander Pushkin by Orest Kiprensky

Alexander Pushkin
Pushkin is celebrated as a national hero in Russia. So much so that his birthday, June 6, is a Russian holiday that commemorates his contributions to Russian literature. Young Pushkin was raised in wealth and splendor replete with servants and mansions. As a child, he loved to hear stories told to him by his grandmother Hannibal about his famous black great-grandfather that came from a faraway land. His memories of his childhood consisted of his grandmother, his nanny and the great earthquake that hit Russia in 1802. He was given a great education and loved the works of Voltaire and Moliere and would stay in his father's library absorbing as much as he could.

RETHINKING THE HISTORY AND MYTHS OF THE PAST

By the time he was eleven, he had mastered the French classics. As a young adult, Pushkin was a radical and was often under surveillance or house arrest for his anti-authoritarian views, opinions or activities. He lived a reckless and daring life and was a notorious womanizer and gambler. In this regard, Pushkin and Dostoevsky were kindred souls that used gambling and other vises to help soothe the demons that chased their literary genius. As in the case of many writers, musicians and artists, these were merely negative reflections of their positive attributes.

Eugene Onegin, Boris Gudunov and *The Captain's Daughter* are considered masterpieces. *Eugene Onegin* is a particularly unique and completed piece that sieves with literary genius. It is most unfortunate, that Pushkin's reckless life eventually led to his downfall. He died in a senseless duel in 1837. He was married to one of the most beautiful women in Russia and this led to a scandal in which he felt he had to defend his honor. His life was short but fruitful.

Duel of Pushkin and Georges d'Anthès

Perhaps more shocking is the prophetic nature of his death. The duel sequence in *Eugene Onegin* written five years before his death mirrors the tragic death of Pushkin with remarkable accuracy. In both cases, the wronged party (Pushkin in fact, Lensky in fiction) was killed in a duel initiated around similar circumstances. In a speech in Moscow honoring the unveiling of Pushkin's statue in 1800, the great Russian author Fyodor Dostoevsky (1821–1881) author of *Crime and Punishment* (1866), T*he Idiot* (1869), *Demons* (1872), and *The Brothers Karamazov* (1880) said the following:

I am needed here, not just by the Friends of Russian Literature, but by our whole party and the whole idea for which we have been struggling for 30 years now. For the hostile party (Turgenev, Kovalevsky, and almost the entire university) is determined to play down the importance of Pushkin as the man who gave expression to the Russian national identity, by denying the very existence of that identity... My voice will carry weight and our side will prevail.

A NEW PERSPECTIVE

Pushkin's statue had been financed by public donations, and immediately became a symbol of their national literary consciousness. There are not only statues of him in Moscow but throughout Russia.

Greatness, like pieces of silver, although tarnished can be polished by the hands of those that appreciate the intrinsic beauty. Great men are not only judged by what they have accomplished but what they enable others to accomplish. In this regard, we must consider Pushkin's greatness. He had a profound influence on Russian culture and thought. He influenced Dostoyevsky who later had a major influence on Western thinkers including Einstein who once said: "Dostoevsky gives me more than any scientist, more than Gauss." Pushkin is usually considered as Russia's national poet and he accomplished the same notoriety for the Russian literary language that Dante accomplished for Italian and Shakespeare for the English language. He is often praised by Russian literary giants and is said to have lifted the Russian language to an unprecedented level. Dostoevsky went as far as to proclaim his superiority over Shakespeare. His effect on Russian literature cannot be denied.

Pushkin wrote: *It is better to have dreamed a thousand dreams that never were than never to have dreamed at all.* He was not only a literary figure but also a symbol of freedom. He was a political revolutionary and it showed in his early works most noted was his *Ode to Liberty*. He was exiled because of his writings and activism during these years. For the rest of his life, he was under constant surveillance by the Russian government because of his radical views.

Perhaps to replicate what Pushkin did for the Russian language in music, his work was emulated in opera by Mikhail Glinka (1804–1857), Modest Mussorgsky (1839–1881), Nikolai Rimsky Korsakov (1844–1908), and Peter Tchaikovsky (1840–1893). He influenced the renowned group of Classical Composers referred to as the "Russian Five". From these five a new group of Russian classical composers such as Igor Stravinsky emerged. Modern Russians are more likely to know more about Pushkin and his works than any other Russian writer. As with Shakespeare, many lines from Pushkin's poems have become proverbs. His words continue to be memorized by Russian school children. In reference to Pushkin, Paul Robeson (1898–1976), the two-time All-American football player, valedictorian of his Rutgers class of 1919 and Ivy League lawyer, in a speech upon his arrival to the United States from the Soviet Union said:

"Here is a white nation which is now doing honor to our poet Pushkin, one of the greatest poets in history, the Soviet people and our proud world possession. Could I find a monument to Pushkin in a public square of Birmingham or Atlanta or Memphis, as one stands in the center of Moscow? No! perhaps one to Goethe, but not to the dark-skinned Pushkin."

RETHINKING THE HISTORY AND MYTHS OF THE PAST

Paul Robeson: American actor, athlete, bass-baritone concert singer, writer, Civil Rights activist, Spingarn Medal winner, and Stalin peace prize laureate

Robeson, a modern-day Pushkin, who sung at the 150th Anniversary of Pushkin's birth, was merely pointing out the serious disjunction between a Communist nation that honored, respected and revered a person of African descent and America—a nation fighting for democracy and freedom around the globe—which refused to pay homage to its people of African descent.

Instead of using Robeson's assessment as an opportunity for introspection, fearful not only of the Communist red scare but of black men like Robeson that demanded equality; they branded him as a Communist, revoked his passport and repelled his accolades—then ostracized him from the American public. During the early years of the Cold War, there was no warm welcome to Pushkin or Robeson, because to do so was to destroy the myth of Jim Crow and the innate inferiority of black people ingrained in the American culture and enforced by its laws. Robeson was the first black actor to play Shakespeare's Othello.

The descendants of these obscure black generals, Thomas Alexander Dumas and Abraham Hannibal, are considered among the best writers in literary history. Most have heard of Dumas, but few have heard of Pushkin. For over a century, outside of their native countries, they were hidden behind a veil of literary whiteness although they were both proud of their African ancestry. Both men excelled during a time when it was forbidden for black slaves to read in antebellum America or to imagine that black men were commanding white men on the battlefield. What a travesty it

A NEW PERSPECTIVE

would have been to world literature if Dumas and Pushkin were forbidden to display their craft.

Dumas once wrote: *So rapid is the flight of our dreams upon the wings of imagination.* Despite the ghost of slavery and racism that haunted every person of African descent from sea to shining sea—antebellum America produced literary figures and polymaths such as Phyllis Wheatley, Frederick Douglass, Martin Delany, Dr. John S. Rock and others whose voices were not muted by the roaring trumpet of those that tried to silence them.

The emergence of African American writers in the 20th century, echoes and confirms Dumas' words: *"Mastery of language affords one remarkable opportunities."*

RETHINKING THE HISTORY AND MYTHS OF THE PAST

The Rise of the Nation of Islam and Malcolm X

Nation of Islam members at Speakers' Corner in Hyde Park, London, March 1999. By No machine-readable author provided. Nrive assumed (based on copyright claims).—No machine-readable source provided. Own work assumed (based on copyright claims)., CC BY-SA 2.5, https://commons.wikimedia.org/w/index.php?curid=1449313

The Nation of Islam (NOI) was founded on July 4, 1930, in Detroit, Michigan, by Wallace D. Fard Muhammad. Although Elijah Muhammad was its leader for decades, Malcolm X greatly influenced the NOI and helped to launch the organization into national and international prominence.

Noble Drew Ali and the Moorish Science Temple
The seeds of the NOI were planted in the soil of the Moorish Science Temple of America (MSTA) founded by Noble Drew Ali (1886–1929) in Newark, NJ in 1913. The establishment of the Canaanite Temple in Newark, NJ two years before Garvey's arrival in 1915 places Noble Drew Ali at the forefront of a major black migration from the South to the North.

Drew Ali was a Freemason and was familiar with the black Shriners (the Ancient Egyptian Arabic Order, Nobles Mystic Shrine) which migrated to Newark about 1901. It is then conceivable that the organization served as a model for Drew Ali's MSTA. There is also evidence that Drew Ali was strongly influenced by *The Aquarian Gospel of Jesus Christ* written by Levi H. Dowling and published in 1908 as well as the writing and dogma of the Rosicrucian (Ancient and Mystical Order Rosae Crucis) or AMORC. From such material, Drew Ali generated the *Circle 7 Koran* and some of the teachings of the Nation of Islam could be traced back to this prime narrative.

A NEW PERSPECTIVE

Drew Ali's combination of Black nationalism and religion was as popular as Garvey's movement and by 1928, Ali had established seventeen temples in fifteen states with Chicago being the largest one. It was at the Detroit temple where Elijah Muhammad was first introduced to the teachings of Islam. It was the belief that Drew Ali was the Seal of God's Prophets although this opposed the Koran which taught that Muhammad was the Seal of the Prophets.

1928 Moorish Science Temple of America in Chicago, Drew Ali dressed in white in the center

Being a Mason, Drew Ali could have also been aware of the works of people like Count Volney (!757-1820) author of *The Ruins of Empires*, Gerald Massey (1826-1907) author of *Ancient Egypt Light of the World* and the prolific Freemason writer and student of Massey, Albert Churchward (1852–1925) author of *Proof that the Nilotic Blacks were the Founders of Ancient Egypt* and their assertion that the black man was indeed the original man and the father of civilization. This was based on anthropology and the belief that Ancient Egypt was a black civilization.

A close friend of the Founding Fathers, Volney wrote the following in his *Ruins of Empires*:

"Those piles of ruins which you see in that narrow valley watered by the Nile, are the remains of the opulent cites, the pride of the ancient kingdom of Ethiopia... There a people, now forgotten discovered while others were yet barbarians, the elements, of the arts and sciences. A race of men now rejected from society for their sable skin and fizzled hair, founded on the study of the laws of nature, those civil and religious systems which still govern the universe "

RETHINKING THE HISTORY AND MYTHS OF THE PAST

The Ruins of Empires was a popular book in its day and was partly translated from French to English by Thomas Jefferson and read by Abraham Lincoln.

Not only was Drew Ali a Mason but so were prominent men in government, such as J. Edgar Hoover, Warren G. Harding, Franklin Delano Roosevelt and Harry Truman. Therefore, they may have also been familiar with the works of Massey and Churchward and recognized some of the aspects of Freemasonry in Drew Ali's movement and considered it an existential threat. We all know of the Shriners, through their work with children hospitals and their parades, but few make the connection between the Shriners and Islam.

If Drew Ali turned certain aspects of Freemasonry and the NOI into a race-based religion, it wouldn't be the first time. Joseph Smith has long been accused of doing the same thing with Mormonism. In addition to rituals that have their birth in Freemasonry, the Mormons believed that black people were the descendants of "the curse of Cain", and therefore unworthy of priesthood. This aspect of the Mormon Church was kept *sub rosa* until they were forced to change their racial dogma in 1978.

It appears that at the turn of the century, with it being the last century of the millennium, the apocalyptic millennium theory of a savior was in full force, with black people like Father Devine (1876–1975), and Sweet Daddy Grace (1884–1960), as well as Marcus Garvey (1887–1940), preaching similar doctrine. This theme resonated with black people many of them former slaves or their progeny. These were also the days of strong occult influence. For example, the teachings of Madame Helen Blavatsky and her Theosophical Society influenced Mahatma Gandhi, Henry A. Wallace (who became FDR's Vice President and the man responsible for putting Masonic Symbols on the Dollar Bill) as well as many within Hitler's Nazi Party. Some scholars argue that the Swastika and the Aryan race theory prevalent in Germany were first introduced by Blavatsky.

Madame Blavatsky also had a profound effect on Gandhi and the independence movement in India which later had a major influence on Martin Luther King. Such teaching may have also influenced Nobel Drew Ali and later Master Fard as there were many spin-offs and interpretations of her teachings outlined in *Isis Unveiled* (1877) and the *Secret Doctrine* (1888). Therefore, the occult aspects of the Nation of Islam could be attributed to the pervasiveness of occultism at the turn of the century. Blavatsky's influence, although often hidden behind a veil of secrecy, on the occult cannot be understated.

A NEW PERSPECTIVE

Madame Blavatsky, born in Russia 1831—died in England 1891

After a member of MSTA who had conflicts with Drew Ali over his number of women and extravagant spending was murdered, Drew Ali was arrested for conspiring in his murder and subsequently, he died while in jail. The absence and death of Drew Ali allowed others within the organization to rise. One such rising star was David Ford, who later became Wallace D. Fard and later Wallace D. Fard Muhammad and later Master Fard.

The Founding of the Nation of Islam
Many NOI members dispute that Fard was a student of Drew Ali, but instead, the incarnation of Allah. Yet the Moroccan Fez wore by Noble Drew Ali, the establishment of Islam and the distribution of temples was adopted by Elijah Muhammad and the Nation of Islam. Religions often spring from the soil of their times. And when we examine the tree of the NOI its roots are apparent.

The changed behavior of Elijah Muhammad confirmed the teaching of Master Fard. Before he was enlightened by him, Elijah was on the verge of becoming an alcoholic. Afterward, he completely stopped drinking. Master Fard's teaching provided three essential things. First, a reason why the white race was so evil. Second, the ability to lift the self-esteem of black people as well as a sense of unity or strength in numbers. Third, a means of steering away from the evils, such as alcohol and drugs that habitually pulled the black race down. These three things not only resonated with Elijah Muhammad, and a young Malcolm, but with tens of thousands of blacks in the following decades.

RETHINKING THE HISTORY AND MYTHS OF THE PAST

Master Fard

Perhaps the oddest and most ironic thing about Master Fard was that he appeared to be a white man, a John Brown so to speak, peaching the destruction of the white race and the freeing of the black race from the shackles of oppression. As part of this philosophy, Fard instructed his members to abandon their slave names, in favor of the letter X for the unknown. Fard also gave his movement the name: The Nation of Islam (NOI). He set up the infrastructure that Elijah Muhammad was soon to inherit. He established The Fruit of Islam (FOI) a para-military group for men, The Muslim Girls Training (MGT) designed to teach women home economics and the University of Islam for the education of children. What Master Fard set up, was a race-based organization akin to the Mormons, a nation within a nation.

However, in 1934, Fard disappeared never to be seen or heard of again. The disappearance of Fard, like the death of Noble Drew Ali, allowed Elijah Muhammad to reshape the movement. There is evidence to suggest that Elijah Muhammad may not have comprehended the source of Drew Ali's dogma as articulated and implemented by Fard. He began to preach that Master Fard was God (Allah) incarnate and that he was the Elijah of the Book of Malachi of the Bible and the Messenger of God.

Henceforth, Fard was God and Elijah was the Messenger of God. Just as Muhammad had received his revelations from Allah in the form of the angel Gabriel, Elijah Muhammad received his revelations from Allah in the form of Master Fard. There were, however, some in the NOI that did not believe that Fard was Allah. Most noted was Elijah Muhammad's brother John. Some claimed that this was a way of Elijah solidifying his power over the NOI after the disappearance of Fard. His son Wallace was also skeptical of the divinity of Fard.

A NEW PERSPECTIVE

Elijah Muhammad

Like the Prophet Muhammad before him, Elijah converted his immediate family and friends to his newly found theology. He later outlined the NOI philosophy in his book entitled: *Message to the Black Man in America,* published in 1965. The following is a listing of the key beliefs that became the theology of the Nation of Islam.

1. The black man was the original man and the father of civilization.

2. The white race is a race of devils grafted by an evil black scientist by the name of Yakub.

3. Yakub was born near Mecca more than six thousand years ago.

4. Yakub taught his followers that there was no God but him and that they would rule the world with a religion-based science known as tricknology.

5. Yakub noticed in his genetic experiments that the further they moved away from blackness the eviler they became.

6. The white race became so evil that finally they were driven away from Mecca into Europe and lived like cavemen.

7. The pig was: part rat, part cat, and part dog and that Muslims should not eat it.

8. Because white people were the incarnation of the devil, they were not allowed to become members of the NOI.

RETHINKING THE HISTORY AND MYTHS OF THE PAST

The bourgeoning of World War I in Europe, the lynching of black people in America along with the rise of the Klu Klux Klan and Jim Crow laws only reinforced such beliefs within the African American community.

We have both retrospection and the introspection of modernity to trace the evolution of the Nation of Islam. It was from the chrysalis of Islam, Freemasonry, Christianity and racist myth that the theology of the Nation of Islam developed; and like a moth, it was driven toward a flame of hate. It was not based on the truth, but rather, the belief in the truth. To its members, the white man was a blue-eyed devil that had an innate hatred for the black man because he knew that the black man was *the original man* and the father of civilization. Although some of the beliefs may seem bizarre, nonetheless, they had the power to transform those that believed in them.

The Influence of Malcolm X on the NOI
It was while in prison that Malcolm became familiar with the stories about the NOI and Elijah Muhammad's divine relationship with Master Fard. Just as Fard's teachings had rehabilitated Elijah in his youth, they begin to rehabilitate young Malcolm. Furthermore, he recalls having a vision of Master Fard while in prison. The acceptance of Master Fard and his Messenger Elijah Muhammad was vital to establishing the hierarchy and rules of engagement within the NOI. Because of his devotion and diligence, Malcolm was able to establish direct correspondence with Elijah Muhammad while in prison. This was a nexus that would prove beneficial after his parole.

Members of Malcolm's family Wilfred, Hilda, Philbert, and Reginald were members of the NOI, and this further established and helped to foster a deeper familial relationship. Perhaps more than anything, it was the aspects of the Marcus Garvey movement that were imbued in them as children by their parents and now transformed into the rhetoric of the NOI that drew the family closer to Elijah Muhammad and his organization. The family believed that their father was murdered because he supported Garvey. With Elijah Muhammad and his family in his corner, Malcolm began to grow both spiritually and intellectually. He was baptized not only into the waters of a new religion but a new way of life and like so many religious transformations before him, he changed his name from Malcolm Little to Malcolm X. Thus, a chapter in his life was now closed and a new one opened.

Although serendipity or perhaps fate brought him to a place where he could develop, his transformation was the result of dedication, God-given ability and persistence. He was not only able to reinvent himself but to fold a turbulent past into a prospective future. Because he had lived the life of the streets and because of his time in foster care and on welfare, he could not only relate to the disenfranchised, but he became

A NEW PERSPECTIVE

proof of the NOI's power to transform. In retrospect, Malcolm was always in training. His early life provided the narrative for his later success.

Malcolm X before a 1964 press conference

He entered the prison as a high school dropout and by the time he left he was a scholar debating among scholars. He became the voice of his people; the chief accuser of the white man's lies and injustice and a leader of his race. However, the road that Malcolm traveled after his parole was not one of Milk and Honey.

Malcolm built the NOI as much as it had built him. Before Malcolm, there were NOI Mosques in Chicago and Detroit, but the NOI presence on the East Coast was small. When Malcolm got out of prison and was sent to the Detroit Mosque, he immediately notices its sparse attendance. He changed the recruiting methods and went out into the streets looking for converts. Building the Detroit Mosque was a family affair and one of Malcolm's brothers became the minister of the Mosque. The truth is that before Malcolm X, the Nation of Islam was a nation in name only with little demographic and national presence. It was through the devotion of Malcolm, that the Mosques in Boston, Philadelphia and New York rose to prominence. Malcolm helped to start the *Muhammad Speaks* newspaper, and he gave the NOI national and later international recognition.

More than any other person, including Elijah Muhammad's sons, Malcolm was responsible for the NOI's growth. He was simultaneously, the chief minister in New York, Philadelphia and Boston before turning the Boston Mosque over to his protégé Louis X (Farrakhan). In addition to being the chief minister, between 1954–1955, Malcolm also founded mosques in Springfield, Massachusetts, Buffalo, NY, Pittsburgh, PA, Newark, NJ and Miami, FL. Although they both were iconoclasts and

RETHINKING THE HISTORY AND MYTHS OF THE PAST

Elijah Muhammad possessed many skills, he was not charismatic, was not a good orator and did not have the young enthusiasm of Malcolm X.

Malcolm could articulate the truth that struck right at the heart of the issue. His rhetoric could be caustic and humorous at the same time. For example, he would say something like this: Weez been robbed, bamboozled, hoodwinked, ... tricked into believing that *the white man's ice is always colder*. Or, *"We didn't land on Plymouth Rock; Plymouth Rock landed on us."* He believed that the Founding Fathers had one tyrant three thousand miles away and they rebelled. But the black man had three thousand tyrants one mile away and was expected to be peaceful and silent. Such juxtapositions of the white man and the black man were among his most effective tools.

His messages were so powerful because he could not only talk the talk, he had walked the walk. In this regard, Malcolm's life was the amalgamation and personification of the black man's life in the white man's world. Although other Civil Rights leaders such as Martin Luther King possessed good oratory skills, it was Malcolm's ability to debate the issues that set him apart.

Even though NOI Mosques were strung up and down the East Coast like pearls on a necklace, it was Mosque №7 in New York that was its center pearl. It was the highest-grossing temple in the country. When Malcolm arrived at the Mosque in 1954, it was just a storefront with few members. This was to become Malcolm's Mosque and the pulpit from which he preached the NOI's agenda. Unlike other cities on the East Coast, New York was a large cosmopolitan city with many Civil Rights organizations competing against each other for membership. It was through the outstanding work of Malcolm and Captain Joseph (Yusuf Shah) that the NOI presence was established and maintained in America's largest city. Malcolm had rescued Captain Joseph from alcoholism and for many years Joseph was his right-hand man. In many ways, Mosque №7 was the icon of Malcolm's evangelism and his ability to attract members to the NOI.

Perhaps Malcolm was the victim of his own success and some within the NOI became jealous of his fame and notoriety. He was seen by many within as being bigger than the organization, and moreover, bigger than Elijah Muhammad. As a result, he had to be put in his place. Members within the NOI as well as the Federal Government began to see him as a threat. They worked in tandem to pull Malcolm down as some members of the NOI covertly worked with law enforcement.

A NEW PERSPECTIVE

Malcolm's departure from the NOI

When Malcolm made "the chicken coming home to roost" statement after President Kennedy's assassination, in November of 1963, along with the scandal within the NOI regarding Elijah Muhammad's affairs with female members within the NOI, it gave his enemies inside and outside the excuse to coalesce and ostracize him from the NOI. After all the talk and rhetoric about blue-eyed devils, the NOI appeared to have a legitimate fear of a government composed of such men.

After his trip to Mecca and Africa, Malcolm was transformed and moved by the vastness and diversity of Islam. He changed his name and grew facial hair, perhaps as a sign of his transformation and independence from the NOI. Many saw this as a sign that Malcolm now believed that he was bigger than the NOI and that he no longer viewed Elijah Muhammad as divine, but rather, as human with human frailties. He had crossed the Rubicon, and he could no longer subscribe to the theology of the NOI. Many of his friends including, Captain Joseph, Muhammad Ali, and Louis Farrakhan, abandoned him and his only supporter within the NOI was Elijah Muhammad's son Wallace. It was Malcolm who was the mentor and spiritual advisor to a young Cassius Clay. Before his fight with Sonny Liston in 1964, not many NOI members believed that Clay could defeat Liston. However, when he became heavyweight champion of the world, they embraced him as one of their own. He changed his name to Muhammad Ali; a name given to him by Elijah Muhammad. His victory and conversion sent shockwaves throughout the sports world.

Muhammad Ali, 1967

RETHINKING THE HISTORY AND MYTHS OF THE PAST

Having the heavyweight champion of the world in your corner was a huge step for the NOI. With Malcolm out of the picture, Ali became their new shining object. Many, however, did not care much for boxing and saw Ali as a cash cow and celebrity that could represent their organization on the world stage. The truth of the matter is that Malcolm had outgrown the NOI. He was an international figure that became the symbol of black oppression around the world. No longer restricted by Elijah Muhammad's myopic view of the world, he was free to seek his own agenda. He accepted, as Wallace D. Muhammad later did, Islam in its orthodox form. Within the Islamic world, the NOI was seen as a pariah and an organization based on myth and not the truth. Their racist theology and the notion that Elijah Muhammad was the Messenger of God was a bridge too far for most traditional Muslims.

In this regard, Malcolm created a nexus between the Middle East and Africa at a time when Africa was revolting against European colonialism. He became a greater threat to those outside of the NOI. While inside the NOI, he could be contained and somewhat controlled. Outside, however, he was free to establish a new organization based on Pan-Africanism and black unity. Furthermore, debunking the theology of the NOI was one thing, but an attack on Islam would alienate America's allies in the Middle East.

Malcolm X's only meeting with Martin Luther King Jr., March 26, 1964, in Washington DC

In America, Martin Luther King was the voice of Southern blacks and a champion of the black Christian movement. Malcolm, however, was the voice of urban oppression and the young. He dispelled the myth that racial discrimination was a Southern thing. He believed in the liberation of his people *By Any Means Necessary* whether it be the ballot or the bullet. Moreover, no longer bounded by the dogma of the NOI, Malcolm

A NEW PERSPECTIVE

and King could combine forces against the oppression of African Americans and perhaps bring a case against the United States to the United Nations.

During the Cold War, the Soviet Union pointed out the racial hypocrisy of the United States. With African nations in rebellion, America's post-World War II inheritance as the standard-bearer of freedom and democracy, along with the bourgeoning of war in Vietnam, America could not afford additional criticism from within. Surveillance on King and Malcolm was conducted by America's Intelligence and Law Enforcement Agencies and some argue that they were viewed, by J. Edgar Hoover, as enemies of the state. Both men were assassinated before their fortieth birthday.

Assassination
The assassination of Malcolm X by Black Muslims on February 21. 1965 at the Audubon ballroom in front of his children and pregnant wife was the end of his earthly journey and a sad day for African Americans. Many argue that his assassination was initiated by the Federal Government and that it was important that he died by the hands of his own people.

Malcolm's life was full of irony and so was his death. It was difficult to find a Mosque that would take his body for service and its was also difficult to find a church. In the end, his body lay in state and his funeral was held at the Faith Temple Church of God in Christ in West Harlem. It was Ossie Davis that delivered Malcolm's Eulogy. Ossie recalls Malcolm's burial:

When we got to the cemetery, the professional grave diggers were standing there with their shovels, but some of the Black brothers said, no, uh uh. We dig this grave. We cover this brother with dirt. And it was a moving moment, and I was proud at that moment to be Black. And proud that my community and people, no matter what had been said by the outside world, said to the brother, we loved you and respected and admired you. And we buried him, and there it is.

To people of African descent around the world, Malcolm was a hero and true to the words of F. Scott Fitzgerald: *show me a hero and I'll write you a tragedy*. His death was a tragedy. Yet, like so many martyrs before him, he gave birth to something greater than himself. The struggle for equality did not die with Malcolm and in the coming years, violence ensued in cities across America. He became the inspiration of the Black Panther Party which started a year after his death.

It is most unfortunate that today, Malcolm's accomplishments are often hidden in the shadows of Martin Luther King, Rosa Parks and other icons of the Civil Rights movement, and at times, the caustic rhetoric of Farrakhan. He was a seminal figure of which any race would be proud to call one of their own. In the aftermath of his death, many members of the NOI bragged about what the NOI did for Malcolm and some

RETHINKING THE HISTORY AND MYTHS OF THE PAST

even boasted about his killing. Yet few recognized what Malcolm had done for the NOI. They viewed him as a traitor, a Judas within their midst, because he had the courage and the fortitude to speak truth to power. He died poor, and everything he had, including his house, belonged to Elijah Muhammad and the NOI. It is left to posterity to judge whether Malcolm betrayed the NOI; or the NOI betrayed Malcolm?

A NEW PERSPECTIVE

RETHINKING THE HISTORY AND MYTHS OF THE PAST

Politics

A NEW PERSPECTIVE

RETHINKING THE HISTORY AND MYTHS OF THE PAST

First Mothers: The Relationship Between American Presidents and Their Mothers

Mary Ball Washington, Mother of George Washington

Much has been written about the First Ladies of the United States and Mary Lincoln was the first to coin that phrase. However, little has been written about the First Mothers—those great women that shaped the lives of many American presidents.

Of the forty-four men that have served as president, Grover Cleveland had two nonconsecutive terms, there are many firsts and similarities. Three out of the first five presidents died on the Fourth of July. John Adams and Thomas Jefferson both died on the fiftieth anniversary in 1826 and James Monroe on Independence Day five years later. John F. Kennedy was the first and only president to have his assassination viewed by the public on television. Franklin D. Roosevelt was the first president, whose mother was able to vote for him for president, James Polk, was the first President to have his photograph taken and Barrack Obama was the first non-white person to hold that office (although there has been some debate regarding the ancestry of Warren G. Harding).

The Matriarchs
It is often said that behind (beside) every great man is a great woman and the presidency of the United States has proven this aphorism. Long before the president set eyes on his future bride and companion in the White House, he gazed into the

A NEW PERSPECTIVE

eyes of his mother and felt her smooth hands across his face. To the First Mother, the president was not the father of the nation, but instead, her little boy now grown. She had the unique pleasure of planting the seed and seeing it grow into the tree that she had hoped it would be. As William Rose Wallace aptly stated: The hand that rocks the cradle rules the world.

In the history of the presidency, there have been three presidents whose paternal father died before they were born: Andrew Jackson, Rutherford B. Hayes, and William Jefferson Clinton. Andrew Jackson's mother, Elizabeth, was a nurse during the Revolutionary War who contracted cholera from a patient and died. Many psychologists believe that Andrew Jackson spent his whole life seeking to become one of those heroes from which his mother had sacrificed her life. Other presidents were molded likewise. For example, Abraham Lincoln's mother, Nancy Hanks, died when he was nine years old, and her death deeply affected him for the rest of his life.

FDR and his mother Sara

Franklin Delano Roosevelt's mother, Sara, constantly looked over his shoulder before and during his presidency and wrote a bestselling book entitled: *My Boy Franklin*. In many ways, Sara Delano could be controlling, using the purse strings of the Roosevelts to exercise control over Franklin, Eleanor and the children. In today's terms, she would be called a Helicopter Mom, who protected her only child like a lioness protecting her cub. She died on September 7, 1941, three months before the December 7, attack on Pearl Harbor. Her last request was to restore the room in which he was born to the way it was on the day of his birth. Perhaps as a symbol of her enduring love for him. This he faithfully executed.

RETHINKING THE HISTORY AND MYTHS OF THE PAST

There are many interesting things about American presidents that are unknown to the general public. For instance, in researching the presidents, I found that the names of the presidents generally fall into two major categories: those that have no middle name, e.g., George Washington, Thomas Jefferson, and Abraham Lincoln and those that have their mother's maiden name as their middle name, e.g., Franklin *Delano* Roosevelt. John *Fitzgerald* Kennedy, Richard *Milhous* Nixon. Harry S Truman could also be considered in that first category as the S does not stand for any particular name, thus a period behind the S is not warranted. Woodrow Wilson also follows this pattern as his full name is Thomas Woodrow Wilson. Millard Fillmore, however, took his mother's maiden name as his first name and John Knox Tyler was the first president to have his mother's maiden name as his middle name.

The trend continues with the sons of presidents that became president. John Quincy Adams was the first son of a president and the first one to have a middle name. He does not have his mother's maiden name, but instead, his grandmother's maiden name: *Quincy* (mother's side). The same is true of the other president who was the son of a president, George Walker Bush, whose grandmother's maiden name was *Walker* (father's side). His father's name was George Herbert Walker Bush, and he passed his mother's maiden name, *Walker*, to his son.

Although there are some exceptions to this rule, e.g., Garfield and Eisenhower both had siblings with their mother's maiden name, the fact remains that many presidents do. Below is a list of presidents that have their mother's maiden name:

6. John *Quincy* Adams 1825–1829 -- grandson of William and Elizabeth (Quincy) Smith- grandmother on mother's side

11. James *Knox* Polk 1845–1849 (son of Samuel and Jane (Knox) Polk

13. *Millard* Fillmore 1850–1853 (son of Nathaniel and Phoebe (Millard) Fillmore

18. Ulysses *Simpson* Grant 1869–1877 (son of Jesse and Hannah (Simpson) Grant

19. Rutherford *Birchard* Hayes 1877–1881 (son of Rutherford and Sophia (Birchard) Hayes

28. Thomas *Woodrow* Wilson 1913–1921 (son of Joseph and Janet (Woodrow) Wilson

32. Franklin *Delano* Roosevelt 1933–1945 (son of James and Sarah (Delano) Roosevelt

35. John *Fitzgerald* Kennedy 1961–1963 (son of Joseph and Rose (Fitzgerald) Kennedy

A NEW PERSPECTIVE

36. Lyndon *Baines* Johnson 1963–1969 (son of Sam and Rebekah (Baines) Johnson

37. Richard *Milhous* Nixon1969–1974 (son of Francis and Hannah (Milhous) Nixon

40. Ronald *Wilson* Reagan 1981–1989 (son of John Nelle Clyde (Wilson) Regan

41. George Herbert *Walker* Bush 1989–1993 (son of Prescott and Dorothy (Walker) Bush

43. George *Walker* Bush 2001–2009 (grandson of Prescott and Dorothy (Walker) Bush grandmother on father's side

One can speculate if such an occurrence is coincidence or providence? At first, I attributed the maiden name trend to the family or conventional tradition of keeping the family name alive. However, after close examination, I found that it was more to it than meets the eye. Although serendipity may play a role, it seemed that the mother was passing to the son more than just a name, but a deep and perhaps subliminal affection. In many cases, the child was the indisputable favorite of the mother

For instance, in the case of Lyndon Baines Johnson (LBJ), his political career was molded by the hands of his mother, Rebekah Baines Johnson. From his early years, she set a high bar for her beloved son; often reminding him of the Baines family tradition of excellence. She not only gave him her maiden name, but her heart. Like many mothers, she lived vicariously through her darling son. Throughout his political career, in the House and the Senate, he often consulted her as if she held a piece of his soul or the ores to the ship that guided him. She died in 1958 before he became president, yet the momentum and the confidence that she imbued in him enabled him to reach the highest political position of president of the United States. He once wrote:

"I am so grateful for having you as my mother—a woman of such fine spirit and unlimited devotion. You have been my inspiration, always, and whatever I become, the credit for all that is good will be yours."

Kennedy and Nixon
Perhaps the story of presidential mothers is best exemplified by the rivalry between Kennedy and Nixon. It is well known that Joseph (Joe) Patrick Kennedy Jr., the eldest son and namesake of the father Joseph, was the one selected to be president of the United States. However, it was the second child, John *Fitzgerald* Kennedy (JFK) the bearer of his mother's maiden name, *Fitzgerald*, who became president of the United States. It was John, or Jack as he was called, that emerged as the World War II hero.

RETHINKING THE HISTORY AND MYTHS OF THE PAST

Moreover, it is believed that his older brother Joe died while taking a dangerous assignment trying to outdo his brother's war accomplishments and fame. Although Joseph Kennedy would prepare all of his sons to be president: no other Kennedy male would become President of the United States. Not Joseph Patrick Kennedy Jr., Robert Francis Kennedy or Edward Moore Kennedy. Well before John and the children were born, the Fitzgerald name was known around Boston. Rose Kennedy (1890–1995), the matriarch of the Kennedy family, was the daughter of the mayor of Boston, John Francis Fitzgerald (1863–1950), also known as "Honey Fitz" (the name that Kennedy gave to the Presidential Yacht).

JFK with his mother Rose

Rose Elizabeth Fitzgerald would have been a catch for any man. Like most elite women of her day, she was raised to be the companion of a great man and to stand behind him. She was bright and pretty, the daughter of one of the most powerful Irishmen in the United States. Joseph Patrick Kennedy was the son of Patrick Joseph "P.J." Kennedy a Boston politician and businessman and sometimes rival of Honey Fitz. Therefore, Rose's marriage to Joseph Kennedy was an Irish Catholic marriage akin to the marriage of Isabella and Ferdinand uniting two powerful Irish-American families, and from this marriage, the Kennedy dynasty was born.

Although Joseph Kennedy was the patriarch of the family and provided financial security, he was not without his faults. He was a notorious womanizer, a failed Ambassador to England and held anti-Semitic sentiments. He also believed that Irish-Americans were oppressed people and often used his wealth, power and prestige to combat such oppression.

A NEW PERSPECTIVE

To Joseph Kennedy, "winning wasn't everything it was the only thing." He imbued in all his children that second place was still a loser. However, Rose did not always stand in the shadows of her husband. She was proud of her Fitzgerald heritage and often reminded the family of it. She was very close to her father Honey Fitz, and perhaps she saw a little bit of Honey Fitz in John or perhaps just as important, molded a little of Honey Fitz into him. Rose recognized that Jack was different from the other children. He was more detached, creative, charming and imaginative. With few places for women to ascend to in those days, all she could hope is to live vicariously through her sons.

When Jack made his bid for Congress in 1946, Rose was there with him along the way. In 1952 when he defeated Henry Cabot Lodge Jr. for the Senate there was no one on the earth happier than his mother. John went on to become the first Catholic president. At his Inaugural Address, she did not comment so much on his speech, but that he stood there without his overcoat. To others in the audience, he was a man and the leader of the free world, but to his mother, he was the little boy that always came late to dinner and forgot the small things. There is a time for a mother to step up and a time to lean back and let the boy be the man. Yet her mind saw things that others were blind to; invisible things seen not by the eyes but by the heart. Such is God's sacred gift to all mothers: to see in their children not what they are but what they can be.

Richard *Milhous* Nixon was not only the presidential opponent of JFK in the 1960 presidential election but in many ways the antithesis and nemesis of JFK. Both men were elected to congress in 1946; both had served in World War II. Both men carried their mother's maiden name and both men were destined to become President of the United States. A Quaker from California, Richard Nixon was the son of Francis and Hannah (Milhous) Nixon. They were not members of the American aristocracy, but rather, blue- collar workers in search of the American Dream. Nixon is quoted as saying in reference to JFK: "When they look at you, they see what they want to be. When they look at me, they see what they are."

JFK was born with a silver spoon in his mouth, he was everything that Nixon was not. He was handsome, articulate, a Harvard graduate, war hero and the perfect candidate for the new age of television. If he needed money, he only needed to turn to his father who had been plotting his course long before he entered politics. His father, an ambassador to England under President Roosevelt, was more than capable of demolishing the financial and political roadblocks of his son.

Nixon, on the other hand, stood in sharp contrast to JFK. He was dull, with a blue-collar persona. Nixon and Kennedy were both nurtured by their mothers, yet the

RETHINKING THE HISTORY AND MYTHS OF THE PAST

reflections of their fathers could be seen in the mirrors of each man. Although Nixon went to Duke Law School, it was Whittier College that seemed to stick to him perhaps because he wanted it to. He was smart enough to go to an Ivy League school, but not rich enough to attend. And this resentment toward Ivy League graduates in general and JFK, in particular, permeated his life.

He was not against the graduates per se, but the privilege of the rich that often came with it. Nixon had pulled himself up by his bootstraps and this became part of his political persona. He rose during the McCarthy era and the Red Scare. He gained fame in Congress as part of the Alter Hisses "witch hunt" and road this fame to become the Vice President under Eisenhower. It was during his vice presidency that the specter of dishonesty that would haunt him the rest of his political life first emerged. Forced to play second fiddle behind Ike for eight years, he almost had to resign his vice presidency in ignominy and Ike seriously considered dumping him. Many simply did not trust Nixon. Harry Truman once said of him:

"Richard Nixon is a no good, lying bastard. He can lie out of both sides of his mouth at the same time, and if he ever caught himself telling the truth, he'd lie just to keep his hand in."

Eventually, the lies and deceit would catch up to Nixon. It was as if Nixon was borne to be the scorn of the nation, while JFK was borne to be the prince charming of a post-World War II nation. Such were the cards that fate had dealt them. Yet amid it all, Nixon was not alone. He had his mother, Hannah, at his side and it was her that helped to raise him from the abyss of disgrace. Of her five sons—Harold, Richard, Donald, Arthur and Edward, she had a special bond with Richard. Everyone else called him Dick except for his mother who called him Richard.

Nixon and his mother Hannah (Richard Nixon Library)

A NEW PERSPECTIVE

There is little doubt that Nixon's strength, his fortitude, his determination to bounce back from adversity time and time again, emanated from his mother. It was Hannah that wrote Ike a letter in defense of her son's character and who gave him a seat and a towel in the brutal ring of politics. After he was defeated by JFK by a narrow margin in the 1960 presidential election, he tried to run for office in his native California and was also defeated there. This seemed to be the end of Nixon's political career. However, true to his nature imbued by his mother, he would rise again. Fortune had dealt the Kennedy family a terrible hand as both Kennedy brothers that were his closest nemesis were assassinated. The nation had changed much in less than a decade. The Vietnam War had been a disaster for Lyndon Baines Johnson and the country needed a new face and that face belonged to Richard Nixon.

Nixon was never one to shy away from confrontation. What plagued LBJ, the Vietnam War protests, and the turbulence of the sixties was something that Nixon thrived on. Perhaps his only regret was that his mother did not live to see him become president. It wasn't long after he took office that he became a target of protests and a symbol of American imperial power. Yet there was a "silent majority" that supported him. However, all of that change with the Watergate scandal. And with Watergate came, once again, the specter of distrust and the moniker "Tricky Dick"; culminating with Nixon's infamous declaration: "I am not a crook" and his subsequent resignation to avoid impeachment.

It is often said: "Nearly all men can stand adversity, but if you want to test a man's character, give him power." Watergate was an event that has become the icon of abuse of power, obstruction of justice and cover-up. Nixon was ahead in every poll and eventually won by a landslide, yet he felt the need to jeopardize it all on a useless break-in. Without his mother at his side, he entered a dark room of disgrace without a window to gaze upon her. Yet, in his resignation from office, his heart went out to his mother and he found a way to touch her soul. He said: "My mother was a saint" and in his lament, he praised her for his success while silently blaming himself for his misfortune. While she was alive, he often stumbled; but after she died, he fell. Yet, the sweet memories of her persisted. On the day of his second inauguration as vice president she wrote this note to him:

Dear Richard,

You have gone far and we are proud of you always—I know you will keep your relationship with your maker as it should be for after all that, as you must know, is the most important thing in this life.

With love, Mother

RETHINKING THE HISTORY AND MYTHS OF THE PAST

Henceforth, Nixon carried this letter in his wallet throughout his political life. And this gave him courage, solace and light against the darkness of his political despair.

The juxtaposition of the political careers of Kennedy and Nixon are just two of the many stories that could be told about the relationship between American presidents and their mothers. It is a case of two political nemeses carrying the maternal family banner embedded in their names and etched in their hearts. The reverence that most presidents held for their mothers is undeniable; often bordering on the veneration of a saint. In fact, the admiration for the mother and the subliminal or overt disdain for the father (Oedipus Complex) is quite common among presidents. Show me a great president and I will show you a great mother is the motif of the presidency. Perhaps the first President of the United States said it best:

"My mother was the most beautiful woman I ever saw. All I am I owe to my mother. I attribute all my success in life to the moral, intellectual and physical education I received from her."

From the beginning of the presidency, it is the mother that has shaped the lives and careers of American presidents. It is the leitmotif not only of those with maiden names but of maiden voyages taken by mothers and sons across a troubled sea. God's sacred gift to humanity was a woman and without her, there would be no humankind. So powerful was this sacred gift that a mother's tender touch transcends the boundaries of death to touch the heart of the living and to bring solace to the troubled soul.

A NEW PERSPECTIVE

RETHINKING THE HISTORY AND MYTHS OF THE PAST

The State of the Union

Union Army Flag, 1863–1865

This essay was written before the 2019 State of the Union Address given by Donald John Trump, the 45th President of the United States of America.

The Founding Fathers of the United States were enlightened men, borne from the Age of Enlightenment, fueled by the fervor of revolution, inspired by the zeal of freedom, and forged by their brotherhood. They laid the foundations and ideals of a new nation that was three-thousand miles from the shores of their ancestry. Guided by the legacy of their European forebears, they established on its shores the laws and creed of this nation, enshrined in a palladium known as the Constitution that guaranteed, as implemented, freedom, justice and equality for its white citizens while denying such rights to its darker denizens.

From the inception of this nation, its leaders have acted contrary to its founding creeds. Four out of the first five presidents were slaveowners. Moreover, the three-fifths rule, embedded in the Constitution, guaranteed that the slave-holding states would hold the levers of power, so much so that, prior to the Civil War, every two-term president was from a slave-holding state. Compromise after compromise failed to render a solution to its slave dilemma, culminating in the bloodiest war fought in the Western Hemisphere. The Civil War ended slavery, but it did not remove the lashes of racism from the body we call America. One needs only to view the slave map of 1861 and the electoral map of 2016 to witness the scars of a much-divided nation. Our enemies know that, despite America's greatness, race remains its Achilles' heel. Therefore, they will not hesitate to use it as a silent weapon to further divide us.

A NEW PERSPECTIVE

For centuries, race has been the skeleton in the closet, dancing in the darkness of this hidden and forbidden room. America's Founding Fathers hoped that slavery would die a natural death, but today the ghost of racism still sits upon slavery's cold grave. The election of an African American president in 2008 was not a panacea to this disease. Instead, we witnessed the better angels of our nature succumb to the racist demons of our past. Fifty years after the Civil Rights movement, we do not uphold Dr. King's dream of a nation in which "a person is not judged by the color of their skin, but by the content of their character." Instead, we live in a country in which color trumps character, and palace intrigue is the news of the day. A nation in which the beacon of freedom remains obscured behind the walls of ignorance, bigotry and prejudice. A nation in which justice is neither rendered equally nor with all deliberate speed.

In an attempt to "Make America Great Again," some turn a blind eye to immorality, incompetence and greed. White Identity Politics has become the shibboleth whispered in the halls of Republicanism. We fail to climb that mountain of freedom as former master and former slave. We fail to teach our children that America is the home of the brave. Instead, many white Americans nostalgically yearn for yesteryear—a time "when movies were in black and white and so was everything else"—a time in which white privilege was an inalienable right, despite how wrong it was. We now live in a time when the lines of demarcation between reality and fiction have blurred and the truth obscured by the myths of our past. We no longer stand for something, and we are willing to fall for anything. In these troubling and turbulent times, "fair has become foul and foul has become fair." We have learned to fear those that do not look like us, or worship the same God by a different name, or choose to love someone of the same sex. We ignore our friends and pay homage to our enemies. We call real news fake and fake news real.

Today, we are shipwrecked on the isthmus of our future, trapped between the shores of our better angels on one side and the demons of the past on the other. Our moral compass no longer points toward truth but toward what is acceptable and convenient. Never in the history of the presidency has so much effort been used to try to justify verifiable inaccuracies and blatant lies. We are in desperate need of a captain that will right our ship of state and not let it sail into the ocean of fallen empires. The question that lingers is whether we will "live together as brothers or perish together as fools."

My fellow Americans, do not fiddle while our great nation burns nor dance to the morbid beat of our demise. **We the people** are too powerful to be led by a ship of fools. We can no longer sit in silence in the theater of the absurd, nor can we fall prey to yellow journalism that fuels the fire of our discontent. We owe it not to ourselves

RETHINKING THE HISTORY AND MYTHS OF THE PAST

but to the ideals of this nation, the forgotten martyrs of our past, and the begotten leaders of our future to right what we know is wrong and contrary to our creed.

Like all presidents before him, history will judge Trump's triumphs and his follies before placing him in the pantheon of greatness, the abyss of failure or somewhere in-between.

A NEW PERSPECTIVE

Appendix

The Twelve Caesars

Emperor	Birth/Death	Reign	Era
1. Julius Caesar	102-44 BCE	49-44 BC Dictator	
2. Augustus	63 BC-14 CE	27 BC-14 CE	Augustan
3. Tiberius	42 BC-37 CE	14-37 CE	Julio-Claudian
4. Gaius Caligula	12-41 CE	37-41 CE	Julio-Claudian
5. Claudius	10 BC-54 CE	41-54 CE	Julio-Claudian
6. Nero	37-68 CE	54-68 CE	Julio-Claudian
7. Galba	3 BC-69 CE	68-69 CE	Year of the four emperors
8. Otho	32-69 CE	69-69 CE	Year of the four emperors
9. Vitellius	15-69 CE	69-69 CE	Year of the four emperors
10. Vespasian	9-79 CE	69-79 CE	Year of the four emperors/ Flavian
11. Titus	39-81 CE	79-81 CE	Flavian
12. Domitian	51-96 CE	81-96 CE	Flavian

A NEW PERSPECTIVE

Timeline in the Early Christian Movement

Event	Timeframe	Note
Caesar Augustus made Emperor Beginning of the *Pax Romana*	23 BCE - 14-CE	Both Paul and Jesus were born during his reign
Life of Jesus	4 BCE to 30 CE	
Life of Paul	5 BCE to 67 CE	
Emperor Tiberius	14 – 37 CE	Jesus crucified during his reign
Emperor Nero	37-68 CE	
Letter of Paul	50- 60 CE	Synoptic Gospel
The conversion of Paul	49 CE	
The Death of Peter, James and Paul	60-70 CE	
Mark	65- 70 CE	The First Synoptic Gospel
Luke, Matthew	80-85 CE	Synoptic Gospel (the birth of Jesus narrative)
John	95 CE	Gospel of John
Thomas, Peter, etc.,	120 CE	Non-Canonical Gospels

RETHINKING THE HISTORY AND MYTHS OF THE PAST

Major dates in the History of Islam

Major dates in the History of Islam	
Event	Date: CE
Birth of Muhammad	570
First verse of the Koran	609
Prophets migration from Mecca to Medina	622
Rightly Guided Prophets	632- 661
Umayyad Caliphate	661-750
Moorish Conquest of Spain	711
Abbasid Caliphate	750- 1258
Spanish Umayyad Caliphate	756-1031
The Fatimids	909-1171
The Seljuqs	1037- 1300
The First Crusade	1096-1099
Saldin's Conquest of Jerusalem	1187
The Mamluks	1252- 1517
The Mongol Conquest of Baghdad	1258
The Ottoman Empire	1299- 1919
The Timurids	1369-1500
Conquest of Constantinople	1453
The Conquest of the Moors	1492
The Safavids	1502-1736
Mogul Conquest of India	1526-1857

A NEW PERSPECTIVE

RETHINKING THE HISTORY AND MYTHS OF THE PAST

Relevant Notes

Lincoln and the Civil War

1. The construction of his cabinet was more about establishing and maintaining equilibrium in an unstable environment than it was about balancing or consolidating rivals. However, some viewed Lincoln's cabinet from a different perspective. It was the Radical Republicans that were most unhappy with the selection of Lincoln's cabinet. They were disheartened with his consolatory policies toward the Border States and by the lack of fellow Jacobins within his cabinet (except for Chase). Represented by Thaddeus Stevens in the House of Representatives and the Senate by "Bluff Ben" Wade, Charles Sumner and Zachary Chandler, they wanted fellow aspirants such as John C. Fremont or Cassius Marcellus Clay as part of Lincoln's cabinet. Horace Greely viewed Lincoln's cabinet as "a web of cunning spiders." And there were others such as Ben Wade and Owen Lovejoy that went even further and described them as "a disgraceful surrender to the South
2. In August 1861, Congress authorized the confiscation of slaves used to aid the rebellion in the First Confiscation Act. On the 30th of that month, Union General Fremont issued a proclamation freeing all slaves in Missouri that belonged to secessionists. In a letter dated September 11, Lincoln ordered Fremont to change his proclamation to conform to the First Confiscation Act https://www.archives.gov/education/lessons/blacks-civil-war
3. The Emancipation Proclamation was a subliminal migration of blacks from confiscated property, the brainchild of General Butler, to free people. After all, slavery was a business, big business, and like it or not Lincoln saw it through the eyes of a businessman. Therefore, profits and losses, as well as public opinion, had to be considered. He presented the Emancipation Proclamation to his cabinet on July 22, 1862.
4. On July 13 of 1862, Lincoln brought on the subject of presidential emancipation before Secretary Seward and Secretary of the Navy Welles as the three rode in a carriage after attending the funeral of Secretary Stanton's infant child. The president said he had "given it much thought and had about come to the conclusion that it was a military necessity essential to the salvation of the Union, that we must free the slaves or be ourselves subdued." Lincoln, at the advice of Secretary Seward, delayed his announcement until the Union army won a major battle. The month of August brought no good news, then on the seventeenth of September McClellan turned back Lee at Antietam. On September 22, 1862, the commander and chief of the army and navy issued the famous proclamation giving his fellow white brothers 100 days to return to the Union or have their slaves freed. [The Real Lincoln, pp. 345, 346]
5. The House passed the measure in January 1865 and it was sent to the states for ratification. When Georgia ratified it on December 6, 1865, the institution of slavery officially ceased to exist in the United States. After the Civil War ended Congress initiated three amendments to the constitution to give blacks equal rights. In December of 1865, the 13th Amendment abolished slavery. It is interesting to note that Lincoln was shot in April of 1865. Therefore, he never lived to see the slaves officially freed. The 14th and 15th amendments guaranteed equal rights. Some of the Border States such as Maryland freed their slaves before the 13th Amendment.

A NEW PERSPECTIVE

6. Some African American historians such as Lerone Bennett Jr. have stated that this clause kept almost 300,000 black people in bondage longer and there is some truth to Bennett's assertion.
7. The counter-argument often used is that Lincoln lacked the constitutional power to free slaves in areas loyal to the United States and thus could only initiate it in areas under rebellion. In retrospect, it is easy to question the motives and tactics behind the wording of the Emancipation Proclamation. To free the slaves, Lincoln had to put on his lawyer's hat and he did not have the luxury of Radical Republicans and abolitionists to write a document without considering the constitutional aspects raised by Democrats and Supreme Court Justices acting on their Southern affinities. Chief Justice Taney's position on slavery had been affirmed in the Dred Scot case
8. It is also important to note that by issuing the Emancipation Proclamation, Lincoln took some of the steam out of the Radical Republican cabal, which in its own right, had been gathering steam throughout 1862. Before the Emancipation Proclamation, there had been a power struggle between the Executive Branch and Congress (mainly the Radical Republicans) best highlighted by the writ of habeas corpus debate. Neither questioned that a dictator was needed during times of war, but the question remained as to "who" would be that dictator Congress or the president. Using an executive order, Lincoln, in effect, proved that in areas where the Constitution was not explicit the power rested with the President and not Congress.
9. Lincoln's innate feeling toward slavery was driven by his sense of moral conscious and an intuitive belief that if it continued it would ultimately have dire consequences for America. What Lincoln was against was the exploitation of labor in all of its incarnations

West Point

10. When retired General of the Army Douglas A. MacArthur made a farewell visit to his alma mater on May 12, 1962, it was to receive the Sylvanus Thayer Medal, the highest honor bestowed by the United States Military Academy. He also needed to share his thoughts on the meaning of the West Point motto.
http://www.thenewamerican.com/culture/history/item/11521-duty-honor-country-douglas-macarthur
11. Lewis Armistead did not graduate from West Point due to an incident just before graduation of his class in 1839. His father got him a commission in the Army at the same time that his classmates graduated. His uncle, Maj. George Armistead commanded Fort McHenry in Baltimore harbor during the War of 1812 and the British bombardment that Francis Scott Key was watching when he was inspired to write "The Star-Spangled Banner." [Fleming: Band of Brothers, p.102] [Waugh: Class of 1846, p.530]
12. The West Point graduating class of 1915 numbered 164. More than a third of that extraordinary class won stars, 59 in all-24 brigadier generals (one star), 24 major generals (two stars), 7 lieutenant generals (three stars), two generals (four stars), and 2 generals of the army (five stars). The two who attained the army's highest possible rank were Dwight David Eisenhower and Omar Nelson Bradley. They joined a very select group. Before World War II only four men had held that rank: Ulysses S. Grant (Class of 1843), William T. Sherman (1840), Philip H. Sheridan (1853), and John J. Pershing (1886)

RETHINKING THE HISTORY AND MYTHS OF THE PAST

[Sear: George B. McClellan, pp.12, 13]
http://americanhistory.si.edu/westpoint/history_6b.html
13. Friction arose when President Nixon wanted to install a monument to Confederate officers at West Point. Seidule explained that the then-superintendent managed to avert the plan, in part by consulting African-American cadets, who in turn conferred with African-American officers, and demonstrating the inherent problems in such a move.
http://philipstown.info/2010/08/15/west-point-retains-mixed-feelings-on-confederate-graduates-historian-says/

Antiquity

Egypt

14. Imhotep is also spelled Imouthes, Imothes, Imutep, etc., his tomb has yet to be discovered. [The Sirius Mystery, pp. 75, 77] Legend has it that this tradition derived from the identification of snakes with the priests of the Greek god Asclepius (Imhotep). [The Chalice and the Blade, p. 70] Imhotep was the god who sent sleep to those in pain, and those who were afflicted with any kind of disease formed his special charge; he was the good physician both of gods and men, and he healed the bodies of mortals during life and superintended the arrangements for the preservation of the same after death. [The Gods of the Egyptians, p. 524] The caduceus is seen on Egyptian monuments with the serpents twisted around a rod on the front of Osiris. [Egyptian Belief and Modern Thought, p. 272] The intertwined serpents known as the caduceus is an emblem of modern medicine. Serpents are not always used as an evil symbol; they are also as a symbol for wisdom.
15. Author unknown and may have been Senuret I or a scribe working for him. However, historians believe that Amemehet was murdered.
16. John Darnell, an Egyptologist in Yale's Near Eastern Languages and Civilization department, and his team have succeeded in doing what most Egyptologists merely dream of: discovering a lost pharaonic city of administrative buildings, military housing, small industries, and artisan workshops
http://www.yalealumnimagazine.com/articles/2979
17. The story regarding the long enslavement of Jews, is popular in our Western society. However, another story, not so popular was told by the Egyptians. For hundreds of years, the native Egyptians were virtual slaves to the Hyksos and their Jewish brothers. Many historians and professors of theology argue if Joseph existed. They believe that the story of Joseph and Potiphar (Gen 39:1-21) is nothing more than a rehash of the Egyptian fable, The Tale of the Two Brothers, Anubis (Anpu) and Bata popular around the 19th dynasty. However, the legend of Joseph may serve as a prototype of the relationship between Jews and the Hyksos during their occupation of Egypt. The Egyptians were the most meticulous of all the ancients when it came to records and there are no records of a Joseph. Nevertheless, there are records of the Hyksos and their treatment of black Egyptians. The famous Egyptian historian Manetho states: "We had a king called Tutimaeus. In his reign, it happened. I do not know why God was displeased with us. Unexpectedly from the East, came men of an unknown race. Confident of victory they

A NEW PERSPECTIVE

marched against our land. By force, they took it, easily, without a single battle. Having overpowered our rulers, they burned our cites without compassion and destroyed the temples of the gods. All the natives were treated with great cruelty, for they slew some and carried off the wives and children of others into <u>slavery</u>. Finally, they appointed one of themselves as king. His name was Salitis and he lived in Memphis and made Upper and Lower Egypt pay tribute to him, and set up garrisons in places which would be most useful to him... and when he found a city in the province of Sais which suited his purpose... he rebuilt it and made it strong by erecting walls and installing a force of 240,000 men to hold it." We also know from various descriptions in the Bible, that if Joseph existed his reign had to be during the Hyksos period. [The Bible as History, p. 87]

18. Some scholars contend that the Hyksos and the Israelites were the same and that the famous Exodus is nothing more than an allegory of the Hyksos expulsion. For example, the Jewish historian, Josephus, described them as "the so-called Shepherds our ancestors"[Black Athena, Vol. II, p. 357]. It is also possible that the Jews, being a tribe of Shepherds liked dwelling in the splendor of Egypt cities and this is why they chose to stay after their friends, the Hyksos were expelled. Or they may have been prisoners of war. It has also been mentioned that the Jews being shepherds would find the building of monuments, temples, etc., harsh and equated this labor with slavery. Some religious scholars believe that the exodus allegory as an experience that is constantly appearing, an exodus from an inner "Egypt" in which we are all slaves. [Jewish Mysticism, p. 19]
19. Again, the origin of this myth lies in the Osirian story. The story of Moses and Jesus echoes the story of Horus (i.e., Set's attempts to destroy the baby Horus). The slaughter of male children by King Herod echoes the pharaoh's execution of the male children of the Hebrews. A comparison of Matt: 2:20 and Exodus 4: 19 reveals that they are virtually identical regarding the return from exile. [Mary in the New Testament, p. 14] We also find the same myth regarding the birth of Abraham. [Hebrew Myths, p. 135]
20. References to the "store cities" of Pithom and Ramesses point to the 19th dynasty between 1308 and 1194. Therefore, the Book of the Dead was present before Moses and the Exodus. [Black Athena Vol II, p. 356] The Book of the Dead or Per-em-hru resides in the British Museum and contains 190 chapters written on one of the finest examples of Egyptian papyri. In this book, the decease declares to the tribunal of 42 gods that he has not committed a series of wrongdoing. According to James Breasted, the scenes of the judgment and the text of the Declaration of Innocence were multiplied on rolls by the scribes and sold to all the people. [Development of Religion and Thought in Ancient Egypt, p. 308]
21. The Pope now is virtually the successor of the Pharaohs. He is a priest and king. He is the thrice crowned. He is the earth personification of Deity, who rules by him. He is the ultimatum of appeal in all questions of faith and morals, as was the Pharaoh. But, until the recent proclamation of the Council at Rome, that the Pope was infallible, the parallel was incomplete; for the deified and adored Pharaoh was assumed to be the Infallible [Bonwick: Egyptian Belief and Modern Thought pp.247, 248]

RETHINKING THE HISTORY AND MYTHS OF THE PAST

22. Amenhetep IV (meaning: Amen is satisfied) changed his name to Akhenaton (meaning: Glory of the Aton) to symbolize his conversion to the one god religion. However, he failed to establish his religion, and in less than 25 years after his death, his temples were in ruins. [Dwellers of the Nile, 224] It has not been determined if Akhenaten was the brother or father-in-law of Tutankhamen systems of Egypt. If by chance, it could ber(King Tut). He may have been both. We do know that Tutankhamen was a brief follower of Akhenaten's religion, as shown by his early name Tutankhaton which was later changed to Tutankhamen. [Tutankhamen, pp. 1,2] Any serious theologian cannot ignore the possible influence of Akhenaton's religion on present-day monotheism. If as the Bible says that Moses was truly wise in all things Egyptian, he had to be aware of the various religious thought that preceded Judaism and its influence would not be ignored just as the influence of Judaism on Christianity and Islam is not ignored.
23. Akhenaten's belief in the One God exceeded that of the Hebrews. The Jews believed that their God (Yahveh) was better than all others not that he was the only God. During hard times, many Jews believed in the gods of their oppressors. Furthermore, there is a polytheistic version of the Creation in Genesis something that Akhenaten would have never considered. Ergo, true monotheism, that is to say, the belief in one Supreme Being of which there are no others, was developed in Egypt.
24. For years the relationship between King Tut and Akhenaten was unclear. However, DNA evidence supports Akhenaten is the father of Tutankhamun. Besides, the mummy of one of Akhenaten's minor wives, Kiya, was linked through DNA as Tut's mother. Further DNA testing reveals that Kiya, also known as the "Younger Lady," was the daughter of Amenhotep III and Tiye. This makes her a sister of Akhenaten. http://www.ancient-egypt-online.com/king-tut.html
25. Greek religion is peculiar in that it had no dogma, no sacred book, no revelation, no permanent, professional priesthood. It did not preach virtue. Its basis was the ritual act, the thing done, the thing which had always been done from immemorial antiquity, in propitiation of, or in thanksgiving to, the mysterious power of life, death, and growth, the sense of whose existence, vast menacing and inscrutable, is in primitive man what first distinguishes him from beast. [The World of Herodotus, pp. 168, 169]
26. The Greeks, nor the Romans, truly understood the spiritual nature of the Egyptian gods. The modern reader must remember that the Egyptian myths unlike the Greek or the Roman cannot be considered as fixed stories. Their function in Egyptian religion was to provide a notation of symbols with which to express ideas. [Egyptian Mythology, p.127]
27. Because Rome was the most important city of the Classical world, the Roman interpretation of Egyptian gods strongly influenced how Europe viewed the Ancient Egyptians. What emerged was a pagan image, although many Christian motifs and rituals were Egyptian at origin. The relationship of Mary and Jesus to Isis and Horus is perhaps the most significant. [Egyptology, p. 102]
28. According to legend, this obelisk was brought from the Temple of the Sun at Heliopolis by Caligula in 37 A.D. In 1586 Pope Sixtus V transported the obelisk from a church which had been built alongside it to the center of St. Peters square. Later the obelisk was topped with a cross. [Splendors of the Christendom, p. 204]

A NEW PERSPECTIVE

29. When Jean-François Champollion deciphered the Rosetta Stone in 1822, he was in effect going back in time linguistically. The hieroglyphic script was indeed phonetic and most importantly, the forerunner of our alphabet reshaped by the Phoenicians, given vowels by the Greeks and handed down to us by the Romans.

Greece and Rome

Greece

30. The most plausible date for the Trojan War is the last half of the 13th Century with the Epic poems written around four- and one-half centuries later. This is an interesting date for the Trojan War as it represents the transition from the Bronze Age to the Iron Age. The
31. Andromeda was the daughter of King Cephus and Queen Cassiopeia of Ethiopia, who had angered Poseidon by claiming she was more beautiful than the Nereids (the sea-nymphs). The sea-god sent a sea monster to torment Ethiopia, and an oracle then said that if Andromache was sacrificed, the monster would leave. The princess was chained to a rock by the sea but was rescued by Perseus who turned the monster into stone after showing it the head of Medusa. Perseus went to king Cephesus to ask for Andromeda's hand, and the king gladly agreed. His brother Phineus was angered though because he had been promised Andromeda. Phineus and his followers tried to take the princess, but Perseus turned them all into stone using Medusa's head. Andromeda eventually became Perseus' wife and queen of Tiryns. The couple founded Midia and Mycenae, and their children were Alcaios, Electryon and Sthenelos. Perseus, Andromeda, Cassiopeia and also Cephus were later turned into star constellations.

http://www.in2greece.com/english/historymyth/mythology/names/andromeda.htm

32. The Mycenaeans were Indo-Europeans who blended into the indigenous Greek population (the Pelasgians) between 2800 BCE and 2000 BCE as far north as Epirus. While city-states had emerged by 1600 BCE (the same time at which Mycenaean culture also appears on Cyprus), the Mycenaeans did not form one nation state but instead banded their independent city states together under one leader in times of trouble. During their own time, they were known primarily as Achaeans, after the Achaea region of Greece. http://www.historyfiles.co.uk/KingListsEurope/GreeceMycenae.htm
33. Heinrich, Schliemann was a German archeologist. In 1876, he unearthed elaborate golden artifacts, including a so styled "Mask of Agamemnon" discovered alongside skeletal remains in shaft graves associated by Schliemann with the ancient civilization of the Myceneans. There are some scholars that believe that the Mask of Agamemnon is a forgery. http://www.age-of-the-sage.org/archaeology/heinrich_schliemann.html
34. Theseus is reported to have been the founder of Athens and the Aegean Sea is named after his father. Unlike most important sites inhabited by the Mycenaeans, Athens did not suffer the catastrophic destruction at the end of the Bronze age. [Martin: Ancient Greece, p.82]
35. The Phoenicians were the first to bring the alphabet to Europe. They called the first letter of the alphabet ox, because the Phoenician word for ox, *aleph*, began with the first letter. The second letter they called house because *beth* was the Phoenician word for house. The words were later to Alpha, Beta, etc. The alphabet, therefore, contains the two

RETHINKING THE HISTORY AND MYTHS OF THE PAST

Phoenician words "ox" and "house." Along with the alphabet, the equipment for using it, that is pen, ink, and paper- for the first time came into Europe. Hence, the word paper from *papyros* and Bible from *bibla* meanings books a derivative of Byblos the Phoenician city from which most of the paper came from. [The Conquest of Civilization, pp. 276, 277]

36. Hesiod was a Greek poet and the earliest author of didactic verse. His two complete extant works are the Works and Days, dealing with the agricultural seasons, and the Theogony, concerning the origin of the world and the genealogies of the gods. Written in the late eighth century BCE by Hesiod, one of the oldest known of Greek poets, Theogony and Works and Days represent the earliest account of the origin of the Greek gods and an invaluable compendium of advice for leading a moral life, both offering unique insights into archaic Greek society. In the Theogony there is a story of Cronus dismembering his father and throwing hos parts into the sea reminiscent of the myth of Seth dismembering Osiris and throwing him into the Nile
http://dictionary.reference.com/browse/Hesiod

Rome

37. The exact date of the formation of Rome is unknown. However, the Romans chose a date of April 21, 753 as the starting point of their history.
38. In the Aeneid, Virgil tells of how the Romans are descendants of a wandering Trojan, Aeneas from the Trojan War that settled in Italy. The Aeneid was a Homeric epic about the adventures of Aeneas, ancestor of Romulus the founder of Rome.
39. The Roman Republic was rested on three pillars: The Executive, the Legislative and the Judiciary branches. It lasted from 500 BCE until 44 BCE. The Executive Branch had two Consuls, elected yearly by the people and had powers equivalent to kings. The Legislative had a Senate whose members served for life, Assembly of the People (included al citizens) and Tribunes of the people (elected annually). The Judiciary acted as the judges and implementers of the law (elected annually). In the 18th century, the French political theorist Montesquieu wrote Spirit of the Laws based on the Roma Republic of which the Founding Fathers
40. Two men emerged from such a bellicose milieu. They were Pompey (106-488 BCE) and Julius Caesar (100-44 BCE). Although he is better known for his military exploits Caesar was also an accomplished writer that had command of the Latin prose as demonstrated by his Commentaries on the Gallic Wars. Pompey was a famous general and his subjugation of the Near East established him as Rome's greatest general. Together with Marcus Licinus Crassus (115-54 BCE), they formed Rome's first triumvirate
41. Queens of Cleopatra's magnitude were nonexistent within the Greco-Roman world. However, despite her alleged beauty (of which Plutarch questions) and obvious intellect, Cleopatra could also be ruthless. According to Josephus, she had her brother Ptolemy XIV assassinated to clear the way for her son Caesarian to inherit the throne. [Tydesley, Cleopatra, p110]

A NEW PERSPECTIVE

42. Cleopatra and Mark Antony were defeated by the forces of Octavian at the Battle of Actium on September 2, 31 BCE
43. He changes his name from Octavian to Caesar Augustus and by the decree of the Senate his official name was: Imperator Caesar *Divi Filius* (son of god) Augustus, which means the invisible incarnation of Caesar, the Son of God and the Blessed one sent by the gods (Messiah).
44. The Augustan era and the Julio-Claudian era that followed it would also herald an era of great Latin literary works. Roman literature did not begin until the second century BCE when many of the Latin writers began to emulate the Greeks. Among them were Marcus Pacuvius (220-130 BCE), Polybuis (202-120 BCE), Panaetius (180-110 BCE), Gaius Lucilus (180-102 BCE), Publius Terentius Afer, or Terrance (195-159 BCE) and Lucuis Accius (170-85 BCE) In fact, in the beginning
45. Virgil wrote of a golden age that would be ushered in by the coming of the divine son. It was clear that Virgil's reference to the divine son was the emperor, Augustus. However, early Christians such as Saint Augustine took this to be a pagan prophecy of the coming of Christ

Religion

Christianity

46. In 1819, Thomas Jefferson completed his book entitled: The Life and Morals of Jesus Christ, a project he started in 1804. This became the Jefferson Bible. He wrote the following regarding his book to Charles Thomson a close friend: "it is a document in proof that I am a real Christian, that is to say, a disciple of the doctrines of Jesus"[A book about the Bible, p.133]
47. According to Elaine Pagels, The Gnostic Gospels describe the Holy Spirit as feminine. Therefore, in conventional Catholic terms, the trinity parallels the myth of Osiris, Isis and Horus as well as Jesus and Mary. [Gnostic Gospels, p. 52]
48. The Roman Catholic Church viewed many of the Classical Greek writings as pagan and destroyed them. Fortunately, they were preserved by the Arabs and eventually brought back to Europe.
49. Many of the great cathedrals and works of art such as the Sistine Chapel were financed by indulgences during the reign of the notorious Renaissance Popes. This was one of Martin Luther's main complaints against the Catholic leadership which later gave rise to Protestantism.
50. Professor Collin Humphrey attempts to explain this contradiction in his book *The Mystery of The Last Supper* based on different calendars. Even if his hypothesis proves to be true it is only one of many discrepancies in the Bible and still does not answer how those present could have mistaken the event. A horizontal rather than a vertical reading of the Gospels will reveal numerous discrepancies. Furthermore, it only addressed people of the known world at the time it was written. I do not think the question of where Native Americans or Chinese was ever answered.

RETHINKING THE HISTORY AND MYTHS OF THE PAST

51. According to Egyptian myth, Horus is the resurrection of the Virgin Mother Isis. Horus, Isis, and Osiris formed a Trinity. Numerous statues were depicting Isis and Horus throughout the Roman Empire. I have also been intrigued by Egyptian symbols within the Western culture such as the obelisk in the middle of Saint Peter's Square. Moreover, I have been intrigued by the number of 3s (trinity) associated with Christ, e.g., three men on the cross, rose in three days, died at 33, preached for three years, sold for thirty pieces of silver, and so forth.
52. If Jesus was born on December 25th then he was conceived nine months earlier making his conception coincide with his resurrection thus completing the circle. I find it to be very ironic how these events are coeval with "pagan" practices and celebrations. December 25th is also the birthday of Osiris.
53. If the Catholic Church was founded on Peter to fulfill a prophecy of Jesus, why not Paul, since he wrote a large percentage of the New Testament and Luke his follower allegedly wrote a substantial part? There were other Hellenized Jews that may have been influenced Paul, most notable is Philo of Alexandria who lived during Jesus' time.
54. Paul, being a Jew and a Roman citizen, was familiar with both Jewish and Hellenistic thinking. Many point to Hellenistic elements of Paul's writings in general and elements of Stoicism in particular. It was perhaps because of this background that Paul was able to truly comprehend and articulate the teaching of Jesus in ways that the disciples could not. There can be no doubt that without Paul, Christianity would not be the religion that it is today.
55. It is the opinion of most scholars that the gospels were all written psedonymically (under a false name) and the names assigned to them later. Mark was the first gospel written and both Luke and Matthew used Mark along with the Q document as references.
56. Because of the precession of the equinoxes, the vernal equinox moves through all the constellations of the Zodiac over the 26,000-year precession period. Presently the vernal equinox is in the constellation Pisces and is slowly approaching Aquarius. http://csep10.phys.utk.edu/astr161/lect/time/precession.html
57. St. Athanasius, Bishop of Alexandria, was the first to list the twenty-seven canonical books of the New Testament. There is much debate on why some of the Gnostic Gospels discovered in Nag Hammadi, Egypt is non-canonical.
58. The Persian emperor Cyrus is honored as the only foreigner in the Bible to be identified as the "messiah" or "anointed one" of YHWH, the Israelite God.1 Isaiah tells us that YHWH spoke, "to his messiah, to Cyrus, whom I [YHWH] took by his right hand to subdue nations before him" (Isaiah 45:1). The title Messiah means "anointed." It is an anglicization of the Hebrew meshiach (jyvm). In Greek, it is rendered Christos (cristos)— English "Christ." http://members.bib-arch.org/publication.asp?PubID=BSBR&Volume=19&Issue=5&ArticleID=3
59. Joseph Campbell defined a classic sequence of actions that are found in many stories. It is also known as the *Monomyth,* a term Campbell coined from James Joyce's Finnigan's Wake. http://changingminds.org/disciplines/storytelling/plots/hero_journey/hero_journey.htm
60. The use of "I am" appears only two times in Mark and Luke, five times in Matthew but forty-six times in John. [Ehrman: The New Testament, p. 162]
61. Pagels points out in her *Book Beyond Belief* that the reference to Jesus being the son of a book in the Synoptic Gospels results from them being read within the context of John.

A NEW PERSPECTIVE

And if for example the Gospel of Thomas was included or replaced John that the perspective would be entirely different. [Pagels: Beyond Belief pp. 37, 38]

62. When Cyrus conquered Babylon, he posed as both a liberator and a supporter of the local gods, and once in power, pursued a careful policy of religious toleration. The most important example of this was his allowing the Jews to return to their homeland. The Babylonian Captivity and the subsequent return to Israel were seen as one of the pivotal events in the biblical drama between Yahweh and his people of Israel. Just as they had been predestined for, and saved from, slavery in Egypt, in the logic of the Bible, it had been prophesied that the Israelites would go into captivity to the Babylonians for their idolatry and disobedience to Yahweh, and then be delivered once more. Thus, unknown to him, Cyrus had fulfilled Jewish biblical prophecy. http://www.examiner.com/article/a-persian-jewish-messiah

63. Joshua 6:20-21 God ordered Joshua to attack Jericho's mighty walled city. God knocked the walls down with sound. Joshua's army slaughtered all the men, women, young and old.

64. In 2 Kings 2 v 23, right after Elisha heals the dodgy water, some kids call him a baldhead. He then turns around and curses them in the name of God... Two bears pitch up and maul 42 of the children. Matt 19:13 Then little children were brought to Him that He might put His hands on them and pray, but the disciples rebuked them. 14 But Jesus said, "Let the little children come to me, and do not forbid them; for of such is the kingdom of heaven." 15 And He laid His hands on them and departed from there.

65. This may be only one perspective of the reasons why Jesus was crucified. We cannot ignore that the conditions and predicament although similar under Roman rule were different than what was experienced under Pharaoh in Egypt. There is much evidence to support that the Romans tried to accommodate its Jewish population and that they respected their religious rites. Coinage in Judea was different than in other reasons as to respect the Jewish religious rites. The government in the region was fairly autonomous as well. Moreover, the Jews were not slaves and Paul a Jew was a Roman citizen as were other Jews.

Islam

66. In Christianity and Judaism, Isaac is to be sacrificed while in Islam it is Ishmael (in Arabic Ismail) who is sacrificed

67. In remembrance of the martyrdom of Ḥusayn, Shī'ite Muslims observe the first 10 days of Muḥarram (the date of the battle according to the Islamic calendar) as days of lamentation. Revenge for Ḥusayn's death was turned into a rallying cry that helped undermine the Umayyad caliphate and gave impetus to the rise of a powerful Shī'ite movement

68. According to historian J.B. Russell, Petrarch devised the term "Dark Ages" in or about 1340 to designate a period between classical times and his own form of modernism. [Gould: Dinosaur in a Haystack, p.40]

69. It was the publication of his book *System of the World* that resulted in his imprisonment. [Cohen, I, Bernard, The Birth of a New Physics, New York: W.W. Norton & Company, 1995 p.63] Galileo made two important contributions to astronomy. The first was the

RETHINKING THE HISTORY AND MYTHS OF THE PAST

invention of the telescope; the second was his consistent advocacy of the Copernican system regarding physical truth. [Toulmin, Stephen and June Goodfield, The Fabric of the Heavens, New York: Harper and Row,1961, p.197] Galileo was indeed lucky. Late in the sixteenth century, The Italian philosopher Giordano Bruno argued that space is filled with infinite numbers of planetary systems inhabited by a multitude of living creatures. For this and other indiscretions, Bruno was burned at the stake. [Lightman, Alan, Time for the Stars, New York, Warner Books,1992, p.13]

70. The Arab-dominated Umayyad dynasty at Damascus was overthrown in 756 by the Abbasids, who moved the caliphate to Baghdad. One Umayyad prince fled to Spain and, under the name of Abd al Rahman (r. 756-88), founded a politically independent amirate (the Caliphate of Cordoba), which was then the farthest extremity of the Islamic world. His dynasty flourished for 250 years. Nothing in Europe compared with the wealth, the power, and the sheer brilliance of Al Andalus during this period.
http://historymedren.about.com/library/text/bltxtspain4.htm

71. It is not often these days that we talk about Arabic mathematics, but the period in which Al-Khwarizmi lived and the House of Wisdom in which he worked, preserved for us most of the Greek and Byzantine mathematics and science that eventually led to the revival of learning in Europe.
http://www.mathsisgoodforyou.com/people/alkhwarizmi.htm

Science and Religion

72. We should also be reminded that throughout history churches have not always been on the right side of history thus proving their fallibility. For example, the Roman Catholic Church (Pope Pius IX Jefferson Davis' Pope) supported the Confederacy and their silence during the Holocaust (Pope Pius XII Hitler's Pope) is well document and has been addressed by the Church. The role of the Catholic Church has from its inception been debated by historians. *The Donation of Constantine* was a document that granted enormous political and spiritual power to the Pope (the bishop of Rome). However, in the 15th century, it was proven to be a forgery by Lorenzo Valla. It does clearly demonstrate the extent that members of the Catholic Church would go to secure power over the kings and denizens of Europe

73. The scientific estimate for the age of the earth is approximately 4.5 billion years old.

74. Galileo held controversial views and he expressed them openly both verbally and in several books. He believed like Copernicus that the earth revolved and around the sun which was inconsistent with church doctrine. Galileo was once a good friend of the pope and before the publication of his book, the pope believe that the two of them had arrived at a compromise. The publication of his book, *Dialogue on the Great World Systems, The Ptolemaic and Copernican* in which he mocked the Church's point of view drove a wedge between the two. Galileo was formally pardoned on October 31, 1992, almost 360 years after his trial.

75. The Spanish Inquisition is a prime example of this behavior. The persecution of Jews and Muslims by the Castilians was particularly brutal. Many were forced to leave, convert or die. In some cases, the eating of pork was required to ferret out true believers of the Christian faith. The seal of the Spanish Inquisition depicts the cross, the branch and the sword.

A NEW PERSPECTIVE

76. Although there have been some conflicts between science and religion for centuries, the problem did not come into clear view until the end of the eighteenth century. Geological discoveries indicated that the earth was not 6000 years old but millions of years old which challenge the Biblical interpretation. Previously it had been the belief, that creation occurred in 4004 B.C. [Jauncey, James: Science Returns to God, Grand Rapids, Michigan: Zondervan Publishing House, 1961, p.19]
77. In presenting the history of man, based on scientific facts, it becomes obvious that history and science conflict with the Bible. For instance, the creation story diametrically opposes the archeological and biological evidence. A similar phenomenon occurred during the Age of Enlightenment when scientists such as Galileo presented theories that conflicted with religious belief. Although they were forced to recant, science eventually prevailed. I believe that the Bible is an inspired book based on information available at the time. Therefore, it cannot be taken literally and is an earnest attempt by humankind to understand its spiritual makeup
78. Nuclear DNA is the type that condenses into chromosomes, re-assorted each time a mother's egg or father's sperm is formed; nuclear DNA from each parent is thus contributed to the new offspring, as egg and sperm fuse. As far as anyone knows, nuclear DNA is the control center for inheritance. But the fact that there is also DNA within mitochondria is fascinating. The sperm is little more than the nucleus with a tail and contributes only its nuclear contents to the new offspring, while the egg is a complete cell. This means that mitochondrial DNA residing in the cytoplasm must be passed to the fertilized egg only from the mother. There is no recombination and reassortment in mtDNA, so any mutations that occur in the mtDNA will be recorded in generation after generation. In other words, mtDNA is a wondrous record of matrilineal evolution. [The Neanderthals, p. 362] African American women, for the most part, have the same mtDNA record as their African counterparts. This is because interracial sex during slavery was primarily one way, from the white male to the black female. Since males contribute nothing to the mtDNA the African lineage survived. [The Search for Eve p. 99].
79. We find that the genetic distance between Africans and non-Africans exceed those found in other international comparisons. This result is exactly what one would expect if the African separation was the first and oldest in the human family. [Scientific America November 1991, p. 106]
80. The British anthropologist Louis Leakey, his wife Mary and their son Richard have made major contributions to the study of human evolution. From 1931 to 1959, Louis and his wife, Mary, worked at Olduvai Gorge, Tanzania reconstructing a long sequence of Stone Age cultures dating approximately 2 million to 100,000 years ago. Richard worked in the OMO area of southern Ethiopia. He found traces of australopithecines as well as fragments of a more advanced hominid, perhaps an early Homo.[Grolier Electronic Encyclopedia, Leakey] Also instrumental in the discovery of early humans are Africans such as Kamoya Kimeu who in 1971 recovered skull and bone fragments 1.5 million years old.[National Geographic, November, 1985 p. 625]
81. Today it is an accepted fact that the world's richest repository of early hominid remains is found in the eroded sediments surrounding northwest Kenyais Lake Turkana. [In the Age

RETHINKING THE HISTORY AND MYTHS OF THE PAST

of Mankind, p. 71] In his autobiography, White African, Dr. Leakey says that as a young student he was told not to waste his time searching for Early Man in Africa since everyone knew he had started in Asia. Dr. Leakey was born and grew up, in Kenya. At the age of 13, he was initiated as a Kikuyu. The Kikuyu people called him the black man with the white face because in their eyes he was more African than European. [White African, p. 5] Dr. Leakey also states that the early experiences with the Kikuyu were invaluable to his success as a fossil hunter.

82. A very well-known example of the effect of mutations on a species is provided by the history of the peppered moth, a well-camouflaged species found widely distributed on the earth, especially in cooler countries like England and Scotland. Naturalists have collected the moth for centuries, noting now and again the appearance of a dark-colored moth among the common off-white members of the species. The off-white camouflage blends extremely well with the lichen-covered trunks of the trees in England and prevents the moth from being taken by birds while resting during the day. This advantage is not possessed by the dark-colored mutants which, because of the ease with which they are discovered by birds, rarely survive. However, this advantage was suddenly reversed in the 19th Century factory some began to blacken the tree trunks and kill lichens in the English midlands, and it is now the light-colored forms that lack the protective coloring and the dark-colored moth that survives. The mutant moths produced offspring with the same characteristics and gradually these became the dominant form of the species. A better example of natural selection could hardly be found. Sickle-cell anemia is another example of a mutation. Many feel that this was a mutation required to survive in the malaria-infested area, hence the rate among Africans in the malarial areas of Africa. [Our Roots, pp. 60, 61]

83. The Vitamin D theory was first outlined by Murray and it has slowly gained adherents as a plausible explanation of why white skin evolved from black skin. [The African Background to Medical Science, p. 44]

84. At the beginning of the last year of the 20th Century, the first sequence of the human genome was completed, the 2.5 billion units that define what we are as a species. This was a significant event because it gave us the ability to map migration patterns and was in effect, a telescope that could be used to peer into our distant human past. In this regard, our genes and not light held the glues to be interpreted. Moreover, the biological evidence seams to track the anthropological evidence previously collected. It was a great step for science and a giant leap for humankind. On this new journey, the human steps are becoming apparent. Our early Homo erectus ancestors left Africa around 1.8 million years ago and settled in the subtropical areas of Central Asia and East Asia, unfortunately, they became extinct. Neanderthals left Africa around 500,000 years ago and also died out. The early Homo sapiens that made it into the Middle East also became extinct. Our current group of humans is the only group to leave descendants to the present day. [Wells: Deep Ancestry, p. 116]

A NEW PERSPECTIVE

Technology

The Drawing of the Electrical Era

85. Abraham Clark was a signer of the Declaration of Independence and an icon of integrity. During the Revolutionary War, his sons were captured by the British. They agreed to release them if Abraham Clark denounced the Declaration of Independence. He chose his country over his progeny and they were brutally tortured on the notorious prison ship *Jersey* known as a "floating Hell". They were released at the end of the war.
86. This photograph is the tenth on the list of most expensive photos and sold in 2004 for $478,000. It was the inspiration for the twins in the famous movie the Shining. You can find the photo here: http://en.wikipedia.org/wiki/Identical_Twins,_Roselle,_New_Jersey,_1967
87. Bob Sumner, also from Roselle, is the nephew of Tony Williams. Bob is the former producer of Def Jam Comedy and is responsible for the discovery of several famous comedians during the last twenty years including Dave Chappelle, Chris Tucker, Bernie Mac, D.L. Hughley, Martin Lawrence and more. Watch Bob Sumner interview here: http://www.youtube.com/watch?v=QErk0mgZW7Y Roselle is also the home of renowned poker player Phil Ivey. His grandfather Lenard "Bud" Simmons was a leader in the Black community and taught Phil how to play poker at a very early age. Phil has established a foundation in his name. Read more about Phil here: http://www.poker-king.com/phil-ivey-profile.php
88. The name New Jersey came from the Isle of Jersey, where Carteret had been Royal Governor when King Charles II and his brother James, Duke of York, sought shelter on the 45 square mile island, during the English Civil War. King Charles II, in 1664, whose claim to New England gave him the power to claim to the southward, being unwilling to sanction the prosperity of the Dutch, as a separate community, granted a patent to his brother James, Duke of York and Albany, of lands in America, including all that the Dutch then held as their New Netherlands. The Dutch reluctantly submitted New York and named after the conquering duke. The Duke of York possessed what is now New Jersey and granted the area to Sir George Carteret, who came from the Isle of Jersey. He intended to name it in honor of his family, Nova Cesaria, but the people preferred to call it by a name they could better understand. (The Indian name of the New Jersey was Scheyichbi.)
89. Charles Edison (August 3, 1890 – July 31, 1969), son of Thomas Edison, was a businessman, Assistant and then United States Secretary of the Navy, and served as the 42nd Governor of New Jersey.
90. There was a significant problem at that time with soot collecting inside electric light bulbs as filaments burned which ultimately made the light bulb turn black. This is not something you would want to happen in a village or city. To resolve this problem, Edison placed a metal plate inside an evacuated light bulb, brought a wire from it outside the bulb, and applied voltage between the wire and the filament in an attempt to attract soot particles to the plate. Thomas Edison in 1883 noticed that electrical current flowing through a light bulb's filament could make the wire so hot that electrons boiled off, sailing through the vacuum inside the light bulb to a metal plate that had a positive

RETHINKING THE HISTORY AND MYTHS OF THE PAST

charge. Ironically, Edison could not find a practical application for the effect that bears his name

91. Roselle Park is also the home of the first concrete house constructed by Thomas Edison. Unlike many of Edison's inventions, the concrete house proved not to be practical.

92. The Edison effect remained on the shelf until 1904 when Professor John Ambrose Fleming went to work for Marconi Radio Company. John Fleming's first assignment was to find a better way to receive radio signals. Fleming began experimenting with the Edison Effect. He discovered that radio waves passing through a vacuum tube created a varying direct current, which could be used as a value or a switch. Lee De Forest read about Flemings' valve and built one himself. The valve Lee De Forest created in 1906 had something new; a grid made of nickel wire which he placed between the filament and the plate. Applying even a small amount of electrical charge to the grid disrupted the flow of electrons from the filament to the plate thus amplifying the original signal. This was the beginning of the vacuum tube and the electronic era.

Black History

African Slave Trade

93. During the lifetime of the Prophet, the good reputation of the Ethiopians was further increased by the kindly welcome accorded to Muslim refugees from Mecca. [Race and Slavery in the Middle East, p. 41] It is well known that Muhammad's companions were sheltered by the emperor of Ethiopia, in Arabic called al- Najashi (Negus) when they fled from Mecca to escape the persecution of the reigning pagan oligarchy. [Ibid., p. 96] After the Prophet's death the Semitic Arabs began to look down on blacks in general. This change in attitude affected even freemen of African ancestry- - even the descendants of the Companions of the Prophet including Bilal. [Ibid., p. 41]

94. The legend of Prester John is well documented in European history. Referred to in Latin as Presbyter Johannes and in French as Pretre Jean, he was known as the king of kings and the lord of lords. The legend of a black Christian prince living on the flank of the Muslim world had excited Europe for nearly three hundred years. The legend started with a letter addressed to Manuel Comnenus, Emperor of Byzantium, it purported to be from a distant ruler who, though hardly modest, styled himself simply Prester --that is, presbyter, or priest. As early as 1340 Prester John was identified with the Negus of Ethiopia. On October 20, 1520, after a grueling overland march of six months, the captain of the Portuguese expedition wrote that " We saw . . . to our great joy the tents and camps of the Prester John." [Mysteries of the Past, p. 209] [The Rise of the Colored Races, p. 151] [The Great Discoveries, pp. 15, 16] For more information the reader is referred to *The Realm of Prester John* by Robert Silverberg.

95. The master of the Liverpool slaver Zong, 1783, caused 133 slaves to be flung overboard alive since they were 'sick and weak, or not likely to live'. He argued that if the slaves should die a natural death on board ship their loss would be borne by the owner, while the underwriters would have to pay if the slaves were thrown living into the sea. [The African Slave Trade, p. 244]

A NEW PERSPECTIVE

96. The Book of Genesis records an instance of Noah cursing his son Ham's descendants to be slaves. Although there is no biblical evidence that Ham was the "father" of African peoples, various Jewish, Christian and Islamic writers came to believe that he was, and their association helped to justify centuries of African enslavement. How conveniently they forgot that the mighty Egyptians were also descendants from Ham. Readers may want to refer to David Goldenberg's book, *The Curse of Ham: Race and Slavery in Early Judaism, Christianity and Islam.* Furthermore, it only addressed people of the known world at the time it was written.
97. Nine out of the first twelve presidents were slave owners. They include George Washington, Thomas Jefferson, James Madison, James Monroe, Andrew Jackson, William H. Harrison, John Tyler, James K. Polk and Zachary Taylor. [A Crash Course in Black History, p. 36]

Pushkin Dumas

98. In 1837 Aleksandr Pushkin died at the age of thirty-seven, from a stomach wound suffered in a duel two days earlier. Though the duel is still something of a mystery, full of drama and social overtones, its specific cause was straightforward enough: a handsome officer in the Tsar's Horse Guards, a beautiful wife who liked to flirt, and salon gossip that had become nasty and public in St. Petersburg.
http://www.todayinliterature.com/print-today.asp?Event_Date=6/8/1880
99. Also known as "The Mighty Five," "The Five," "The Russian Five" or "The Mighty Little Heap;" it refers to a group of Russian composers of the 19th century who wanted to establish a nationalist school of music. The group was formed in the 1860s and the nickname Moguchaya Kuchka (Russian for "The Mighty Little Heap") came from critic Vladimir Stasov. Here are the members of "The Mighty Handful." The composers of "the Five"/"the Handful" were Mussorgsky, Borodin, Rimsky-Korsakov, Cui, and Balakirev.

NOI and Malcolm X

100. Early Prophets of the Mormon Church taught that this mark of Cain was black skin. They were also said to have believed that the real curse on all who bore the mark of Cain was that, they would be forbidden to attain Mormon priesthood.
http://www.religionnewsblog.com/5323/the-untold-story-of-the-mormons
101. Brigham Young cited the curse of Ham or Canaan often. Quoting the "prophet" You must not think, from what I say, that I am opposed to slavery. No! The Negro is dammed and is to serve his master till God chooses to remove, the curse of Ham...." On another occasion he stated: We consider [slavery] of divine institution, and not to be abolished until the curse pronounced on Ham shall have been removed from his descendants"[Mormonism's Negro Doctrine, p. 57]
102. The first edition of the Muhammad Speaks appeared in December 1960. [Collins: Seventh Child, p.114]
103. Cassius Marcellus Clay was the name of a Southern Abolitionist and cousin of the well-known Henry Clay
104. Although Muhammad Ali sided with Elijah Muhammad against Malcolm, after Elijah Muhamad died and the NOI was taken over by his son Wallace, he like Wallace denounced that Elijah Muhammad was the Seal of the Prophets and that Fard was Allah.

RETHINKING THE HISTORY AND MYTHS OF THE PAST

105. Ronald Stokes was a Black Muslim that was killed by police in Los Angeles. Malcolm wanted some type of retaliation, but Elijah Muhammad refused.
106. Ali would later write in his autobiography entitled: The Soul of a Butterfly "that turning his back on Malcolm was one of the mistakes that I most regret in my life. I wished I'd been able to tell Malcolm I was sorry, that he was right about so many things. But he was killed before I got the chance. "
107. Malcolm's two brothers were members of the Nation of Islam at the time of Malcolm's murder. And they were forbidden by the Honorable Elijah Muhammad from attending his funeral. Moreover, they had to prostrate themselves before the Honorable Elijah Muhammad and an assembly of Muslims to denounce their brother.

A NEW PERSPECTIVE

RETHINKING THE HISTORY AND MYTHS OF THE PAST

References

1. Adas, Michael, *Islamic & European Expansion*, Temple University Press, Philadelphia, PA, 1993
2. Adkins, David, and Lesley, *The Keys to Egypt*, HarperCollins, New York, 2000
3. Al- Faruqi, Ismail, Raji, *Islam and Other Faiths,* Islamic Foundation, Leicester, UKLeicester, UK
4. Alexander, Caroline, *The War that Killed Achilles,* Viking, 2009
5. Alexander, Paul, J., *The Ancient World to A.D. 300,* Macmillan Publishing, New York, 1968
6. Alexander, Stephon, *The Jazz of Physics, Basic Books*, New York, 2016
7. Alfred, Cyril, *Akhenaten,* Thames and Hudson, New York, 1988
8. Alfred, Cyril, *The Egyptians,* Thames and Hudson, New York, 1987
9. Al-Hassani, Salim T.S., *1001 Inventions,* National Geographic, Washington DC, 2012
10. Allama Sir Abdullah, Al Mamun Al-Suhrawardy, *The Sayings of Muhammad*, John Murray, London, 1980
11. Anderson, Bernhard, W., *Understanding the Old Testament,* Prentice-Hall, Englewood, Cliffs, NJ, 1966
12. Anderson, Fred, *The War that Made America,* Penguin Books, New York, 2005
13. Anderson, Nancy, Scott and Anderson, Dwight, *The Generals,* Alfred Knopf, New York, 1998
14. Angelo, Bonnie, *First Mothers,* William Morrow, New York, 2000
15. Armstrong, Karen, *A Short History of God*, Alfred A, Knopf, New York,1993
16. Armstrong, Karen, *A Short History of Myth*, Cannongate, New York,2005
17. Armstrong, Karen, *Islam,* The Modern Library, New York, 2000
18. Armstrong, Karen, *Jerusalem,* Alfred A, Knopf, New York, 1996
19. Armstrong, Karen, *Muhammad*, Phoenix Press, London 1991
20. Armstrong, Karen, *The Battle for God*, Alfred A. Knopf, New York,2000
21. Armstrong, Karen, *The Case for God,* Alfred A. Knopf, New York,2009
22. Armstrong, Karen, *The Holy Wars*, Anchor Books, New York, 2001
23. Assmann, Jan, *The Mind of Egypt*, Metropolitan Books, New York, 1996
24. Attenborough, David, *The Mediterranean World and Man*, Little Brown and Company, Boston,1987
25. Baines, John, and Mallek, Jaromir, *Cultural Atlas of Ancient Egypt*, Checkmark Books 1980
26. Baldwin Art, *Inventing the Century,* Hyperion, New York, 1995
27. Baring, Anne, and Cashford, Jules, *The Myth of the Goddess,* Penguin Books,1993
28. Barman, Ben, *John the Believable Gospel,* Friendly Press, Bristol England, 1994
29. Barr, Stringfellow, *The Will of Zeus,* Barnes and Nobles, New York, 1962
30. Beatty, John, L., and Johnson, Oliver, A, *Heritage of Western Civilization,* Prentice Hall, Englewood Cliffs, New Jersey, 07623
31. Bell, Madison, Smartt, *Toussaint Loverture*, Pantheon Books, New York, 2007
32. Berg, Richard and Stock, David, *The Physics of Sound,* Pearson Prentice Hall, Upper Saddle River NJ, 2005
33. Bernal, Martin, *Black Athena Vol. I,* Rutgers University Press, New Brunswick, N.J.,1987
34. Bernal, Martin, *Black Athena Vol. II,* Rutgers University Press, New Brunswick, N.J., 1991

A NEW PERSPECTIVE

35. Boatner, Mark, M., *The Civil War Dictionary,* David McKay Company, INC. New York, 1959
36. Bonekemper, Edward, H., *How Robert E. Lee Lost the Civil War,* Sergeant Kirkland's Press Fredericksburg, Virginia, 1998
37. Borg, Marcus, J., and Crossan, John, Dominc, The First Paul, HarperOne, 2009
38. Borg, Marcus, J., *Jesus,* HarperSanFrancisco, San Francisco, 2006
39. Boritt, Gabor, *The Gettysburg Gospel*, Simon & Schuster, New York, 2006
40. Bowle, John, *Man Through the Ages,* Little, Brown & Company, Boston, MA, 1962
41. Bradford, Ernle, *Hannibal*, McGraw- Hill, New York,1981
42. Branch, Taylor, *The King Years,* Simon &Schuster, New York,2006
43. Brier, Bob, Houdin, Jean- Pierre, *The Secrets of the Great Pyramid*, Smithsonian Books HarperCollins, New York, 2008
44. Budge, E.A. Wallis, *Egyptian Magic,* Dover Publications, INC, New York,1971
45. Budge, E.A. Wallis, *Osiris and the Egyptian Resurrection vol. 1,* New York: Dover Publications, Inc., 1973
46. Budge, E.A. Wallis, *The Egyptian Book of the Dead,* New York: Dover Publications, Inc., 1967
47. Bulfinch, Thomas, *Myths of Greece and Rome*, Penguin Books, New York, 1979
48. Bunson, Matthew, *Encyclopedia of the Roman Empire,* Facts on File, New York, 1994
49. Burbank, Jane and Copper, Frederick, *Empires in World History*, Princeton University Press, Princeton, NJ, 2010
50. Burckhardt, Jacob, *The Greeks and Greek Civilization,* St Martin's Press, New York, 1998
51. Burke, James and Ornstein, Robert, *The Axemaker's Gift*, G.P. Putnams and Sons, New York, 1995
52. Burleigh, Nina, *Mirage,* HarperCollins, New York, 2007
53. Campbell, Joseph, *Creative Mythology,* Penguin Compass, New York, 1991
54. Campbell, Joseph, *Hero with A Thousand Faces,* Princeton University Press, N.J., 1973
55. Campbell, Joseph, *Primitive Mythology,* Penguin Compass, New York, 1987
56. Campbell, Joseph, *The Power of Myth*, Doubleday, New York, 1988
57. Campbell, *The Mythic Image,* MJF Books, New York, 1974
58. Canby, Courtlandt, *Lincoln and the Civil War,* Laurel Edition, 1958
59. Cantor, Norman, F. *Antiquity*, Perennial, New York, 2003
60. Canvendish, Richard, *Mythology,* Crescent, New York, 1987
61. Carroll, James, *Constantine's Sword*, Houghton Mifflin Company, New York, 2001
62. Cartledge, Paul, *The Greeks*, BBC, London, 2001
63. Carwardine, Richard, *Lincoln,* Alfred A, Knopf, 2006
64. Case, Brian and Britt, Stan, *The Harmony Illustrated Encyclopedia of Jazz*, Harmony Books, New York,1987
65. Casson, Lionel, *Ancient Egypt,* Time Incorporated, New York, 1965
66. Castle Books, Battles *and Leaders of the Civil War, Volume III*, Edison, NJ, 1995
67. Cator, Norman, F., *Alexander the Great*, HarperCollins, New York, 2005
68. Catton, Bruce and William, *Two Roads to Sumter*, Castle Books, 2004
69. Catton, Bruce, *Reflections of the Civil War,* Berkley Books, New York, 1981
70. Ceram, C.W., *The March of Archaeology,* Alfred A. Knoph, New York, 1966
71. Cerny, Janroslav, *Ancient Egyptian Religion,* Hutchinson's University Library, London, 1952

RETHINKING THE HISTORY AND MYTHS OF THE PAST

72. Chamoux, Francois, *The Civilization of Greece,* Simon and Shuster, New York, 1965
73. Champollion, Jacques, *The World of the Egyptians,* Minerva, Geveve, 1989
74. Clark, John, Henrik, *Malcolm X,* The Macmillan Company, Toronto, 1969
75. Clarke, Lindsay, *The War of Troy,* St. Martin's Press. New York, 2004
76. Cohen, Jon, *Almost Chimpanzee,* Henry Holt & Company, New York, 2010
77. Cole, Sonia, *The Prehistory of East Africa,* The American Library of World Literature, Inc., New York, 1965
78. Collier, Joy, *The Heretic Pharaoh,* Dorset Press, New York, 1970
79. Collins, Rodnell, *Seventh Child,* Carol Publishing Group, Secaucus, NL, 1998
80. Combellack, Frederick, M., *Quintus of Smyrna: The War at Troy,* Barnes and Nobles, New York,1998
81. Conot, Robert, *A Streak of Luck,* Seaview Books, New York, 1979
82. Cooney, Kara, *The Women Who Would be King,* Crown, New York, 2014
83. Corssan, John, Dominic, *Who Killed Jesus,* HarperSanFrancisco, San Francisco, CA, 1995
84. Cotterell, Arthur, *The Encyclopedia of Ancient Civilizations,* The Rainbird Publishing Group Limited, NewLimited, New York, 1980
85. Cox, Earnest S., *Lincoln's Negro Policy,* Richmond, 1972
86. Craughwell, Thomas, J., *Failures of the Presidents,* Fair Winds Press, Beverly, MA, 2008
87. Crossan, John, Dominic and Reed, Johnathan L., *In Search of Paul,* HarperSanFrancisco, 2004
88. Crossan, John, Dominic, *Jesus,* HarperSanFrancisco, San Francisco, CA, 1994
89. Crossan, John, Dominic, *The Historical Jesus,* HarperSanFrancisco, 1991
90. Crossan, John, Dominic, *Who Killed Jesus,* HarperSanFrancisco, San Francisco, 1995
91. Crowe, Charles, *The Age of Civil War and Reconstruction,* 1830-1900, The Dorsey Press, Homewood IL, 1966
92. Cruden, Robert, The *War That Never Ended,* Prentice- Hall INC, Englewood Cliffs, New Jersey, 1973
93. Cunliffe, Barry, *Rome and Her Empire,* McGraw Hill Book Company, New York, 1978
94. Current, Richard, N., *Lincoln and The First Shot,* J.B. Lippincott Company, New York, 1963
95. David, Rosalie, *The Egyptian Kingdoms*, Elsevier Phaidon, New York, 1975
96. Davidson, Basil, *African Kingdoms,* Time-Life Books, New York, 1966
97. Davidson, Basil, *The Black Man's Burden*, Times Book, New York, 1992
98. Davidson, Basil, *The Lost Cities of Africa,* Boston: Little, Brown and Company, 1987
99. Davis, Burke, *The Civil War, Strange and Fascinating Facts*, Wings Book, New York, 1996
100. Davis, David, Brion, *Ante-Bellum,* Harper and Row, New York, 1967
101. Davis, Kenneth, C. *Don't Know Much About the Bible*, Eagles Books, New York 1998
102. Davis, Kenneth, C., *Don't Know Much about the Universe,* HarperCollins Publishing, New York, 2001
103. Day, William, *Genesis on the Planet Earth,* Yale University Press, New Haven, CT, 1984
104. De Selincourt, Aubrey, *The World of Herodotus,* North Point Press, San Francisco, 1982
105. Deacon, Terrence, *The Symbolic Species,* W.W. Norton & Company, New York, 1997
106. Denny, Frederick, Mathewson, *An Introduction to Islam,* Macmillan Publishing Company, New York,1985
107. DiLorenzo, Thomas, *The Real Lincoln*, Ransom House, New York,2002

A NEW PERSPECTIVE

108. Dimont, Max, I., *Jews, God and History,* The New American Library, New York, 1964
109. Diodorus, Siculus, *Book I.*
110. Diop, C.A., *Civilization or Barbarism,* Lawrence Hill Books, New York, 1991
111. Diop, C.A., *Pre-colonial Black Africa,* Lawrence Hill Books, Connecticut, 1987
112. Diop, C.A., *The African Origins of Civilization: Myth or Reality,* Connecticut, Lawrence Hill Books, 1974
113. Donald, David, Herbert, and Holzer, Harold, *Lincoln in the Times,* St Martin's Press, New York, 2005
114. Donald, David, Herbert, Jean Harvey Baker, Michael F. Holt, *The Civil War and Reconstruction,* W.W. Norton and Company, Inc., New York. 2001
115. Donald, David, Herbert, *Lincoln at Home,* Simon & Schuster, New York, 1999
116. Donald, David, Herbert, *Lincoln,* Simon & Schuster, New York, 1995
117. Donovan, James, *A Terrible Glory,* Little Brown and Company, New York, 2008
118. Drake, St. Clair, *Black Folk Here and There Vol. II*, Center for Afro-American Studies, University of California, Los Angeles, 1990
119. Drower, Margret, *Flinders Petrie,* The University of Wisconsin Press, 1995
120. Dryden, John, *Plutarch's Lives,* Modern Library, New York, 1975
121. Dudley, Donald, The Romans, Barnes and Noble, New York,1993
122. Dunning, William, A., *Essays on The Civil War and Reconstruction,* Harper Touchbooks, New York,1965
123. Durant, Will, *Caesar and Christ,* Simon & Schuster, Inc. New York, 1944
124. Durant, Will, *Our Oriental Heritage,* Simon & Schuster, Inc. New York, 1954
125. Durham, Michael, S., *Desert Between the Mountain,* Henry Holt & Company, New York, 1997
126. Ehrman, Bart, D, *Jesus Interrupted*, HarperOne, New York, 2009
127. Ehrman, Bart, D., *God's Problem,* HarperOne, 2008
128. Ehrman, Bart, D., *How Jesus Became God,* HarperOne New York, 2014
129. Ehrman, Bart, D., *Misquoting Jesus,* HarperSanFrancisco, San Francisco, 2005
130. Ehrman, Bart, D., *The New Testament,* Oxford University Press, Oxford, 2004
131. Eisenhower, John S.D., *So Far from God,* Random House, New York, 1989
132. Entine, Jon, *Abraham's Children,* Grand Central Publishing, New York,2007
133. Evanzz, Karl, *The Messenger,* Pantheon Books, New York, 1999
134. Fairclough, Adam, *Better Day Coming,* Viking, New York,2001
135. Fehrenbacher, Don, E., *Abraham Lincoln,* The New American Library, New York, 1964
136. Fehrenbacher, Don, E., *The Leadership of Abraham Lincoln,* John Wiley & Sons, Inc, New York, 1970
137. Fenster, Julie, M., *The Case of Abraham Lincoln,* Palgrave, Macmillan, New York, 2007
138. Finley, M.I., *The Greek Historians,* The Viking Press, New York,1959
139. Fleming, Candace, *The Lincolns,* Eastern Acorn Press, *The Negro in the Civil War,* Easton Acorn Press, 1988
140. Fletcher, Richard, *The Cross and the Crescent*, Viking, New York, 2003
141. Flood, Charles, Bracelen, *1864, Lincoln at the Gates of History,* Simon &Schuster, New York, 2009
142. Foote, Shelby, *The Civil War,* Random House, New York, 1974
143. Forrest, W.G., *The Emergence of Greek Democracy,* McGraw Hill, New York, 1966
144. Forty, Jo, *Ancient Egyptian Pharaohs*, PRC Publishing Ltd, London, 1998,

RETHINKING THE HISTORY AND MYTHS OF THE PAST

145. Fosdick, Harry, Emerson, *The Man from Nazareth,* Harper & Brothers, New York,1949
146. Foster, Genevieve, *Augustus Caesar's World, 44 BC to AD 14,* Beautiful Feet Books. Sandwich, Massachusetts, 1947
147. Fox, Robin, Lane, *The Classical World,* Basic Books, New York, 2006
148. Fraknoi, Andrew, *The Universe,* Banton Books, New York, 1987
149. Frazer, James, G., *The Golden Bough,* The Macmillan Company, New York, 1951
150. Frazer, James, George, *The New Golden Bough,* Anchor, Books. Garden City, New York,1961
151. Freeman, Charles, *The Greek Achievement,* Viking, New York, 1999
152. Freke, Timothy, Gandy, Peter, *Jesus and the Lost Goddess,* Three Rivers Press, New York,2001
153. Freke, Timothy, Gandy, Peter, *The Jesus Mysteries,* Three Rivers Press, New York, 1999
154. Frenandez-Armesto, Felipe, *Civilizations,* Simon & Schuster, New York, 2001
155. Freud, Sigmund, *Moses and Monotheism,* Vintage Books, New York, 1937
156. Friedel, Robert, and Israel, Paul, *Edison's Electric Light,* The John Hopkins University, 2010
157. Gallagher, Gary, W., *Lee, the Soldier,* University of Nebraska Press, Lincoln, Nebraska,1996
158. Gardner, Alan, *Egypt of the Pharaohs,* Oxford University Press, Oxford, 1961
159. Garfinkle, Norton, *Lincoln and the Coming of the Civil War,* D.C. Heath and Company, Boston, MA, 1959
160. Garrison, Webb, *Lincoln's Little War,* Rutledge Hill Press, Nashville Tennessee, 1997
161. Geer, Walter, *Campaigns of the Civil War,* Konecky & Konecky, Saybrook CT, 1926
162. Gibbon, Edward, *The Decline and Fall of the Roman Empire,* The Modern Library, New York, 2003
163. Gieuppe, Riciotti, The *Age of Martyrs,* The Bruce Publishing Company, Miwaukkee, WI, 1959
164. Goguel, Maurice, *Jesus and the Origins of Christianity, Vol II,* Harper Touchbooks, New York, 1960
165. Goldenberg, David, *The Curse of Ham: Race and Slavery in Early Judaism, Christianity and Islam*, Princeton University Press, Princeton, NJ
166. Gomez, Michael, *Black Crescent,* Cambridge University Press, Cambridge, New York, 2005
167. Goodman, Martin, *Rome and Jerusalem*, Alfred A. Knopf, New York, 2007
168. Goodwin, Doris, Kearns, *Team of Rivals,* Simon& Garrison, Webb, *Unknown Civil War,* Cumberland House, Nashville TN, 2000
169. Grabsky, Phil, *I, Caesar,* BBC Books, London, 1997
170. Grant, Michael, *A Social History of Greece and Rome,* Scribner, New York, 1992
171. Grant, Michael, *Cleopatra,* Barnes and Noble, New York,1972
172. Grant, Michael, *Founders of the Western World*, Charles Scribner's Sons, New York, 1991
173. Grant, Michael, *Saint Peter,* Scribner, New York, 1994
174. Grant, Michael, *The Ancient Mediterranean,* Penguin Books, New York, 1969
175. Grant, Michael, *The Fall of the Roman Empire,* Simon & Schuster, New York, 1997
176. Grant, Michael, *The Jews in the Roman World,* Barnes and Noble, New York, 1973
177. Grant, Michael, *The Rise of the Greeks,* Phoenix Press, London, 1987

A NEW PERSPECTIVE

178. Grant, Michael, *The Twelve Caesars*, Charles Scribner's Sons, New York, 1975
179. Graves, Robert, *The Greek Myths*, Penguin Books, New York,1960
180. Green, Peter, *The Parthenon,* Newsweek Book Division, New York, 1973
181. Green, Roger, Lancelyn, *Tales of Ancient Egypt,* Puffin Books, New York, New York, 1983
182. Grier, Rosey, Rosey, *an Autobiography: The Gentle Giant*, Harrison House (August 1986)
183. Guelzo, Allen, C. *Lincoln's Emancipation Proclamation*, Simon & Schuster, New York, 2004
184. Gul, E., and Koner, W., *The Greeks,* Senate, Middlesex UK, 1994
185. Gullan, Harold, I, *Faith of Our Mothers,* William B. Eerdmans Publishing Company, Grand Rapids, Michigan, 2001
186. Guthrie, W.K.C., *The Greeks and Their Gods*, Beacon Press, Boston, MA, 1971
187. Hadas, Moses, The *Complete Works of Tacitus,* The Modern Library, New York, 1942
188. Haley, Alex, *The Autobiography of Malcolm X*, Ballantine Books, New York,1964
189. Hamblin, Dora, Jane, *The Etruscans,* Time-Life Books, New York,1975
190. Hamilton, Edith, *The Greek Way,* W. W. Norton & Company, New York, 1993
191. Hamilton, R., *Ancient Egypt Kingdom of the Pharaohs,* Barnes and Noble, New York, 2005
192. Hamlyn, Paul, *Egyptian Mythology*, Tudor Publishing Company, New York, 1965
193. Hansberry, William L., *Africa and Africans As Seen by Classical Writers,* Howard University Press, Washington D.C.,1977
194. Hansen, Harry, *The Civil War,* New American Library, New York, 1991
195. Harmon, Nolan, B, *The Interpreters Bible*, Abingden Press, New York, 1955
196. Harrington, Wilfrid, J., *The Gospel According to Luke*, Newman Press, New York, 1967
197. Herbert, Sandra, *Charles Darwin and the Question of Evolution*, Bedford/St Martins New York,2011
198. Herndon, William, *Life of Lincoln*, Da Capo Press, Inc., New York, 1942
199. Hicks, Maurice, J, Roselle, *New Jersey Site of Thomas Alva Edison's First Village Plant*
200. Hill, Peter, P., *Napoleon's Troublesome Americans,* Potomac Books, Washington D.C.,2005
201. Hillerbrand, Hans, J/, *Man and Ideas in the Sixteenth Century*, Rand McNally &Company, Chicago, 1969
202. Hillstrom, Kevin, Hillstrom, Laurie, Collier, *American Civil, War*, UXL, Detroit, MI, 2000
203. Holland, Tome, *RVBICON,* Doubleday, New York, 2003
204. Holzer, Harold, and Shenk, Joshia, Wolf, *In Lincoln's Hand,* Bantam Books, 2009
205. Holzer, Harold, *Lincoln and the Power of the Press,* Simon & Schuster, New York,2004
206. Holzer, Harold, *Lincoln at Cooper Union,* Simon & Schuster, New York,2014
207. Holzer, Harold, *The Civil War in 50 Objects,* Viking, New York,2013
208. Hood, Sinclair, *The Minoans,* Praeger Publishers, New York, 1971
209. Hopper, R.J., *The Early Greeks,* Harper and Row, New York, 1977
210. Horowitz, Mitch, *Occult America,* Bantam Books, New York,2009
211. Howard, Martin, *Egyptian Pharaohs,* Fall River Press, New York, 2009
212. Hughes, William, *Western Civilization, Volume 1*, The Dushkin Publishing Group, Guildford, CT, 1987

RETHINKING THE HISTORY AND MYTHS OF THE PAST

213. Islamic Affairs Department, *Islam A Global Civilization,* The Embassy of Saudi Arabia, Washington, DC
214. James, Jamie, *The Music of the Spheres*, Grove Press, 1993
215. Jeans, James, *Science & Music*, Dover Publications, New York,1968
216. Johnson, Luke, T., *The Writing of the New Testament,* Fortress Press, Philadelphia, 1986
217. Johnson, Paul, *A History of Christianity,* Simon &Schuster, New York, 1976
218. Jonathan, M., *Ancient Canaan and Israel,* Oxford University Press, London, 2004
219. Jones, George, Thaddeus, *Music Theory*, HarperResources, New York, 1974
220. Jones, Howard, *Abraham Lincoln and the New Birth of Freedom,* University of Nebraska Press, Lincoln, 1999
221. Jordan, Paul, *The Riddles of the Sphinx*, New York University Press, New York, 1998
222. Keller, Werner, *The Bible as History,* Batam Books, New York, 1981
223. Kennedy, Hugh, *When Baghdad Ruled the Muslim World,* Da Capo Press, Cambridge MA, 2004
224. Kesich, Veselin, *The Gospel Image of Christ,* St Vladimir's Seminary Press, 1992
225. Khalidi, Tarif, *Images of Muhammad,* Doubleday, New York, 2009
226. Khalidi, Tarif, *The Muslim Jesus,* Harvard University Press, Cambridge, MA, 2001
227. Kolchin, Peter, *American Slavery, 1619-1877,* Hill and Wang, New York, 1993
228. Kutler, Stanley, *Abuse of Power*, The Free Press, New York, 1997
229. Lane-poole, Stanley, *The Story of the Moors in Spain,* Baltimore: Black Classics Press, 1886
230. Lewis Bernard, *Islam and the West*, Oxford University Press, New York, 1993
231. Lewis, Bernard, *A Middle East Mosaic,* Random House, New York,2002
232. Lewis, Bernard, *Islam and the West,* Oxford University Press, New York, 1993
233. Lewis, Bernard, *The Middle East,* Touchstone Books, New York ,1995
234. Lewis, Bernard, *The Muslim Discovery of Europe,* W.W. Norton & Company, New York, 2001
235. Lewis, Lloyd, *Myths after Lincoln*, Grosset and Dunlap, New York, 1957
236. Lewis, Naphtali and Reinhold, Myer, *Roman Civilization Volume I,* Columbia University Press, New York, 1990
237. Lowry, Rich, *Lincoln Unbound,* HarpersCollins, New York, 2013
238. Loy, Gareth, *Musimathics: The Mathematical Foundations of Music (Volume 1)*, The MIT Press, Cambridge, MA, 2011
239. Loy, Gareth, *Musimathics: The Mathematical Foundations of Music (Volume 2)*, The MIT Press, Cambridge, MA, 2011
240. Ludwig, Emil, *Abraham Lincoln,* Fawcett Publications, INC, New York, 1956
241. Luttwak, Edward,N., *The Grand Strategy of the Roman Empire*, The John Hopkins University Press, Baltimore, MD, 1976
242. Lyons, Eugene, *David Sarnoff,* Harper and Row, New York, 1966
243. MacGregor, Neil, The British Museum, *A History of the World in 100 Objects*, Viking, New York, 2010
244. Mack, Burton, *The Lost Gospels,* Harper San Francisco, 1993
245. MacQuitty, William, *Tutankamun,* Jarrold & Son, Norwich, UK,1976
246. Malone, Dumas and Rauch, Basil, *Crisis of the Union,* 1841 -1877, Appleton- Century-Crofts, New York, 1960
247. Mann, Charles, C., *1491,* Alfred A. Knopf, New York, 2005

A NEW PERSPECTIVE

248. Mann, Charles, C., *1493,* Alfred A. Knopf, New York, 2011
249. Marble, Manning, *Malcolm X*, Viking, New York,2011
250. Martin, Thomas, R., *Ancient Greece*, Yale University, New Haven, 1996
251. Marty, Martin, *Martin Luther,* Viking Books, New York, 1976
252. Massey, Gerald, *A Book of the Beginning,* ECA Associates, New York, 1990
253. Massey, Gerald, *Ancient Egypt, The Light of the World,* ECA Associates, New York, 1990
254. Massey, Gerald, *The Natural Genesis,* S. Weiser, New York, 1974
255. Matthews, Christopher, *Kennedy & Nixon*, Touchstone, New York, 1996
256. Meacham, John, *The Soul of America*, Random House, New York, 2018
257. Mertz, Barbara, *Temples, Tombs & Hieroglyphs*, William Morrow, New York, 2007
258. Meyer, Jeffery, E, *Myths in Stone University* of California Press, Berkley, 2001
259. Meyer, Jeffery, E, *Myths in Stone,* University of California Press, Berkley, 2001
260. Middlebrook, Ron, *Scales & Modes in the Beginning*, Centerstream Publications Anaheim Hills, CA
261. Miers, Earl, Schence, *Lincoln Day by Day,* Morningside, Dayton Ohio, 1991
262. Miers, Earl, Schenck, *The Great Rebellion,* The World Publishing Company, New York,1958
263. Miles, Jim, *Forged in Fire,* Cumberland House, Nashville, TN, 2000
264. Miller, Kenneth, R., *Finding Darwin's God,* Cliff Street Books, New York,1999
265. Miller, William, Lee*, President Lincoln*, Alfred A. Knopf, New York, 2006
266. Milles, Jack, *Christ*, Alfred A. Knopf, New York, 2001
267. Milles, Jack, *God*, Alfred A. Knopf, New York, 1995
268. Mokhtar, G., *General History of Africa II Ancient Civilizations,* University of California Press, California, 1990
269. molin, Lee, *The Life of the Cosmos,* Oxford University Press, Oxford, 1997
270. More, Jasper, *The Land of Egypt*, B.T. Batsford Ltd, London, 1980
271. Moulton, Carroll, *Ancient Greece and Rome,* Volume 1, Charles Scribner's Sons, New York, 1998
272. Moulton, Carroll, *Ancient Greece and Rome,* Volume 2, Charles Scribner's Sons, New York, 1998
273. Moulton, Carroll, *Ancient Greece and Rome,* Volume 3, Charles Scribner's Sons, New York, 1998
274. Moulton, Carroll, *Ancient Greece and Rome,* Volume 4, Charles Scribner's Sons, New York, 1998
275. Mullins, Ron, *Jazz Piano Voicing,* Hal Leonard, Milwaukee, WI, 2002
276. Murray, Margaret, *The Splendor That Was Egypt*, Dover Publications, INC. Mineola, New York, 2004
277. Neely, Mark, E., *Lincoln and the Triumph of the Nation*, University of North Carolina Press, Chapel Hill, NC, 2011
278. Nevins, Allan*, War for the Union,* Konecky & Konecky, 1960
279. Nolan, Albert, *Jesus Before Christianity*, Orbis Books, New York, 1993
280. O'Reilly, Kenneth, *Black Americans the FBI Files,* Carroll & Graf, Publishing, New York,1994
281. Oates, Stephen, B., *Abraham Lincoln, The Man behind the Myth*, HarperPerennial, New York, 1994
282. Oates, Stephen, B., *The Approaching Fury,* HarpersCollins, New York, 1997

RETHINKING THE HISTORY AND MYTHS OF THE PAST

283. Oates, Stephen, B., *The Whirlwind of War*, HarpersCollins, 1998
284. Oates, Stephen, B., *With Malice Toward None*, A Mentor Book, 1977
285. Olson, Steve, *Mapping Human History*, Houghton Mifflin Company, New York, 2002
286. Osman, Ahmed, *Moses and Akhenaten*, beat & Company, Rochester, Vermont, 2002
287. Paludan, Phillip, Shaw, The *Presidency of Abraham Lincoln,* University Press of Kansas, 1994
288. Papahatzes, Nicos, *Mycenae-Epidaurus Tiryns-Nauplion, Clio Editions*, Athens, 1978
289. Pareti, Luigi, *The Ancient World Volume II*, Harper and row, New York, 1965
290. Patterson, Gerald, A., *Rebels from West Point*, Doubleday, New York, 1987
291. Patterson, Stephe, J., *The God of Jesus*, Trinity Press International, Harrisburg, PA, 1998
292. Payne, Robert, *The Splendor of Greece,* Harper & Row, New York, 1960
293. Pelikan, Jaroslav, *Jesus Through the Centuries,* Mary Through the Centuries, History Book Club, New York,1985
294. Peraino, Kevin, *Lincoln and the World*, Crown Publishers, New York, 2013
295. Perret, Goeffrey, *Lincoln's War*, Random House, New York, 2004
296. Peters, F.E., *The Harvest of Hellenism,* Simon & Schuster, New York, 1970
297. Pierce, John, R., *The Science of Musical Sound*, Scientific American Library, New York, 1983
298. Rawlins, Robert, and Bahha, Nor Eddine, *Jazzology*, Hal Leonard, Milwaukee, WI, 2005
299. Reader's Digest, *The World's Last Mysteries*, Readers Digest, New York, 1978
300. Redford, Donald, B., *Akhenaten, the Heretic King*, Princeton University Press, Princeton, NJ, 1984
301. Reeves, Nicolas, *Akhenaten, Egypt's False Prophet,* Thames & Hudson, New York, 2001
302. Reiss, Tom, *The Black Count*, Crown Publishers, New York, 2012
303. Reston, James, Jr., *Dogs of God*, Doubleday Books, New York, 2005
304. Richardson, Donald, *Greek Mythology for Everyone*, Avenel Books, New York,1984
305. Robbins, Alexandra, *Secrets of the Tomb*, Little, Brown and Company, New York, 2002
306. Robert James Branham, *"I Was Gone on Debating": Malcom X's Prison Debates and Public Confrontations,* Argumentation and Advocacy 31, Winter 1995
307. Roberts, J.M., *Rome and the Classical West, Volume 3*, Oxford University Press, New York, 1999,
308. Roberts, Paul, William, *In Search of the Birth of Jesus,* Riverhead Books, New York,1995
309. Robertson, James, I., Jr. *Jackson and Lee*, Rutledge Hill Press, 1995
310. Roland, Charles, P., *An American Iliad*, Mc Graw-Hill, New York, 1991
311. Safire, William, *Lend Me Your Ears*, W.W. Norton & Company, New York,1992
312. Sasson, Jack, M, *Civilizations of the Ancient Near East,* Charles Scribner and Sons, NewSons, New York, Volumes II and IV 1995
313. Scarre, Chris, *Chronicle of Roman Emperors,* Thames and Hudson, New York, 1995
314. Schuchhardt, Carl, *Schliemann's Discoveries of the Ancient World*, Avenel Books, New York, 1979
315. Sears, Stephen, W., *George B. McClellan,* Ticknor & Fields, New York, 1988
316. Sears, Stephen, W., *Lincoln's Lieutenants,* Houghton Mifflin Harcourt, New York, 2017
317. Shabazz, Ilyasah, *Growing Up X,* The Ballantine Publishing Group, New York,2002
318. Sheinkin, Steve, *Two Miserable Presidents,* Roaring Brook Press, New York,2012
319. Shenk, Joshua, Wolf, *Lincoln's Melancholy,* Houghton Mifflin Company, New York,

A NEW PERSPECTIVE

2005
320. Shenkman, Richard, *Legends, Lies, & Cherished Myths of American History,* New York, Perennial Library, 1989
321. Sheridan, Michael, *Romans,* St martin's Press, New York, 1994
322. Silver, Daniel, Jeremy, *The Story of Scripture,* Basic Books, New York, 1990
323. Silverberg, Robert, *Akhnaten The Rebel Pharaoh,* Chilton Books, New York, 1964
324. Silverberg, Robert, *The Realm of Prester John,* Ohio University Press, 1996
325. Smith, Carter, Smithsonian, Institute, *Presidents All You Need to Know,* Hylas, Publishing, 2004
326. Smith, Morton, *The Ancient Greeks,* Cornell University Press, Ithaca, New York,1960
327. Spence, Lewis, *Ancient Egyptian Myths and Legend,* Dover Publishing, New York, 1990
328. Spong, John, Shelby, *Jesus for the Non-Religious,* HarperSanFrancisco, San Francisco, CA, 2007
329. Spong, John, Shelby, *Why Christianity Must Change or Die,* HarperSanFrancisco, San Francisco CA, 1998
330. Spoto, Donald, *The Hidden Jesus,* St Martin's Press, New York, 1998
331. Stanford, W.E., Luce, J.V., *The Quest for Ulysses,* Praeger Publishing, New York,1974
332. Stapleton, Michael, *Greek and Roman Mythology,* Peter Bedrick Books, New York, 1986
333. Starr, Chester, *The Roman Empire 27 B.C. –A.D. 476,* Oxford University Press, Oxford, 1982
334. Steindorff, George, and Seele, Keith C., *When Egypt Ruled the East,* University of Chicago Press, Chicago, 1942
335. Strickland, William, *Make It Plain,* Viking, New York,1994
336. Sykes, Bryan, *The Seven Daughters of Eve,* W. W> Norton & Company, New York, 2001
337. Tabor, James D, *The Jesus Dynasty,* Simon & Schuster, New York, 2006
338. Tattersall, Ian, *Becoming Human,* Harcourt Brace and Company, New York, 1998
339. Throckmorton, Burton, H, *Gospel Parallels,* Thomas Nelson Publishing, New York,1979
340. Troyat, Henri, *Pushkin,* Doubleday & Company, Inc. New York, 1970
341. Tucker, r., Whitney, *The Descendants of the Presidents,* Delmar Printing Company, Charlotte, North Carolina, 1975
342. Tyldesley, Joyce, *Nefertiti,* Viking, New York, 1998
343. Ulansey, David, *The Origins of the Mithraic Mysteries,* Oxford University Press, Oxford, 1989
344. Vandenberg, Phillip, *The Mystery of the Oracles,* MacMillan Publishing Co, INC, New York, 1979
345. Velikovsky, Immanuel, *Rameses II and His Times,* Doubleday and Company, New York, 1978
346. Vermeule, Emily, *Greece in the Bronze Age,* The University of Chicago Press, Chicago, 1972
347. Veronica, *Egyptian Mythology,* Peter Bedrick Books, New York, 1982
348. Vicchio, Stephen, J., *Jefferson's Religion,* Wif & Stock Publishers, Eugene, Oregeon, 2007
349. Volney, C.F., *The Ruins of Empires,* Black Classics Press, Baltimore, 1991
350. Walbank, F.W., *The Hellenistic World,* Harvard University Press, Cambridge, MA, 1993
351. Walen, Richard, *The Founding Father,* The New American Library, New York, 1964
352. Walker, Williston and Norris, Richard A., *A History of the Christian Church,* Charles

RETHINKING THE HISTORY AND MYTHS OF THE PAST

Scribner's Sons, New York, 1970
353. Walter Dean Myers, *Malcolm X,* Scholastic INC, New York,1991
354. Washington, Ethel, *Union County Black Americans* ISBN 0738536830, 9780738536835
355. Wead, Doug, *The Raising of a President,* Atria Books, New York, 2005
356. Wells, Evelyn, *Hatshepsut,* Doubleday & Company, Garden City, NY,1969
357. Wert, *The Sword of Lincoln,* Simon & Schuster, New York, 2005
358. Wheeler, Joe, *Abraham Lincoln A Man of Faith and Courage,* Howard Books, New York, 2008
359. Whitt, Terrence, *Our Undiscovered Universe,* Adrian Publishing Corporation, Melbourne, 2007
360. Wilczek, Frank, Devine, Betsy, *Longing for Harmonics,* W.W. Norton & Company, New York
361. Wilkinson, Phillip and Philip, Neil, *Mythology,* Metro Books, New York, 2007
362. Willers, Michael, *Algebra,* Fall River Press, New York, 2009
363. Williams, C.S.C., *The Text and Cannon of the New Testament,* Gerald Duckworth & CO. LTD, London, 1960
364. Williams, John, *Africa, Her History, Lands and People,* Cooper Square Publishers, Inc., New York, 1962
365. Williams, Juan, *Eyes on the Prize,* Penguin Books, New York, 1987
366. Williams, T., Harry, *Lincoln and the Radicals,* The University of Wisconsin Press, Milwaukee, WI, 1965
367. Wilson, A.N., *Jesus A Life,* W.W. Norton & Company, New York,1992
368. Wilson, A.N., *Paul,* W.W. Norton & Company, New York,1997
369. Wilson, Ian, *Jesus: The Evidence,* New York: Harper & Row, 1941
370. Wilson, John, A, *The Culture of Ancient Egypt* Phoenix Books, The University of Chicago Press, Chicago, Il,1951
371. Winn, Ralph B., *A Concise Lincoln Dictionary,* New York: Philosophical Library
372. Winston, William, *The Works of Flavius Josephus,* G. Auld, London, 1820
373. Wolff, Daniel, *How Lincoln Learned to Read,* Bloomsbury, New York, 2009
374. Wood, Joe, *Malcolm X,* St Martin's Press, New York,1992
375. World Book Encyclopedia, Inc., *World Book of America's Presidents,* Chicago IL, 1982
376. Wrangham, Richard, *Catching Fire,* Basic Books, New York, 2009
377. Wright, N.T., The *Challenge of Jesus,* InterVarsity Press, Downers Grove, Illinois, 1999
378. Wright, Robert, *God, The Evolution,* Little Brown and Company, New York, 2009
379. Wunderlich, Hans, Georg, *The Secret of Crete,* Macmillan Publishing Company, New York, 1974
380. X, Malcolm, *On Afro-American History,* Pathfinder Press, New York, 1970

A NEW PERSPECTIVE

RETHINKING THE HISTORY AND MYTHS OF THE PAST

Acknowledgments

The author is extremely grateful to the many family members and friends for giving him the fortitude to compile this book and to pursue a writing career. The author wishes to extend his acknowledgments to the following individuals: First and foremost, to my wife Jeanne Royal Singley of 35 plus years; whose patience and endearing support is written on each page in ink only visible to me. To my two sons: Bradford and Adrian, for putting up with their dad all these years and for making me so proud to be their father. To my loving parents, Lawson and Willie Mae Singley (both deceased); whose love, wisdom and guidance I will always cherish. To my uncles, particularly my Uncle Johnny (deceased) aunts, cousins and grandparents (Grandmother and Mommy Essie both deceased), many of them loss but not forgotten, whose perception is also compiled within the confines of this book.

To my sisters and brothers: Edward Singley (deceased), Margret Griggs (deceased), Brenda Wright (deceased), Robert Singley (deceased), Gloria Riley, Mary Crump (deceased), Linda McDaniel, David Singley and especially my older brother Amin Rasheed (Roger Singley) who was always there when I needed him and to their progeny. I would like to extend my appreciation to my Sister-in-laws: Helen Rasheed and Kitty Singley (deceased), Brother-in-law Joseph McDaniel (deceased), and to the entire Singley family. Their support was not only vital to this book but to my life. Gratitude is also extended to my godparents, Sister Ruthie and Brother Chester, for their help in raising me. My appreciation is also extended to my wife's family, Lester McDaniel and Barbara Hughes and the McDaniel and Hughes siblings.

The number of individuals that helped me during my life is far too great to acknowledge without citing some and omitting others. However, there were some that had an enduring impact that warrant special recognition: From my college days: Steve Throne and James G. Spady, whose enlightening conversation and mentorship opened my eyes to a world hitherto unseen. Special thanks to my dearest friends, Jesse Brown, James Spigner, James Grant, Willie Dash, Bill Hart, Dr. Erasmus Feltus (deceased), Jimmy Martin and Charles Cook (deceased) who mentored me during my first job. A special thanks to Lynn Worthy, Alex Tatum, Jesse Brown, Steve Throne and Professor Joseph Kennedy for their review of my work and their faith in my abilities. To Mabel Elizabeth Singletary for her help in getting this book published. To the members of Mount Calvary Church of God in Elizabeth, NJ that prayed for me when I was sick and for providing me with a religious background.

A NEW PERSPECTIVE

To my team of doctors particularly: Dr. Frekko, Mrs. Frekko and their daughters, Dr. Bass, Dr. Lin, Dr. Juarbe, Dr. Baek, Dr. Lieberman and Dr. Melki. To the citizens of the town of Roselle, NJ (the first town in the world to have an electrical infrastructure). My appreciation is also extended to the following individuals: Mr. Frazier who kept on me about publishing my writing, Mrs. Roberts who gave me money for running errands as a child and families like the Sumners, Cooks, Simmons, etc., that formed a neighborhood that was the laboratory for my learning.

To my enduring friends and former coworkers, particularly my former secretary Alice Baker, former managers, John Bigelow, Alan Dunn, Randy Cline and longtime coworkers that supported me in this and other efforts: Mary Lott, Dick Alban, Laveer Jovel, Steve Becraft, Verna Wright, Jim Rader, Dave Epler, Steve Frinak, Jim Hanlon, Paul Gantz, Steve Williams, Stu Benner, Tim Bresnan, Douglas Smith (deceased), Bob McKay, Bob Peters, Dick Roberts, Scott Pettygrove, Zach Stern, Dale Mann, Dale Dahlke, Jeff Shires, Barry Constantine, Bahman Salamat, Jeff Dobek, Jim Burck, John Murphy, Bill Smith, Greg Kneer, Terry Fogle, Mark Mowen, Kevin Graul, Gary Bell, Brendan Regan, Mark and Cathy Flinchbaugh, Melvin Pierce, Pat Howley, Lee Lusby, Ralph Lee, Lenny Jacobs, John Sill, Rob Strain, Frank Hornbuckle, Wyatt Bell, Ken Grish, Jerry Carbone, Daun Green, Don Muller, Ed Kozlosky, Gordon Whitney, Rod Miller, Richard Mugg, Krista Ochlech, Ben Burt, Mike Zeher, Al Hughes, Don Eenigenburg, Wynn Aung, Carl Slutsky, Tim Malac, Stu Mullan, Tim Burns, Joe Colburn, R.T. Stokes, Mike Janes, Mark Beatson, Carmela Young and the employees at Fairchild Space and Defense, Orbital Sciences, Smith Industries, General Electric and so many others that have offered support and encouragement during this endeavor. To the many workers at Friends of the Library Montgomery County, MD and to the Sickles family long-time owners of the Book Alcove and relatives of the Civil War general Dan Sickles for providing me with inexpensive books and for encouraging me to continue to write.

Thanks, is also given to the following friends whose discussions helped in this endeavor. Gene Limb, Mark Edwards, Edward Fortney, Earl Spence, Earl Jenkins, Derrick Carr, Bristol Martin, Steve Cooper, Stephan Shin, Marcus (Doc) Coleman, Vince Coleman, Lenny Chornock, Dr. Gary Greenbaum (deceased) Robert White, Mike Slater, Joe Hasshen, Marcelo Flores, Stu Keeler, Grandville Smith, Earl Meadows, Tommy Arnold, Paul Kane, Kevin Kistler, Cameron Dryden, Reuben Smith, Calton Hall, Russ (40) Deshields, Greg Estep, Trenton Holmes, Cameron Simmons, Matt Fremin, Mike Wigal, Kevin Sinai, Heath Marshall, Kevin Correa, Leroy Gettinger, Mark Alan Hill, Kenny Jenkins, Lloyd McMillian, Jimmy McMillian, Steve Bender, Don Frost, Crispian Kirk, Chalk Dawson, Rashida Anderson, Kathy

RETHINKING THE HISTORY AND MYTHS OF THE PAST

Amidon, Brian Hackett and Boyd Thomas. Gratitude is also extended to my fellow coworkers, staff and students at Rocky Hill Middle School, Clarksburg, Maryland. Specifically, Daphne Williams, Marion Martin, Olivia Reyes, Marc Cosby, Kimberly Wiltshire, Allen Ambush, the Montgomery County Public School (MCPS) staff at Clarksburg, Northwest and Watkins Mill High Schools; Martin Luther King Middle School and to Dr. Karl Reid of the National Society of Black Engineers (NSBE).

To the Washington Independent Review for helping to improve my writing skills and to Chris Matthews of MSNBC, David Maraniss Associate Editor of the Washington Post and Roger Williams of New England Publishing Associates, INC. for their comments on writing and the literary business. I also want to thank my classmates and teachers at Abraham Clark High School and Drexel University for providing me with intriguing dialogue and a good educational foundation. I would like to mention some of my Drexel colleagues specifically, Alton Knight, Colvin Bert, Gwen Evans, Derese Fisher, Alfred Taylor, Don Hinson, John Greene, David Adams (deceased) Mike Wright and Ray Gibson (deceased). Finally, I am grateful to my homeboys "the brothers": Lynn Worthy, Dr. Albert Ford, Kevin Williamson, Alex and Willis Tatum. Together we proved that little black boys who dare to dream can become doctors, lawyers, historians and engineers. The journey has been long, but it has also been joyous.

Let me end by saying that I know there are some that deserve personal recognition that I have failed to mention. To them I offer my sincere apology.

The Singley Family

Made in the USA
Coppell, TX
16 December 2020